LOUISIANA LAW OF SALE AND LEASE

A PRÉCIS

THIRD EDITION

ALAIN LEVASSEUR
Professor of Law, Emeritus
Louisiana State University
Paul M. Hebert Law Center

DAVID GRUNING
William L. Crowe, Sr. Professor of Law
Loyola University New Orleans
College of Law

With the Assistance of Mahogane Reed

CAROLINA ACADEMIC PRESS
Durham, North Carolina

ISBN: 978-1-63283-954-1 (Print)
ISBN: 978-1-63283-955-8 (eBook)

Carolina Academic Press, LLC
700 Kent Street
Durham, North Carolina 27701
(919) 489-7486
www.cap-press.com

2022 Printing
Printed in the United States of America

LOUISIANA LAW OF SALE AND LEASE
A PRÉCIS

Louisiana Code Series

CIVIL CODE SERIES

LOUISIANA POCKET CIVIL CODE
2016

LOUISIANA CIVIL CODE PRÉCIS SERIES

LOUISIANA LAW OF OBLIGATIONS IN GENERAL
ALAIN LEVASSEUR
3RD ED. 2016

LOUISIANA LAW OF CONVENTIONAL OBLIGATIONS
ALAIN LEVASSEUR
2ND ED. 2016

LOUISIANA LAW OF SALE AND LEASE
ALAIN LEVASSEUR & DAVID GRUNING
3RD ED. 2016

LOUISIANA LAW OF TORTS
FRANK MARAIST
2010

LOUISIANA LAW OF SECURITY DEVICES
MICHAEL H. RUBIN
2ND ED. 2016

LOUISIANA LAW OF PROPERTY
JOHN RANDALL TRAHAN
2012

LOUISIANA LAW OF PERSONS
Forthcoming

LOUISIANA LAW OF SUCCESSIONS
Forthcoming

About the Authors

Professor Alain Levasseur is a graduate of the Universities of Paris (France) and Tulane. He was an associate with the Paris firm of Mudge, Rose, Guthrie & Alexander for a while but left the firm to become a technical assistant at the World Bank in Washington, D.C. Professor Levasseur taught at Tulane Law School from 1970–1977 when he joined the LSU Law Faculty. He is a member of the International Academy of Comparative Law, the Société de Législation Comparée, the Louisiana State Law Institute; he serves on the editorial or advisory boards of the American Journal of Comparative Law, the Revue Trimestrielle de Droit Civil, the Revue Générale de Droit, the Foro de Derecho Mercantil, and e-Competitions. He is president of the Louisiana Chapter of the Association Henri Capitant and of the International Association of Legal Methodology. He has published extensively in the fields of Comparative Law, Civil Law (Civil Law System/Tradition, Obligations, Contracts, Sale/Lease), EU/EC Law, US Law (in French with Dalloz). He has been a regular visiting Professor at the Universities of Aix-Paul Cézanne and Lyon III.

David Gruning is the William L. Crowe, Sr., Distinguished Professor of Law at Loyola University, New Orleans. He graduated magna cum laude from Tulane Law School, is a member of the Order of the Coif, and was articles editor of the Tulane law review. He practiced law in New Orleans, before joining the Loyola law faculty in 1986. He was a visiting professor at the University of Montreal, Faculté de Droit, from 2001-2003. He presently serves on several committees of the Louisiana State Law Institute on civil and commercial law, and is a member of the American Law Institute.

Table of Contents

Part I:

Louisiana Law of Sale

INTRODUCTION

The contract of "Sale" was not the first known contract whereby persons would transfer things — their ownership in particular — to others. "Barter" was the prior form of transferring things of value. Under the contract of "barter" each party would consider the thing she delivered to the other party as the "equivalent" of the thing she was receiving. It was, therefore, an exchange made without the use of money. Today, we know this form of contract as "*Exchange*." This latter contract is defined as follows in **Louisiana Civil Code article 2660:**

"Exchange is a contract whereby each party transfers to the other the ownership of a thing other than money.

Ownership of the things exchanged is transferred between the parties as soon as there is agreement on the things, even though none of the things has been delivered.

If it is the intent of the parties that the transfer of ownership will not take place until a later time, then the contract is a contract to exchange."

Thus, when "money" came to be used as a substitute for a thing previously "exchanged" for a thing, the contract of "*Sale*" was created. Today "Sale" is, quantitatively speaking, the most common type of contract we enter into in our daily lives and probably the principal means used to transfer all sorts of things to others. It is so common that on many occasions, we do not even think about it. For example, "minors" — children under the age of eighteen — enter into contracts of sale without the "legal capacity" to do so when they use money to purchase a soft drink or snacks in a coin operated machine! There is little doubt that this same minor "wanted" that drink and expressed his or her consent to acquire it by dropping money into the slot which, in turn, was quite willing to "accept" that money.

The contract of sale is defined as follows in Louisiana Civil Code article 2439: **"Sale is a contract whereby a person transfers ownership of a thing to another for a price in money.**

The thing, the price, and the consent of the parties are requirements for the perfection of a sale."

It is most important to state at the outset that, just like *Exchange, Sale* is but a kind or a type of "Contract or Conventional Obligation." To place "Sale" within its context, it suffices to read **La. C.C. art.** 2438, the lead Article under "Title VII. Sale," which provides that: **"In all matters for which no special provision is made in this title, the contract of sale is governed by the rules of the titles on Obligations in General and Conventional Obligations or Contracts."** This means that, before attempting to identify the specific features of a contract of sale in a given contract and, even more so, before looking into the transfer of ownership or an issue of warranty, it is essential to ascertain whether a "contract" exists at all. Indeed, if there is no valid contract entered into under the rules of Conventional Obligations, there can be no sale at all because there is no "contract." Thus, it is only after one has clearly established the existence of the four requirements for a valid contract to exist (consent, capacity, cause, and object) that one can turn to ascertaining whether this "nominate"[1] contract of sale does exist because the contract does meet the specific requirements of a contract of sale exists.[2] Should one come to the conclusion that all the requirements of a sale have not been met, one might then look into the possible existence of another nominate contract, such as a lease, or even into the existence of an innominate contract, a *sui generis* contract, devised by the parties for themselves.

An analysis of the contract of sale in the Louisiana Civil Code will lead us, in Chapter One, to identify the types of contracts or pre-contracts which may be entered into before a contract of sale is actually perfected. In Chapter Two we will focus on the perfection of a contract of sale and in Chapter Three we will describe the many different effects that flow from a contract of sale.

---

[1] Because it has a **name** in the Civil Code.

[2] See *infra* for the legal requirements for a contract of sale to be perfect, p. 17.

Chapter 1

AGREEMENTS PREPARATORY TO A SALE OR PRE-CONTRACTS

La. C.C. art. 2439 defines the contract of sale and lays down the requirements for a binding contract of sale in these terms:

> **"Sale is a contract whereby a person transfers ownership of a thing to another for a price in money.**
>
> **The thing, the price, and the consent of the parties are requirements for the perfection of a sale."**

In other words, and as a general principle, a contract of sale transfers the ownership of "a thing" from one party to the other who pays "a price" in money for that "thing." In addition, the two parties must have intended to enter into a sale by expressing their consent to that effect. This requirement of consent to enter into a sale is most important to identify because parties to what may have become, in the course of time, a contract of sale, may have previously entered into other kinds of contracts, nominate or innominate, in anticipation of, or in preparation for that sale. There exist three most common types of pre-contracts or contracts meant to prepare the parties to enter, later on, into a contract of sale.

The Louisiana Civil Code lists these pre-contracts as: the "Option"[3], the "Contract to Sell"[4] and "the Right of First Refusal."[5] Because the "contract to sell" is the most commonly used pre-contract and because it is almost the necessary step to be taken before entering into a sale, particularly in the sale of immovables, we shall deal with it first although it is listed after "Option" in the Civil Code.

Article 1
Contract to Sell

Two Code articles describe two different "contracts to sell." According to **La. C.C. art. 2623:**

> **"An agreement whereby one party promises to sell and the other promises to buy a thing at a later time, or upon the happening of a condition, or upon performance of some obligation by either party, is a bilateral promise of sale or contract to sell. Such an agreement gives either party the right to demand specific performance.**

[3] La. C.C. art. 2620–2622.

[4] La. C.C. art. 2623–2624.

[5] La. C.C. art. 2625–2626.

A contract to sell must set forth the thing and the price, and meet the formal requirements of the sale it contemplates."

This type of contract to sell is also referred to as a **"bilateral contract to sell"** or as **"a bilateral promise of sale."**

The other type of contract to sell is described as follows in **La. C.C. art. 2624:**

"A sum given by the buyer to the seller in connection with a contract to sell is regarded to be a deposit on account of the price, unless the parties have expressly provided otherwise.

If the parties stipulate that a sum given by the buyer to the seller is earnest money, either party may recede from the contract, but the buyer who chooses to recede must forfeit the earnest money, and the seller who so chooses must return the earnest money plus an equal amount.

When earnest money has been given and a party fails to perform for reasons other than a fortuitous event, that party will be regarded as receding from the contract."

It is a contract to sell with earnest money.

§ 1.1.1. BILATERAL CONTRACT TO SELL OR BILATERAL PROMISE OF SALE.

A. Formation and Validity.

In such a contract the two parties exchange promises: one promises to sell some "thing" to the other who promises to buy that "thing." Agreement on the "thing" that should be sold eventually is a first essential requirement for the validity of the contract to sell. There occurs, here, an exchange of wills without any performance. If at the time of the exchange of the reciprocal promises, the parties contemplate the future transfer of a movable thing, the *consensual* contract to sell is binding without any requirement of a writing. On the other hand, if the "thing" that the parties have in mind as being the future object of the seller's obligation to deliver to the buyer is an immovable, then the contract to sell will have to **meet the formal requirements of the sale** contemplated.

Such a contract to sell does not require, for its validity, that it be limited in time. In other words, a contract to sell does not have to set a "term", or time limit, for the parties to decide whether or not to proceed to the next step, i.e., enter into the sale. As a result, in theory, a contract to sell can be "open" for as long as the parties want it to be open. However, it is likely that the parties to such a contract will agree on an extinctive term[6] and set a time limit to the waiting period. The parties can also agree on the occurrence, or not, of a suspensive condition as stipulated in **La. C.C. art. 1767.** In the absence of either a term or a condition, one party or the

---

[6] La. C.C. art. 1777; *see* Précis, Louisiana Law of Obligations in General, by Alain A. Levasseur, Charlottesville: LexisNexis, 2006, p. 29 to 39.

other is not likely to wait indefinitely under a contract to sell, and be held hostage for any length of time, because that same contract gives each party the right to demand specific performance, that is to say the right to compel the other party to make up her mind about entering or not into the sale itself.

A second essential requirement for a valid bilateral promise of sale or contract to sell is an agreement on the price of the "thing." Since this contract is bilateral, imposing obligations on both sides,[7] it is perfectly logical to require that, if the object of the seller's obligation, the "thing", be identified, the object of the buyer's obligation, the "price", be also set forth in the contract to sell.[8] Thus, the two major requirements for the contract of sale — the thing and the price[9] — are met in this preliminary contract to sell, making it easy for any one of the two parties to demand specific performance, that is to say, to transform the contract to sell into a sale.

B. Effects.

The effect of a contract to sell between the parties is stated in **Louisiana Civil Code article 2623** as giving **"either party the right to demand specific performance."** According to the general rule stated in **article 1986, "[u]pon an obligor's failure to perform an obligation to deliver a thing, or not to do an act, or to execute an instrument, the court shall grant specific performance plus damages for delay if the obligee so demands. If specific performance is impracticable, the court may allow damages to the obligee.**

Upon a failure to perform an obligation that has another object, such as an obligation to do, the granting of specific performance is at the discretion of the court."

It follows that a *contract to sell* vests in either party the right to demand that an instrument of sale be executed. Thus, depending on the circumstances of each case and, particularly, the behavior of the parties, a court could, in its *discretion* and unless impracticable, "force" a sale upon the parties, make the seller actually sell and deliver a title to the buyer.[10] In such a case the court's judgment will stand in lieu of a contract of sale between the parties. However, because the drastic effect of specific performance of an obligation to do means that the obligor's freedom is seriously infringed upon, the courts might be reticent to resort to such a remedy. Should that be the case, the damages that should then be granted to the other party — presumably the buyer — ought to be sufficient to truly compensate that party for the loss of a right that had an agreed-upon monetary value. Promises legally and lawfully entered into should be upheld. Since obligations to pay money are obligations to "give" or deliver a thing, it follows that **"[u]pon an obligor's failure to perform an obligation to deliver a thing, . . . the court shall grant specific performance plus damages for delay if the obligee so demands. If**

---

[7] La. C.C. art. 1908.

[8] La. C.C. art. 2623.

[9] La. C.C. art. 2439.

[10] Obligation to give on the part of the seller.

specific performance is impracticable, the court may allow damages to the obligee."[11]

As regards the effects of a contract to sell vis-à-vis third persons, **article 2629** provides that a "**. . . contract to sell that involves immovable property is effective against third persons only from the time the instrument that contains it is filed for registry in the parish where the immovable is located."**

If the "thing" referred to in the contract to sell is a movable, then such a **"contract to sell that involves movable property is effective against third persons who, at the time of acquisition of a conflicting right, had actual knowledge of that transaction." (La. C.C. art. 2629.)** One can speculate here, as regards the meaning of the adjective "actual." Does it mean that a third person must have been informed *directly* by the seller? The buyer? Should this be the meaning of "actual" in the sense of subjective knowledge, it is likely that very few contracts to sell movable property would be rescinded on the ground of this *actual* or subjective knowledge by and at the expense of a third person. Furthermore, it is possible that sellers would be enticed, even encouraged, to sell the movable property to a third person for a higher price without that third person having any subjective knowledge that the same movable property had been previously promised to be sold to a buyer, party to a contract to sell.[12]

One could also read "actual knowledge" to mean presumed or constructive knowledge as knowledge arising from the circumstances suggesting that the third person should know or should have known. Under this interpretation many more third persons would be taking a risk of not being protected should they acquire the movable property from the seller. On the other hand, the buyer in the contract to sell would be better protected in his expectations to become the owner of that same movable property he contracted to buy in the preliminary bilateral promise to sell he negotiated with the seller.

Another effect of the contract to sell is the impact that this contract has on the timing of the valuation of lesion.[13] In this respect, **article 2590** states that: **"To determine whether there is lesion, the immovable sold must be evaluated according to the state in which it was at the time of the sale. If the sale was preceded by . . . a contract to sell, the property must be evaluated in the state in which it was at the time of that contract."**

Although it may appear obvious, it is still worth stating that the the creation of the contract of sale has no retroactive effect to the date of formation of the contract to sell. As will be explained below, the transfer of ownership of the thing from the seller to the buyer occurs at the time of the sale itself and does not operate back to the date of the contract to sell. But the price of the immovable is set at the time of the contract to sell and it will be carried over into the sale itself which justifies that lesion be determined at the time the price was fixed, i.e., at the time of the contract to sell. This is all the more so since the contract to sell gives rise to the right to

---

[11] La. C.C. art. 1986.

[12] *See* La. C.C. art. 518, 523.

[13] On Lesion, see *infra*, p. 31; La. C.C. art. 2589.

demand specific performance with no legitimate contractual way out. Note that **article 2595** states that, **"The action for lesion must be brought within a peremptive period of one year from the time of the sale."** This peremptive period is not applicable to a contract to sell because no ownership has been transferred to the buyer; the *latter* has nothing to return to the party "seller" in a contract to sell.

§ 1.1.2. BILATERAL CONTRACT TO SELL OR BILATERAL PROMISE OF SALE WITH EARNEST MONEY.

Louisiana Civil Code article 2624 reads as follows: **"A sum given by the buyer to the seller in connection with a contract to sell is regarded to be a deposit on account of the price, unless the parties have expressly provided otherwise.**

If the parties stipulate that a sum given by the buyer to the seller is earnest money, either party may recede from the contract, but the buyer who chooses to recede must forfeit the earnest money, and the seller who so chooses must return the earnest money plus an equal amount.

When earnest money has been given and a party fails to perform for reasons other than a fortuitous event, that party will be regarded as receding from the contract."

Before looking at the two different meanings and purposes that may be attached to a sum of money given in a contract to sell — either as a deposit on account of the purchase price or as earnest money — a few words need to be said about the three meanings that legal history offers as to the purposes of putting money down in a contract to sell.

One meaning is to look at the money put down as the "price" one is willing to pay to "reserve the right not to proceed" with the sale; it could be analogized to the purchase of the right not to buy. In a sense we are dealing with a contract to sell that includes a "suspensive condition"[14] consisting in one party or the other deciding not to proceed with the sale and acting either unilaterally by withdrawing from the contract to sell or acting in defense to a demand made by the other party to enter into the sale. Such a contractual relationship can also be understood as having created a "facultative obligation."[15]

Another meaning that has been given to an amount of money put down is that of the "*denier à Dieu*", in the sense that the amount of money is evidence or proof before God of the parties' definite intent to enter into the sale. It appears like a "seal" on the parties" intent. Usually this amount of money would be small and somewhat symbolic. This is because its true "moral" purpose is not related to the actual market value of the thing and its price as they are referred to in the contract to sell. The independent legal and moral nature of this amount of money leads to the consequence that it is not to be considered as partial payment of the price of the thing.

---

[14] La. C.C. art. 1767; *see* Précis, Louisiana Law of Obligations in General, p. 40.

[15] *See* Précis, Louisiana Law of Obligations in General, p. 77.

The third meaning given to an amount of money put down is that of a down payment towards the full price. It amounts to some sort of a "division" of the buyer's obligation to perform indivisibly vis-à-vis the seller, i.e. to pay the price in a lump sum.[16]

Louisiana Civil Code article 2624, in its first paragraph, has brought about a major change in the Louisiana jurisprudence that prevailed until the revision of the law of sale by Act 841 of 1993. Despite the clear statement of former article 2624, second paragraph, and until the legislative revision of 1993, the jurisprudence was "determined" to look at any money put down as "earnest money" even when the parties to a contract to sell would specifically refer to the money put down by the buyer as "down payment on account of the purchase price" or when they would state that "this amount of money is not to be considered as earnest money." That jurisprudence is now history and the courts are instructed to consider that **"[a] sum given by the buyer to the seller in connection with a contract to sell is regarded to be a deposit on account of the price, unless the parties have expressly provided otherwise."**[17]

The phrase **"[u]nless the parties have expressly provided otherwise"** implies that the parties must stipulate **that a sum given by the buyer to the seller is earnest money.**[18] As such, neither party can be compelled to enter into the sale. In light of the past jurisprudential perspective on earnest money, parties to a contract to sell are encouraged to expressly and unequivocally refer to a sum of money put down as earnest money when it is so intended.

In a sense, therefore, earnest money is the price one is willing to pay to secure one's freedom not to be compelled to enter into the sale and, thus, to get out of the contract to sell as planned when earnest money was given. As **Louisiana Civil Code article 2624** states that **"the buyer who chooses to recede must forfeit the earnest money, and the seller who so chooses must return the earnest money plus an equal amount."** The third paragraph of the same article adds that **"[w]hen earnest money has been given and a party fails to perform for reasons other than a fortuitous event, that party will be regarded as receding from the contract."**

If a fortuitous event prevents a party from performing, most likely when the seller is unable to deliver the thing because of the fortuitous event, the parties should be returned to the *status quo ante*, the situation they were in before they entered into the contract to sell. Thus, the buyer who gave a sum as earnest money should receive his money back, and nothing more.

One should not look at the forfeit of earnest money or the payment of an equal amount as the same thing as the payment of "damages." A party who exercises a right, as that party does when earnest money has been given, is not penalized when forfeiting the earnest money but is actually carrying out her own free will to the fullest extent under the form of the right to get out of the contract to sell. Hence the

---

[16] La. C.C. art. 1816; on indivisible and divisible obligations see Précis, Louisiana Law of Obligations in General, p. 80.

[17] La. C.C. art. 2624 first paragraph.

[18] La. C.C. art. 2624 second paragraph.

suggestion that earnest money creates a "facultative obligation" for both parties.[19]

§ 1.1.3. OPTION.

An *Option* is a contract between the grantor of the Option and the grantee. The Option contract must, therefore, meet the requirements for any valid contract. Such a contract of Option creates a "unilateral" obligation on the part of the grantor who is actually the only one of the two parties to be bound by an obligation: to keep the Option open for as long as agreed in the contract. The grantee or beneficiary is under no obligation towards the grantor since he has the choice to exercise or not the Option. An Option can also be referred to, therefore, as a "unilateral promise" to sell, in contrast with the contract to sell which is also known as a "bilateral promise" to sell.

The law governing "Option" can be found in two main sets of Civil Code articles; they are Louisiana Civil Code articles 1907, 1908 and 1933 under Conventional Obligations and articles 2620 to 2622 as well as 2628 to 2630 under Sale. After an analysis of the requirements for a valid Option to exist, we will turn to the effects of the Option and, lastly, to the assignment of an Option.

A. Requirements for a Valid Option.

Louisiana Civil Code article 1933 defines an Option as being **"a contract whereby the parties agree that the offeror is bound by his offer for a specified period of time and that the offeree may accept within that time."** Another **article, 2620** within the context of a Sale, describes that same contract as follows: **"An option to buy, or an option to sell, is a contract whereby a party gives to another the right to accept an offer to sell, or to buy, a thing within a stipulated time.**

An option must set forth the thing and the price, and meet the formal requirements of the sale it contemplates."

Referred to as *contract* in both articles, a first requirement that must be met by an Option is that of the free and informed "consent" of the parties to that contract, as is the case of all contracts. Vices of consent, such as error or fraud, may carry with them the relative nullity of the contract. Likewise "capacity" is required from both parties but we believe that the capacity to enter into an Option contract to buy or sell need not be the full capacity required to actually enter into a sale. For example, the party granting or selling an Option need not be the owner, yet, of the "thing" on which the Option bears. Where article 2620 requires that the Option sets forth **the thing**, that "thing" may be a "future thing" not in existence at the time the Option is granted or sold. Indeed, according to article 1976, **"[f]uture things may be the object of a contract."** Thus, someone may grant or sell an Option on a future thing and not have, at the time of the Option, the capacity to dispose of the thing . . . not in existence yet. Such a situation is very common on the futures market and the stock market.

---

[19] *See* Précis, Louisiana Law of Obligations in General, 3rd Edition (LexisNexis 2009), p. 77.

The cause in the Option contract being **the reason why a party obligates himself,**[20] there is a valid objective cause in the purchase and sale of an Option. This is not to say that the contract of Option could not be considered null because of an unlawful subjective cause or reason.

As to the "object" of the Option contract, that object is the Option itself, thus an incorporeal thing, a right, which is movable or immovable according to the nature of the thing on which the Option bears.

Both Louisiana Civil Code articles 1933 and 2620 require that there be a "specified time" or a "stipulated time" within which the Option is to be accepted. In other words, the parties must have agreed on an "extinctive term"[21] within which the Option must be exercised and accepted or rejected. The Civil Code does not set a limit to the time or term as far as an Option on movables are concerned. On the other hand, **article 2628** states that **"[a]n option . . . that concerns an immovable thing may not be granted for a term longer than ten years. If a longer time for an option . . . has been stipulated in a contract, that time shall be reduced to ten years . . .** " However, the same article goes on to state that **"if the option . . . is granted in connection with a contract that gives rise to obligations of continuous or periodic performance, an option . . . may be granted for as long a period as required for the performance of those obligations."**

If an Option bears on a movable thing the contract of Option is a consensual contract which is valid by the mere exchange of the wills of the parties. On the other hand, an Option that bears on an immovable thing **must . . . meet the formal requirements of the sale it contemplates.**[22] As **La. C.C. art. 1839** states: **"A transfer of immovable property must be made by authentic act or by act under private signature. . . .** "

An issue that has plagued the jurisprudence for a long time is whether or not the Option itself must have a price. For reasons pertaining to a poor drafting of former Code articles 2462 and 2463, the Louisiana jurisprudence had transposed the legal regime of a contract to sell with earnest money to an option with a price. Today, there is no longer any reason to equate one to the other. Under the Civil Code of today, an Option need not have a price to be valid. Neither Code articles 1933 nor 2620 require that there be a price for the Option itself. This does not mean that, the Option being a thing of value, the parties to the contract of Option may not enter into a contract of sale of the Option and agree on a price for that Option. Under no circumstances should that price for the Option be considered as "earnest money". In an Option contract, as will be explained below, the buyer acquires, at no charge or after having paid a price, the absolute right to buy or not to buy. That is the exclusive choice that the buyer has and the seller is bound to sell the "thing" to the buyer should the latter decide to exercise the Option to buy. The seller cannot be allowed to pay to the buyer an amount of money equivalent to the price as earnest money; that would defeat the whole purpose of the Option which is

[20] La. C.C. art. 1967.

[21] On extinctive term see Précis, Louisiana Law of Obligations in General, p. 28 *et seq.*

[22] La. C.C. art. 2620.

to bind the seller to sell to his buyer who exercises the Option.

B. Effects of an Option.

The principal effect of an Option is described in Louisiana Civil Code article 2621 but there are other effects of the Option that are mentioned in other Code articles.

Article 2621 states: **"The acceptance or rejection of an offer contained in an option is effective when received by the grantor. Upon such an acceptance the parties are bound by a contract to sell. Rejection of the offer contained in an option terminates the option but a counteroffer does not."**

The receipt theory — receipt by the grantor/seller — applies to the acceptance or the rejection of the Option as exercised by the grantee/buyer. Since the grantor/seller was irrevocably bound to sell, it is legitimate to put him in control of the timing of formation of the next contract to be entered into, the sale or the contract to sell, or to let him off the hook should the grantee/buyer "opt" not to buy. "Actual receipt" of the acceptance or rejection by the grantor/seller, in the sense of the latter taking possession of the grantee's means of communication of the acceptance or rejection, should mean "presumed knowledge" of that acceptance or rejection of the Option. Indeed, "receipt" cannot mean actual subjective knowledge, otherwise the grantor/seller could delay, at will, the formation of the next contract between himself and the grantee/buyer by postponing reading the grantee's letter, fax, etc. We find here, and for identical reasons, the same rule as the rule applicable to an irrevocable offer as stated in article 1934.[23]

"Upon . . . acceptance [of the offer contained in the option] the parties are bound by a contract to sell," states **Code article 2621 § 1**, whereas **"[r]ejection of the offer contained in an option terminates the option but a counteroffer does not" (La. C.C. art. 2621 § 2)**. Should an acceptance by the buyer of the offer contained in an option granted by the seller always and automatically lead to the formation of a contract to sell? Should this be a rule of public order or could the parties to the Option contract provide otherwise, i.e. that upon exercise of the option the parties will be bound by a *contract of sale*? Why have "necessarily" a three step process: Option, first step, turned into a Contract to sell, second step, turned into a Sale, third step? We do not believe that the "rule" stated in Code article 2621 § 1 should be read as a rule of public order; the parties to the option contract should be free to agree otherwise. Indeed, how much sense does it make to move from a contract with a required "specified or stipulated time", i.e. the option, to a contract to sell which, under the Civil Code is "unlimited" in time? Since the Option contains all the necessary requirements of the actual Sale, thing and its price, and form if required, the parties to an Option contract should be allowed to go directly from the Option, step one, to the Sale, step two. Going through the intermediary step of a contract to sell should not be "legally" required (particularly not by the courts) as it is not even necessary.

Among the other effects of an Option, we will mention three.

---

[23] *See* Précis on Louisiana Law of Conventional Obligations, p. 33.

A first additional effect is stated in **Code article 2629** in these terms: **"An option, right of first refusal, or contract to sell that involves immovable property is effective against third persons only from the time the instrument that contains it is filed for registry in the parish where the immovable is located.**

An option, right of first refusal, or contract to sell that involves movable property is effective against third persons who, at the time of acquisition of a conflicting right, had actual knowledge of that transaction."

With respect to the scope of application of this article to an Option we would make, here, the same comments we made above in the context of the contract to sell.[24]

A second additional effect of an Option is that, if the Option itself could be divided between multiple grantees/buyers under the form of "shares in the Option", the **"Right to exercise an option, and the right of first refusal are indivisible. When either of such rights belongs to more than one person all of them must exercise the right."**[25] It follows that all the co-owners of an Option must agree "together" to exercise "indivisibly" their "one" right to accept the Option.

A third effect to mention deals with the connection between Option and Lesion. We read in **Code article 2590** that **"[t]o determine whether there is lesion, the immovable sold must be evaluated according to the state in which it was at the time of the sale. If the sale was preceded by an option contract, or by a contract to sell, the property must be evaluated in the state in which it was at the time of that contract."** Again, the same comment as was made above under Contract to sell could be made here.[26]

C. Assignment of an Option.

An Option, being a thing of value, falls in the patrimony of the grantee/buyer and becomes an heritable right.[27] However, the parties may have agreed to make the Option a strictly personal right of the grantee/buyer in which case **its performance can be enforced only by the obligee** (the grantee/buyer of the Option) **or only against the obligor** (the grantor/seller of the Option).[28] Assuming the Option is heritable, it can, because of its monetary value, be assigned or transferred to a third person. Should an assignment take place, **"The assignor of an option to buy a thing warrants the existence of that option, but does not warrant that the person who granted it can be required to make a final sale. If, upon exercise of the option, the person who granted it fails to make a final sale, the assignee has against the assignor the same rights as a buyer without**

---

[24] See *supra* on actual knowledge versus constructive knowledge, p. 6.

[25] La. C.C. art. 2630. The concepts of divisible and indivisible obligations are described in Louisiana Civil Code articles 1815 to 1819. *See* Précis, Louisiana Law of Obligations in General, p. 80 *et seq.*

[26] *See supra*, p. 6; on Lesion, see *infra*, p. 31.

[27] La. C.C. art. ; *see* Précis, Louisiana Law of Obligations in General, p. 21 *et seq.*

[28] La. C.C. art. 1766 § 1.

warranty has against the seller."[29] The same rule can be found in the Code articles on Assignment of Rights,[30] particularly in **article 2646: "The assignor of a right warrants its existence at the time of the assignment.**

The assignor does not warrant the solvency of the debtor, however, unless he has agreed to give such a warranty."

To warrant the existence of an option does not mean that the assignor of the Option warrants that the grantor/seller of that option will actually consent to enter into a contract to sell or a sale. Should that be the case the assignee's right of recovery is limited to the amount of the price, if any, he paid for the assignment. The same rule is applicable in the case of an exclusion of warranty against eviction under Code article 2503.[31]

Since an Option can be assigned for the reasons given above, an important question must be raised here: can the creditors of the grantee/buyer of an Option substitute themselves to their debtor, the grantee/buyer, and be allowed to exercise the Option in its place? We believe that such creditors, like in the case of a sale at a lesionary price, should be allowed to bring a Revocatory action (or Pauliana action) under Civil Code articles 2036–2043 or an Oblique action under Civil Code article 2044, unless, of course, the Option had been made strictly personal to the grantee/buyer.[32]

§ 1.1.4. RIGHT OF FIRST REFUSAL.

The *right of first refusal* is defined as follows in **article 2625: "A party may agree that he will not sell a certain thing without first offering it to a certain person. The right given to the latter in such a case is a right of first refusal that may be enforced by specific performance."**

Such an agreement can stand alone as a contract of first refusal or it can be included as a provision in a principal contract, such as a contract of lease. The *right of first refusal* is also known as "pacte de préférence" because a party is given a "preference" over others in being the first one to be offered, by the seller, the right to buy a certain thing. The Civil Code articles on the *right of first refusal* are articles 2625 to 2630. We will describe first the concept and the legal requirements of the *right of first refusal* before considering its effects.

A. Concept and Requirements.

Like the contract of Option, the agreement that provides for a *right of first refusal* creates only one obligation. That obligation is imposed on the grantor of that right to "first offer" a certain thing to the other party to the contract, the grantee. The latter is under no obligation, in return, meaning that she is not bound

---

[29] La. C.C. art. 2622.

[30] La. C.C. arts. 2642–2654. On Assignments of rights, see *infra*, p. 23.

[31] *See infra*, p. 64.

[32] On the Revocatory, or Pauliana, Action and the Oblique Action, see Précis on Louisiana Law of Conventional Obligations, p. 119 *et seq.*

to "accept" the "first offer to be made by the grantor" to buy the thing in preference to someone else. Therefore, an agreement or contract granting a *right of first refusal* is, like an Option contract, a unilateral contract.

The *right of first refusal* creates an obligation to do[33] on the grantor, i.e. the obligation to make his "first offer" to the grantee/beneficiary of the *right of first refusal.*

If the thing to be offered first to the grantee is an immovable, the *right of first refusal* will have to be granted by a written instrument and it cannot be extended or be open **for a term longer than ten years**[34]. However, **"if [the option or] the right of first refusal is granted in connection with a contract that gives rise to obligations of continuous or periodic performance, [an option or] a right of first refusal may be granted for as long a period as required for the performance of those obligations."**[35] So, if the *right of first refusal* has been granted by a provision in a contract of lease of an immovable which has a twenty year term, the validity of the *right of first refusal* will borrow from the validity of the principal contract of lease.

Strangely enough, the Code articles do not require that, as far as movable things are concerned, the *right of first refusal*, as a principal contract, be granted for a "specified or stipulated time" as is required for an Option under article 2620. Considering that Code article 2628 treats the *right of first refusal* in the same manner as the Option to the extent that immovables are concerned, we suggest that this "equal" treatment of two very similar concepts be extended to an application of the stipulated time provision in article 2620 to a *right of first refusal* bearing on movables. However, one can also say that in the absence of a specific legal provision applicable to a *right of first refusal*, a reasoning by analogy, or *ubi eadem ratio idem lex*, may not be appropriate. In the latter case, there would be no requirement of a "stipulated time" in a principal contract of first refusal bearing on a movable.

To avoid any controversy, should the "grantor" of an option bearing on a movable wish to be "released" from his obligation to keep the option open until the grantee decides to exercise the option, the grantor should include an extinctive term in the option. The shorter the term, the quicker the grantor will be free to negotiate again.[36]

Does Does Civil Code article 2625 make the *right of first refusal* strictly personal to the grantee where it refers to **"a certain person"**? Is that **"certain person"**, the grantee, denied the right to assign or transfer his *right of first refusal* to others? Again, because of the analogy that exists between Option and *right of first refusal*, article 2622 on Option could be extended to the *right of first refusal.* Very important in this respect is **article 1765 § 2** which provides that **"every obligation is deemed heritable as to all parties."** Furthermore, under **article**

---

[33] La. C.C. arts. 1756, 1986.

[34] La. C.C. art. 2628.

[35] La. C.C. art. 2628.

[36] For an explanation of "term," see Précis on Louisiana Law of Conventional Obligations, p. 28 *et seq.*

2642, "[a]ll rights may be assigned." Therefore, as a matter of principle, a *right of first refusal* should be considered heritable and assignable unless **"the contrary results from the terms or from the nature of the contract"**[37] or unless the *right of first refusal* should fall in **"the exceptions of those (rights) pertaining to obligations that are strictly personal."**[38] It follows that the parties, the grantor most likely, can make the *right of first refusal* "personal" to the first grantee-offeree so that the latter could not transfer or assign that right to others.

B. Effects of the Right of First Refusal.

The grantor of a *right of first refusal* **"may not sell to another person unless he has offered to sell the thing to the holder of the right on the same terms. . . . "**[39] In addition, **Civil Code article 2625** states, in part, that the *right of first refusal* **"is a right . . . that may be enforced by specific performance."** We are led to describe the *right of first refusal* as imposing on the grantor an obligation not to do, i.e. not to sell to another before offering to sell to the grantee, rather than an obligation to do, i.e. sell to the grantee first. The reason behind this suggestion is that **article 1986** tells us that **"upon an obligor's failure to perform an obligation . . . not to do an act or to execute an instrument, the court shall grant specific performance plus damages for delay . . . "** whereas **"upon failure to perform an obligation. . . . to do, the granting of specific performance is at the discretion of the court."** It is a definite advantage to the grantee of a *right of first refusal* to look at it as creating on the grantor an obligation not to do, not to sell to anyone without first offering to sell to him, and as requiring that the grantor execute an instrument, i.e. the contract to sell or the contract of sale which is to follow the exercise of the *right of first refusal.* However, the actual exercise of the *right of first refusal* is subject to two suspensive conditions: one suspensive condition consists in the grantor intending to sell at all, and the second condition consists in the grantee agreeing to buy **"on the same terms** (as those offered to another person)**, or on those specified when the right was granted if the parties have so agreed."**[40] Essentially, since there is already an agreement as to the "thing" that may be sold, the **same terms** of the sale will bear on the price or the modalities of payment — whatever the **same terms** of the offer made to **another person** may be. Once the seller-grantor has fulfilled his obligation to **offer to sell the thing to the holder of the right of first refusal**, the latter must **"accept within ten days from the time it is received if the thing is movable, and within thirty days from that time if the thing is immovable."**[41]

Should the grantee of the *right of first refusal* accept the offer made by the grantor, this acceptance manifested by the positive exercise of the right amounts to the expression of consent by the grantee to enter into the sale. This expression of

---

[37] La. C.C. art. 1765; on heritable obligations, see Précis, Louisiana Law of Obligations in General, p. 21 *et seq.*

[38] La. C.C. art. 2642.

[39] La. C.C. art. 2626; on suspensive condition, see Précis, Louisiana Law of Obligations in General, p. 40.

[40] La. C.C. art. 2626.

[41] La. C.C. art. 2627 § 1.

consent does not have retroactive effect to the time the *right of first refusal* had been granted because a new contract comes into existence, a contract to sell most likely, upon exercise of the *right of first refusal*. In addition, it is at that time of the exercise of that right that the capacity of the former grantee, now buyer, to enter into a sale must be determined.

On the other hand, the grantee may not have been in a position to exercise his *right of first refusal* because, maybe, he could not afford to buy the thing "on the same terms" as those negotiated with another person. If that sale to another person does take place, that sale will be valid and binding on the former grantee of the *right of first refusal* (assuming there was no fraud in that contract of sale). However, should the grantor not enter into a sale **"with a third person within six months, the right of first refusal subsists in the grantee who failed to exercise it when an offer was made to him."**[42] There is much wisdom in this article 2627: it is meant to deter a grantor of a *right of first refusal* to enter into a fictitious sale at a high price with a fictitious buyer so as to deter the grantee from exercising his right and "force" him to give it up for ever.

As far as third parties are concerned, the same Code article 2629 which applies to Option and to Contract to sell, applies also to the *right of first refusal*. The same observations as have been made under the Contract to sell can be made here.[43]

As regards the determination of *Lesion* in the context of a *right of first refusal*, Civil Code article 2590 makes no reference, and rightfully so, to that right. Indeed, at the time the *right of first refusal* is granted, there has been yet no offer by the grantor to sell to another person; so no price for the thing can exist until an offer is made. At that time the grantee may decide to exercise his *right of first refusal* and turn that right into a contract to sell or a sale. It is at that time that article 2590 will become applicable.[44]

---

[42] La. C.C. art. 2627 § 2.

[43] *See supra*, p. 6 *et seq.*

[44] On lesion, see p. 31.

Chapter 2

PERFECTION OF A CONTRACT OF SALE

A contract of sale requires, for its perfection, a **"thing, [a] price and the consent of the parties"** (**La. C.C. art. 2439**). Besides these listed requirements that make up a contract of sale, **"In all matters for which no special provision is made in this title, the contract of sale is governed by the rules of the titles on Obligations in General and Conventional Obligations or Contracts"** (**La. C.C. art. 2438**). Therefore, we will address below both the general requirements for a valid contract as they apply to a sale, and the special requirements of a contract of sale. These requirements, general and special, are: capacity, consent, thing, price, and, in particular instances, form.

Article 1
Capacity

There is not much to add here, as concerns the contract of sale, to the requirement of capacity to enter into any contract as this element of a contract is governed articles 1918 to 1926 and as we are reminded by article 2438 above. For our purpose, it is appropriate to cite **Civil Code article 1918**, the general article on Contractual Capacity: **"All persons have capacity to contract, except unemancipated minors, interdicts, and persons deprived of reason at the time of contracting."**

One should be aware also of the restrictions that matrimonial regimes may impose on the capacity of spouses to enter into contracts of sale. For example, under the matrimonial regime of community property, **Civil Code article 2346** states: **"Each spouse acting alone may manage, control, or dispose of community property unless otherwise provided by law." Article 2347(A)** adds that **"[t]he concurrence of both spouses is required for the alienation, encumbrance, or lease of community immovables, standing, cut, or fallen timber, furniture or furnishings while located in the family home, all or substantially all of the assets of a community enterprise, and movables issued or registered as provided by law in the names of the spouses jointly."**

The only restriction that appears in the Civil Code under the Title of Sale on the capacity of some persons to enter into a contract of sale is mentioned in **article 2447**. It reads as follows: **"Officers of a court, such as judges, attorneys, clerks, and law enforcement agents, cannot purchase litigious rights under contestation in the jurisdiction of that court. The purchase of a litigious right by such an officer is null and makes the purchaser liable for all costs, interest, and damages."** We will consider this article in its proper context when we comment below on things that may be sold.

Article 2
Consent

There does not exist, in the first twelve Chapters under the Title Sale, a reference to this requirement of consent for the perfection of a contract of sale. The reason is the same as that given above about capacity which is that, since a sale is a contract, **"the contract of sale is governed by the rules of the titles on Obligations in General and Conventional Obligations or Contracts." (La. C.C. art. 2438.)** Thus, as regards "consent," one should be familiar with Civil Code articles 1927 to 1964 on Conventional Obligations in order to be able to discuss the existence or not of this requirement in a contract labeled as a sale and analyze its integrity.

However, it appears that the major changes brought into the Louisiana law of sale by the Acts of 1993 added a new chapter, Chapter 13 "Sales of Movables," to the former structure of the law of sale. Several of the articles of this new Chapter (Arts. 2601 to 2617) do refer to consent, under different forms, as a requirement for the perfection of this type of contract of "sale of movables." Although not stated unequivocally in these articles and their comments, it is beyond doubt that they have been strongly inspired and influenced by the Convention on Contracts for the International Sale of Goods (or CISG) and by the UCC. It will be necessary, therefore, to look into these two sources to find help and guidance in interpreting these articles. Furthermore, with the exception of three or four of these articles which refer to "merchants" or to things "in transit," the bulk of the articles should apply to all sales of movables in application of the rule of interpretation which provides that where the law does not distinguish we are not to make distinctions (*ubi lex non distinguit nec nos distinguere debemus*).

For the sake of clarity we will divide these articles, and many others, into two broad categories. One category will deal with contracts of sale of movables between lay persons and the second category will deal with contracts entered into **between merchants.** (La. C.C. art. 2601 § 2.) In between these two categories, references will have to be made to contract of sale between a layperson on one side and a merchant on the other side.

§ 2.2.1. CONSENT IN CONTRACTS OF SALE OF MOVABLES BETWEEN LAY PERSONS.[45]

According to **Louisiana Civil Code article 2601 § 1: "An expression of acceptance of an offer to sell a movable thing suffices to form a contract of sale if there is agreement on the thing and the price, even though the acceptance contains terms additional to, or different from, the terms of the offer, unless acceptance is made conditional on the offeror's acceptance of the additional or different terms. Where the acceptance is not so conditioned, the additional or different terms are regarded as proposals for modification and must be accepted by the offeror in order to become a part of the contract."** Three different scenarios can be contemplated under this article. In the first instance a

---

[45] La. C.C. arts. 1927 to 1947; 2601 § 1, 2602.

sale is formed upon acceptance of the thing and the price; in this instance, the acceptance is the mirror image of the offer and the rules on revocable and irrevocable offers would then apply. In the second instance, a sale is formed even though the acceptance, by the offeree, contains terms additional to or different from the terms of the offer **unless acceptance is made conditional on the offeror's acceptance of the additional or different terms** contained in the offeree's acceptance. There is, in the offeror's accepting the additional or different terms contained in the offeree's acceptance, a suspensive condition consisting in the offeror expressing his own acceptance in good faith (La. C.C. arts. 1759, 1770, 1772). There will be, then, retroactivity of the perfection of the contract of sale as of the moment of acceptance by the offeree.[46] The third type of sale contemplated is that resulting from a "counter-offer" made by the offeree in the form of the additional or different terms of his counter-offer requiring the consent or acceptance of the original offeror for the perfection of the sale. In this case, the offeror's consent or acceptance is not the equivalent of a suspensive condition and has, therefore, no retroactive effect.

Article 2602 adds to articles 1927 and 1939 to 1942 as regards the sale of movables where it reads that **"a contract of sale of movables may be established by conduct of both parties that recognizes the existence of that contract even though the communications exchanged by them do not suffice to form a contract. In such a case the contract consists of those terms on which the communications of the parties agree, together with any applicable provisions of the suppletive law."** We assume that for article 2602 to apply, the parties need not be merchants as the wording of the article does not restrict its application to merchants. These parties must have previously agreed on the thing and the price which are essential for the perfection of a sale as per articles 2601 and 2439 in particular, but the communications between these parties did not amount to an agreement on other provisions of their contract of sale. As concern a type of "conduct" on the part of both parties that would lead to establishing the existence of a sale between them, one may want to look at articles 8 and 9 of the CISG and at the UCC § 2-207. However, we will state again here that the wording of article 2602 is not restricted to "merchants."

§ 2.2.2. CONSENT IN CONTRACTS OF SALE BETWEEN MERCHANTS: LSA-C.C. ART. 2601 § 2.

Subparagraph 2 of article 2601 states as follows: **"Between merchants, however, additional terms become part of the contract unless they alter the offer materially, or the offer expressly limits the acceptance to the terms of the offer, or the offeree is notified of the offeror's objection to the additional terms within a reasonable time, in all of which cases the additional terms do not become a part of the contract. Additional terms alter the offer materially when their nature is such that it must be presumed that the offeror would not have contracted on those terms."**

---

[46] One should point out here the difference between this paragraph of article 2601 and article 1943-3.

This subparagraph calls for two comments, at least. First of all, the Civil Code does not contain a definition of the concept of "merchant." We can come up with some idea of who a merchant might be when we put together Civil Code articles 524 and 2466; in other words, a merchant under the Civil Code is someone who "customarily sells similar things" or who "habitually sells" movables "of the kind."[47] The UCC, on the other hand, provides the following definition of merchant in section 2-104,: "Merchant means a person that deals in goods of the kind or otherwise hold itself out by occupation as having knowledge or skill peculiar to the practices or goods involved in the transaction. . . . " A Louisiana Civil Code understanding of this concept will have to be provided by the courts.

A second comment bears on the meaning to be given to "materially" since it is important for the perfection of a contract of sale between merchants to decide whether **"the additional terms alter the offer materially."** Again, the Civil Code does not provide any guidance. However, it should be obvious that additional terms that would bear on the thing and the price might "alter the offer materially" as agreement on these two essential elements of a contract of sale is necessary for the perfection of the contract. Beyond the thing and the price we can, again, find some guidance as to the meaning of "materially," as well as "additional or different," in article 19 of the CISG.

Article 3
Things that may be Sold

§ 2.3.1. NATURE OF THINGS.

Louisiana Civil Code article 2448 states that **"[a]ll things corporeal or incorporeal, susceptible of ownership, may be the object of a contract of sale, unless the sale of a particular thing is prohibited by law."** As regards the "nature" of the things which can be sold and therefore become susceptible of ownership, reference must be made to Book II of the Civil Code and, in particular, to articles 448, 453, 454, 461, 462, 470, 471, and 473. The indivisibility of a thing is not an obstacle to the transfer of that thing by all the co-owners in indivision or to the transfer of an **"undivided share" (La. C.C. art. 480)**. Besides, whatever the nature of the thing, **article 1971** adds some important adjectives which must fit the thing before it can become the "object" of any contract and, *a fortiori*, a sale: **"Parties are free to contract for any object that is lawful, possible, and determined or determinable."**

To the general statement of **article 2448** referring to **[a]ll things**, there are "things" that cannot be sold or that can be sold only under strict regulations. One can think of prescription drugs, for example. Besides prohibitions or restrictions that can be found in the Revised Statutes, La.R.S. 56:327(A) for example, the Civil Code states that **"[t]he succession of a living person may not be the object of a**

[47] Any difference between "customarily" and "habitually"? U.C.C. section 2-104(1) defines a "merchant" as "person who deals in goods of the kind or otherwise by his occupation holds himself out as having knowledge . . . "

contract other than an antenuptial agreement. Such a succession may not be renounced." **(La. C.C. art. 1976-2.)**

§ 2.3.2. EXISTENCE OF THINGS.

Must a thing be in existence to be the object of a contract of sale? The answer to this question is found in the answer to another question that relates to the "effects" of a contract of sale. That other question can be phrased as follows: does a contract of sale transfer the ownership of the thing agreed upon *immediately, as soon as the parties agree on that thing and its price?* As will be established below, the answer is no. If a contract of sale has for one of its *essential* (in the sense of being of the *essence*) effects to transfer ownership, that transfer does not have to take place immediately. The Civil Code does provide for examples of contracts of sale in which the transfer of ownership is delayed or suspended. Since it is not of the essence of a contract of sale to transfer ownership *immediately*, parties to a sale can exercise their contractual freedom to do as they wish with the timing of the transfer of ownership, as long as they remain within the parameters of legal order. A contract of sale can, therefore, bear on a thing not in existence at the time the parties enter into the sale. The Civil Code gives three examples of such "non-existing things" at the time of the sale.

§ 2.3.3. FUTURE THING.

Civil Code article 1976-1 on Conventional Obligations or Contracts and **article 2450** on the law of Sale state that **"[f]uture things may be the object of a contract"** and particularly **"of a contract of sale."** The purchase of a truck to be fitted by the seller within a few months according to the needs and expectations of the buyer can be a sale of a future thing — the specially outfitted truck. The phrase "can be a sale" is suggestive of the possibility for the contract to be some other contract than a sale, such as a contract for services. To draw the distinction, one must ascertain the true intent of the parties as to the nature of the contract they did intend to enter into. One can be guided in this decision by a comparison of the costs of the two things, the corporeal thing (the truck, the cabinet, etc.) and the services. The more expensive item should determine the nature of the contract. One can also attempt to make a distinction between the principal thing and "its" accessory thing. It may be that the nature and the amount of services surrounding the making of the corporeal thing make the services an accessory to the principal corporeal thing such as to be merged into the latter with the result that a sale would be considered as the contract intended by the parties.

When a "future thing" is the object of a contract of sale **"the coming into existence of the thing is a condition that suspends the effects of the sale." (La. C.C. art. 2450.)** In other words, the sale is perfect at the time it is entered into, it does bind the parties, but its effects, mainly the transfer of ownership, will not occur until some time in the future. The same article adds that the coming into existence of the thing **is a condition that suspends the effects of the sale.** Such a condition is, therefore, a suspensive condition[48] with the "legal effect" that the occurrence of that suspensive condition will have a "retroactive effect" to the time of perfection of the sale which means that the purchaser will be considered to have been the owner of the future thing from that same prior time of the perfection of the sale.

Should the coming into existence of the future thing fail to occur, the purchaser will have to choose between several possible remedies. The availability of these options will depend on whether the seller was at fault in the performance of its obligation to "deliver," or whether a fortuitous event prevented the seller from being able to carry out its obligation.[49]

One can point to paragraph one of Louisiana Civil Code article 2458 as another illustration of a sale of a future thing because the thing sold is not susceptible of being transferred until **"the seller . . . weights, counts or measures the things."**

A comparative note is worth making here. Whereas the Louisiana Civil Code considers the sale of a future thing as a "sale" with the suspended but retroactive effect of the transfer of ownership, the UCC in its article 2-105(2) states that: "[A] purported present sale of future goods or of any interest therein operates as a contract to sell."

§ 2.3.4. HOPE.

Strictly speaking the sale of a hope is neither the sale of a non-existing thing nor the sale of a future thing. It is necessary, however, to briefly address this type of sale to distinguish it from the sale of a future thing and to make it clear that the parties to the sale of the hope are selling an existing thing, the hope, and not the future materialization of that hope. **Civil Code article 2451** describes this sale in these terms: **"A hope may be the object of a contract of sale. Thus, a fisherman may sell a haul of his net before he throws it. In that case the buyer is entitled to whatever is caught in the net, according to the parties" expectations, and even if nothing is caught the sale is valid."** The sale of a hope is an aleatory contract which **Civil Code article 1912** defines in these terms: **"A contract is aleatory when, because of its nature or according to the parties" intent, the performance of either party's obligation, or the extent of the performance, depends on an uncertain event."** Fishermen who contract with the captain of a charter boat to go on a fishing trip do understand that, in exchange for the amount of money they pay the captain, they only purchase the expectation or hope of catching a lot of fish, to make the trip worth their money, time, or pleasure. On his side, the captain will not guarantee a great catch as he is not willing to turn the aleatory contract of his selling a hope to the fishermen into a synallagmatic commutative contract of a sale of a "future thing," a great catch, as he has no control over such a catch. The fishermen will bear the loss in the sense that they will have paid a price for, maybe, no fish at the end of the day.

Since the "hope" is the thing bought, the object of the contract of sale, it is like an incorporeal thing that exists at the moment the sale is entered into with that sale

---

48 *See* Précis, Louisiana Law of Obligations in General, p. 40.

49 La. C.C. arts. 1873–1878.

carrying immediately one of its essential effects, the transfer of ownership of that hope, to the fishermen. Having delivered, by mutual consent, the object of the contract of sale to the fishermen at the same time ownership was also transferred, the captain is now under an obligation to do something — take the fishermen on the fishing trip. Should the captain breach this obligation, and be at fault, he will have to pay damages to the fishermen.

The major differences between the sale of a future thing and the sale of a hope emphasize the importance of properly distinguishing one from the other. Contrasting the elements of a truly commutative contract with the elements of an aleatory contract can help make this distinction.

§ 2.3.5. SALE OF A RIGHT OR ASSIGNMENT OF A RIGHT?

A right, when it is not personal, is an "incorporeal thing" which, under article 2448 **may be the object of a contract of sale**. This presents a problem of interpretation, which hides a problem of substantive law.

The problem can be briefly stated as follows: the formal structure of the Civil Code places the institution known as "Assignment" in a Chapter 15 entitled "Assignment of Rights" which, itself, is placed under Title VII, Sale. The question or problem is then the following: is an Assignment of Rights the same thing as a Sale of Rights? Does the greater formulation of a "Title" in the Code, "Sale" in this particular instance, include necessarily the lesser title, that of a "Chapter", "Assignment" in this instance? If so, then the only way a right could be disposed of, transferred onerously, would be by means of a contract of Sale which contract would carry this special name Assignment when the thing sold is of the nature of a "right."

For several reasons — two of which will be given here — we must look at "Assignment" as a contract of a different nature from that of a contract of sale and, thus, placed under the wrong title in the Louisiana Civil Code.[50]

One first reason is found in the formal structure of a Civil Code and in the names given to the Titles, Chapters, and Sections, appearing in the Code. Those names are not part of the "law" of the Code because its division in Titles, Chapters, and Sections are not part of the Law. They are in the Code only for the sake of organization and structure, so as to facilitate the reading of the Code.[51] Only the substance of the Code articles themselves are "law." They are like provisions of an Act of the Legislature, a statute, which explains why they are cited as sources of law by the jurisprudence whereas the titles of chapters or sections are not. On the basis of that first reason, we can move the Chapter on Assignment out from under "Sale"

[50] This topic "Assignment" properly belongs to "Transfer of Obligations", Chapter 4, in "Obligations in General" Title III, Book III. Actually it should belong under Title IV, Conventional Obligations since an Assignment is a contract which transfers a right from one party to another. For the same reason, "Assumption of Obligations" listed under the same Chapter 4 Transfer of Obligations under Obligations in General, Title III, should also be a part of "Conventional Obligations" as a mode of transfer of an obligation from one party to another. Such a restructuring would place the contractual transfer of a right, "assignment", opposite to the contractual transfer of an obligation, "assumption".

[51] La. R.S. 1:13. Headings to sections, source notes, and cross references are given for the purpose of convenient reference and do not constitute part of the law.

and place it elsewhere in the Civil Code where it would fit much better on account of the substantive law it actually incorporates.

This is the second reason not to equate Assignment with Sale. Indeed, a reading of all the articles that appear under Assignment[52] do not refer to and do not use the word "sale." The only exception is article 2652 which has for its title "Sale of litigious rights." But we know now that titles are not part of the law and, in addition, a reading of that single article shows that the verb used in the article is not "to sell" or "sold" or "selling" but "assigned" or "assignee" or "assignment." Since the substance of the law incorporated in the article prevails over the title of the same article, we can only conclude that the wrong title-name was given to that article. Still, if the verb used in this single article, the verb "assign," is the same as the verb used in all the articles under "Assignment," it means that an Assignment is, and should be, something other than a Sale. To illustrate the broad scope of application of this concept of Assignment, beyond its application to Sale only, one needs only read articles 2711 and 2713 under Lease. **Article 2711** states, in part, that **"The transfer of the leased thing does not terminate the lease . . ."** and **article 2713** states, in part, that **"The lessee has the right to sublease the leased thing or to assign or encumber his right in the lease. . . . "** In other words, an assignment is a mode of transfer as article 2711 provides. It should be pointed out also, and it will be emphasized below, that neither the Code articles on Assignment (except for Art. 2652) nor the Code articles on Lease do require that a price be paid for the transfer or assignment to be valid. An assignment of a right can occur either onerously, by an onerous contract, or gratuitously, by a gratuitous contract in which case we have a donation. In a narrow sense, an assignment is usually an onerous transfer or transaction.

A. Notion of and Requirements of an Assignment.

Briefly stated, an assignment is merely a transfer by a "creditor/assignor" of his right against his "debtor/assigned" to a third person who is the "assignee." By such an assignment, the creditor/assignor will usually receive cash from the assignee *before* the creditor/assignor could have claimed performance from his obligor. So, from a business point of view, the creditor receives its money from somebody other than his debtor and the latter is now faced with another and different creditor who received the same right the original creditor had against that same debtor. Although we now have a different creditor, we do not have a "new contract" different from the contract that existed between the original creditor and his debtor. Assignment is not novation and, as we stated in a previous Précis, there is room in the law for both institutions not only because parties should have the freedom or right to choose one institution over the other, but also and most importantly because the legal effects of an assignment are different from those of a novation.[53] For that reason alone, one party/creditor may want to choose assignment over novation or vice versa.[54]

---

52 La. C.C. arts. 2642–2654.

53 La. C.C. arts. 1879–1885.

54 *See* Précis, Louisiana Law of Obligations in General, p. 142–151.

As regards the requirements for an assignment, they are those of a contract, mainly consensual unless the right transferred is an "incorporeal immovable" in which case the contract of assignment would have to be in writing. As far as the right assigned is concerned, **"All rights may be assigned, with the exception of those pertaining to obligations that are strictly personal. . . . " (La. C.C. art. 2642.)** Upon the assignment of a "principal" right, the accessories to that right will automatically be assigned without any need for the parties to so stipulate **(La. C.C. art. 2645).**

For an Assignment to be valid or effective and, therefore enforceable, it is important that the debtor be informed that he will be facing a different creditor from the one to whom he thinks he is indebted. Under **Civil Code article 2643, "[t]he assignment of a right is effective against the debtor and third persons only from the time the debtor has actual knowledge, or has been given notice of the assignment.**

If a partial assignment unreasonably increases the burden of the debtor he may recover from either the assignor or the assignee a reasonable amount for the increased burden."

"Actual knowledge", (La. C.C. art. 2643) or "knowledge" (La. C.C. art. 2644) of the assignment by the debtor, or "notice" (La. C.C. arts. 2643 & 2644) of the assignment by the debtor will determine the right of performance of that debtor. It should be noted that "acceptance" of the assignment by the debtor is not required. He need only be aware of the assignment. An unaware, uninformed debtor may render his performance to his original creditor and that performance will extinguish the obligation *vis-à-vis* both that creditor as assignor, his assignee as well as third persons.[55] The knowledge or notice of the assignment is particularly important to a debtor under an obligation subject to a term in favor of the creditor since the latter can call on the obligor at any time. On the other hand, when the term is in favor of the debtor/obligor he will be protected at least until the expiration of the term.

B. Effects of an Assignment Between the Parties.

— Transfer of a right.

The essential effect of an assignment of a right is the transfer to the assignee of the very same right and its accessories, such as security rights, that belonged to the grantor/assignor.[56] The assignee is vested with the assignor's right as a result of subrogation.[57] It is exactly the same contractual obligation that existed originally that is "assigned". There lies a fundamental difference with novation which is the extinguishment of an existing obligation by the substitution of a new

---

[55] La. C.C. art. 2644.

[56] La. C.C. arts. 2642 & 2645.

[57] La. C.C. art. 2642. On Subrogation, see Précis, Louisiana Law of Obligations in General, p. 103–116.

one.[58]

Although article 2642 states that **"the assignee is subrogated to the rights of the assignor against the debtor,"** an important difference should be maintained between subrogation and assignment. As we stated in a previous Précis,[59] "both under conventional subrogation and legal subrogation, a subrogated obligee would not recover more from the obligor than the amount he paid the original obligee either because the law says so under article 1830 or because the original obligee can still exercise his right for the balance." On the other hand, "the raison d'être of an assignment of rights is the transfer or sale by an obligee to an assignee of the rights and claims the obligee holds against the obligor . . . An assignment of rights is likely to be an act of speculation. It is an act of purchase made by an assignee who, for the assignment to him of a right belonging to another, the assignor, pays a price which may be unrelated to the nominal value of the obligation which is bought. The price is often a discounted price reflecting the assignee's main motivation of gambling or speculating on the difference in value between the price he agrees to pay and the amount that he expects to collect from the obligor. . . . " Thus, in an assignment of rights, the assignee or buyer is entitled to receive from the original debtor the *full* payment that the latter owed his creditor, now assignor, regardless of the price the assignee paid that assignor for the assignment of the right.

There is one exception mentioned in the Civil Code under **article 2652** when the sale or assignment bears on a litigious right. In this particular instance, and because of the raison d'être of litigious redemption, **"the debtor may extinguish his obligation by paying to the assignee [only] the price the assignee paid for the assignment, with interest from the time of the assignment. . . . "** The assignee is not entitled to collect from the debtor a greater amount than he himself paid to the assignor.

— Warranty owed by the assignor.

When an assignment is onerous and commutative, the assignee expects something in return for the price or its equivalent that he pays or transfers to the assignor. Such is the purpose of the warranty the assignor owes his assignee.

Louisiana Civil Code article 2646 provides for a warranty of law: **"The assignor of a right warrants its existence at the time of the assignment.**

The assignor does not warrant the solvency of the debtor, however, unless he has agreed to give such a warranty." This warranty extends not only to the right itself, or the main object of the contract, but to the accessories, such as security rights, also. The assignor can only warrant the existence of the right at the time it is assigned, and not beyond. Should the right no longer exist after it has been assigned, and for causes that are beyond the control of the assignor, the assignee will have to bear the loss. In addition, the assignor does not warrant the solvency of the debtor at the time the assignee will seek payment from the debtor.

---

[58] La. C.C. art. 1879. On Novation, see Précis on Louisiana Law of Obligations in General, p. 142–151.

[59] Précis, Louisiana Law of Obligations in General, p. 114.

This is where the speculative element of an assignment comes in and why the assignee will pay the assignor a price inferior to the amount of the debt owed by the debtor.

An assignor may also, by contract, **"[warrant] the solvency of the debtor . . . at the time of the assignment only"**; he may also, provided he does it expressly, **"warrant the future solvency of the debtor." (La. C.C. art. 2648.)** In the event of a breach of such warranty, the assignor will be liable to pay back to the assignee the price the latter paid for the assignment. An assignor cannot be presumed to be willing to take on the risk of having to pay more to the assignee, which he would have to do if he had to pay the entirety of the debt owed by the debtor, than the price he received from his assignee. Along the same line is the statement made in **article 2649** to the effect that **"[w]hen the assignor of a right did not warrant the solvency of the debtor but knew of his insolvency, the assignee without such knowledge may obtain rescission of the contract."** Here again, the contract will be rescinded and the assignor will have to return to his assignee the price he received from the latter.

Since a right in a succession may have a monetary or patrimonial value, such a right can be assigned unless, like other rights, such an assignment has been prohibited. **(La. C.C. art. 2653.)** Should a right in a succession be assigned, the **"person who assigns his right in the estate of a deceased person, without specifying any assets, warrants only his right of succession as heir or legatee." (La. C.C. art. 2650.)**

It goes without saying that the assignor's obligation of warranty extends to his own personal action to the extent it would be detrimental to the assignee. Hence, **"[w]hen the debtor, without knowledge or notice of the assignment, renders performance to the assignor, such performance extinguishes the obligation of the debtor and is effective against the assignee and third persons." (La. C.C. art. 2644.)**

C. Effects of an Assignment vis-à-vis Third Parties.

The debtor is a third party to the assignment until that debtor has **"actual knowledge or has been given notice of the assignment." (La. C.C. art. 2643.)** So, until the debtor knows that he has been "assigned" another creditor, the assignee, and that his original creditor is no longer entitled to receive payment from him, that debtor is a third person. Such is the essence of Civil Code article 2644 referred to above. On the other hand, once the debtor has knowledge of the assignment (La. C.C. arts. 2643–2644), he becomes a party in a contractual relationship with the assignee for the same obligation he owed his original creditor. The debtor can raise against the assignee the same exceptions and defenses he could have raised against the original creditor/assignor before he had knowledge or had been notified of the assignment. In other words, following this traditional principle of wisdom or adage, the creditor/assignor could not transfer to his assignee more rights than he had against the debtor. However, it is most important to restate here what was said elsewhere about Compensation[60]: the assignee (transferee) would suffer a

[60] Précis, Louisiana Law of Obligations in General, p. 158–166.

prejudice if the debtor were allowed to raise the defense of compensation that could have occurred between himself and the assignor (transferor) before the assignment took place.

The creditors of both the assignor and the assignee must also be considered third parties. As far as the first set of creditors is concerned, it is in their interest that their debtor's rights, the assignor here, remain in the assignor's patrimony because as the property of their debtor they are, in a sense, their common pledge (La. C.C. arts. 3133–3134). These creditors could possibly seize these rights and be paid out of the proceeds of their sale. The assignor's creditors have nothing to worry about until they have actual knowledge or have been given notice of the assignment. (La. C.C. art. 2643.) Subsequently to having knowledge or having received notice of the assignment, these creditors may then come in conflict with another set of creditors, those of the assignee. From that point onward, the latter set of creditors should prevail over the former.

§ 2.3.6. THING OF ANOTHER.

"The sale of a thing belonging to another does not convey ownership." (La. C.C. art. 2452.) Note that the article does not state that "there is no sale" but only that **the sale does not convey ownership.** In such a sale, a thing exists but, at the time of the sale between the buyer and the seller, the thing belongs to a person other than the seller, which explains why the seller cannot convey the ownership of the thing. This sale is not to be considered as the same thing as a sale of a thing that does not exist, except that the thing does not exist as the object of the seller's ownership at the time of the sale. Article 2452 does not state either that the sale is null, because it has no object; again it merely states that "ownership" is not conveyed. In other words, the sale is valid, it is perfect, it exists but it can have no effect yet, i.e. transfer ownership, because the object sold is not yet owned by the seller. It is expected by the parties that, somehow, the seller will have to acquire that thing at some point in time in the future to transfer its ownership to the buyer. Such a sale looks very much like a sale under the suspensive condition that the seller acquires the ownership of the thing so as to transfer it to the buyer. Should the seller be in breach of his obligation to acquire the thing when delivery of it is owed to the buyer, he will be liable to pay damages to the buyer.[61]

Article 4
Price

Besides requiring "consent" and "thing" for the perfection of a contract of sale, article 2439 requires a "price." This requirement is then described as follows by **Civil Code article 2464: "The price must be fixed by the parties in a sum either certain or determinable through a method agreed by them. There is no sale unless the parties intended that a price be paid.**

---

61 The Civil Code gives examples of such a sale in Louisiana Civil Code articles 521 and 522. Besides, such sales are very well known in the stock market, the commodities market . . .

The price must not be out of all proportion with the value of the thing sold. Thus, the sale of a plantation for a dollar is not a sale, though it may be a donation in disguise."

The price must be payable in a sum of money and not under the form of goods or other things, otherwise another contract than a sale would be created; it could be an exchange (La. C.C. arts. 2660–2667), or giving in payment (also known as *dation en paiement*),[62] but it would not be a sale. In this respect, the law of sale in Louisiana is different from the law of sale of the UCC article 2-304 which provides that (1) *The price may be made payable in money or otherwise; . . . in whole or in parts in goods . . .* On the other hand, like the Louisiana Civil Code, the CISG requires that the buyer pay the price for the goods and that the price be fixed or determined (Arts. 53, 56).

§ 2.4.1. FIXED PRICE OR DETERMINABLE PRICE.

A price fixed in a "certain" sum can be fixed by common agreement of the parties or by one party, the seller in most instances, with the consent, express or tacit, of the buyer, as any buyer-consumer is fully aware.

A price is "determinable" when the parties agree on a "method" which will lead to the determination of the price the buyer will pay. That method may consist in adding several prices one to the other, in multiplying a quantity of things by the price of individual items, or by reference to a market. That method may also consist in calling on a third person to determine the price, as suggested by **article 2465: "The price may be left to the determination of a third person. If the parties fail to agree on or to appoint such a person, or if the one appointed is unable or unwilling to make a determination, the price may be determined by the court."** Article 2465 on price as the object of the buyer's obligation is similar to article 1974 on the determination of the quantity of the object (or "thing") of an obligor'sobligation — the seller in our case. "Thing" sold and "price" paid should be given the same treatment as the two objects of two obligations created by a synallagmatic commutative contract, in this instance a contract of sale.

A major innovation brought to the law of sale by the revision of 1993–95 is the ***open price*** policy as stated in **Civil Code article 2466: "When the thing sold is a movable of the kind that the seller habitually sells and the parties said nothing about the price, or left it to be agreed later and they fail to agree, the price is a reasonable price at the time and place of delivery. If there is an exchange or market for such things, the quotations or price lists of the place of delivery or, in their absence, those of the nearest market, are a basis for the determination of a reasonable price.**

Nevertheless, if the parties intend not to be bound unless a price be agreed on, there is no contract without such an agreement."

Such a policy has been in use in the common law for a long time and has been formally recognized by UCC article 2-305, a few excerpts of which are given here:

---

[62] La. C.C. arts. 2655–2659; *see infra*, n.158, p. 90.

"The parties if they so intend may conclude a contract for sale even if the price is not settled. In such a case the price is a reasonable price at the time of delivery if: (a) nothing is said as to the price; (b) the price is left to be agreed by the parties and they fail to agree; (c) the price is to be fixed in terms of some agreed market. . . . " The similarity between this article of the UCC and Louisiana Civil Code article 2466, quoted above, is also most striking in another respect; the second paragraph of Louisiana Civil Code article 2466 reads similar to paragraph 4 of UCC article 2-305: "If, however, the parties intend not to be bound unless the price is fixed or agreed and it is not fixed or agreed, there is no contract. . . . "

To conclude, it must be emphasized that article 2466 concerns only "movables," that these "movables" must be of the kind the seller habitually sells, which means that the seller must be a "merchant," i.e. someone who habitually sells these movables, that the parties must have intended that a price be agreed upon and that they intended that the price be a reasonable price at the time and at the place of delivery.[63] The CISG also validates the open price policy in its article 55.

§ 2.4.2. OUT OF PROPORTION PRICE.

Civil Code article 2464 states that "**[t]he price must be fixed by the parties in a sum either certain or determinable through a method agreed by them. There is no sale unless the parties intended that a price be paid.**

The price must not be out of all proportion with the value of the thing sold. Thus, the sale of a plantation for a dollar is not a sale, though it may be a donation in disguise." It is worth pointing out that the article states "out of ***all*** proportion" and not merely "out of proportion." Is the example given of the **sale of a plantation for a dollar is not a sale,** an illustration of what an out of **all** proportion price is? Is that the extent of the discrepancy in the evaluation which must prevail? What if the plantation were sold for ten dollars? It is our opinion that the example given of the sale of a plantation for a dollar is meaningless if taken literally, if used as an express benchmark. As Pothier wrote: "A price which bears no proportion to the actual value of the thing sold, is not a real price; as if one sells a considerable tract of land for a crown; for, as the price is only the estimation of the parties in regard to the value of the thing, a sum, which bears no proportion to that value, cannot pass for a serious estimation, nor consequently for a real price. . . . "[64] Furthermore, it cannot be considered as a real price when placed in the context of the Civil Code and its civil law institutions, particularly the commutative nature of the contract of sale.

But the question remains: when is a price an out of all proportion price? We must start with the fundamental premise that a sale is a commutative contract out of which each party expects to receive the equivalent, at least subjectively speaking, of what that party gives. In other words, the buyer expects, in his own determination and evaluation, that the price he pays is the equivalent, in value, of the thing he

---

[63] Which is the place of the seller, unless otherwise agreed by the parties; *see infra*, Obligations of the seller, p. 55.

[64] R.J. Pothier, *Traité du Contrat de Vente, Treatise on the Contract of Sale*, translation by L.S. Cushing, Charles C. Little and James Brown, MDCCCXXXIX, Part I. Sect. II #19, p. 12.

receives from the seller. That is the reason why an action in warranty is given to a buyer who has purchased a defective thing; this action will enable the buyer to "get his money's worth." Such is the normal and reasonable expectation of any buyer. Beyond the commutative nature of the contract of sale, we can find some guidance in some articles of the Civil Code. For example, article 2589 grants the seller of an immovable who sold that immovable for less than one half its fair market value the right to have the sale rescinded on the ground of lesion. It is reasonable to assume, from this article, that "less than half the fair market value" could be considered an out of all proportion price. **Civil Code article 2492** formulates a different method of calculating the difference in value between an immovable sold at the rate of so much per measure and the price for it: **"if . . . the seller is unable to deliver the full extent specified in the contract, the price must be proportionately reduced."** The commutative aspect of the contract of sale is, in this particular case, very strongly enforced. That is not the case, however, of a sale per aversionem under Civil Code article 2495[65] according to which there can be neither an increase nor a reduction in the price regardless of the extent of the discrepancy in the **surplus or shortage of the actual extension of the immovable.**

These examples of "value" of a thing, movable or immovable, vary widely and do not offer much guidance with respect to the existence of a common understanding as to the definition of an out of all proportion price, not only in sales of immovables, in which instances specific Code articles seem to take care of the matter, although in different ways, but mostly in sales of movables about which we find no specific illustrations in the Civil Code. This lack of illustrations should not deter the Louisiana Courts from giving their proper legal meaning to the inherent commutative nature of the contract of sale: a price should not be out of all proportion because each party, in her own mind and for herself, intends to receive the equivalent of what she gives. Buyers of movables, in particular, should not be forced to hide behind claims based on vices of consent, for example, or lack of fitness, to seek the nullity or the modification of a contract of sale in which the price paid is obviously, because "objectively," out of all proportion with the market value of the thing received.

Article 5
Lesionary Price and Rescission for Lesion Beyond Moiety

Civil Code article 2589 states that **"The sale of an immovable may be rescinded for lesion when the price is less than one half of the fair market value of the immovable. Lesion can be claimed only by the seller and only in sales of corporeal immovables. It cannot be alleged in a sale made by order of the court.**

The seller may invoke lesion even if he has renounced the right to claim it."

Lesion is a remedy whose origin and foundation are somewhat controversial, which may explain its very narrow scope of application and the strict conditions that must be met for an action in lesion to be available.

---

[65] On sale per measure, *per aversionem, see infra*, p. 62.

§ 2.5.1. CONDITIONS AND SCOPE OF APPLICATION OF THE ACTION IN LESION.

Lesion is a remedy available only to a seller of a corporeal immovable and only in sales other than judicial sales. The seller cannot renounce the action in lesion until after the sale has taken place. Should the seller then renounce the action in lesion he will be considered as having confirmed (La. C.C. art. 1842) the contract of sale which he could have challenged because of the relative nullity of that contract. Besides the seller, his "successors," may bring the action that the seller had. But, in the event there are several successors, **"each successor may bring the action for lesion only . . . for that share of the immovable corresponding to his right." (La. C.C. art. 2600.)** Creditors of the seller should have the same right of action against the buyer either under the *Pauliana action* (La. C.C. art. 2036) or the *oblique action* (La. C.C. art. 2044).

Because the action in lesion has a monetary value, and although the Civil Code is silent on this point, the action should be available to those parties who hold rights over their debtor's patrimony, such as the creditors of a debtor who would be selling a corporeal immovable at a lesionary price. The creditors should have the right to have the immovable returned to their debtor's patrimony, where they can then seize it, as a result of their bringing a *revocatory or Pauliana action* (La. C.C. arts. 2036–2043) or an *oblique action* (La. C.C. art. 2044).

As regards the scope of application of lesion, **article 2590** states that **"[t]o determine whether there is lesion, the immovable sold must be evaluated according to the state in which it was at the time of the sale. If the sale was preceded by an option contract, or by a contract to sell, the property must be evaluated in the state in which it was at the time of that contract."** Since most contracts of sale of a corporeal immovable follow a contract to sell that immovable, lesion will be determined on the basis of the value of the immovable at the time the contract to sell was entered into. The same will apply if an option was the first contract entered into, then followed by a contract to sell, that contract itself being followed by the sale; lesion will be determined at the time the option was entered into. Regardless of the number of contracts that may have preceded the sale, the action for lesion can be brought only after the sale and it **"must be brought within a peremptive period of one year from the time of the sale." (La. C.C. art. 2595.)**

§ 2.5.2. EXERCISE OF THE ACTION AND RIGHTS OF THE PARTIES.

It is most important to stress that the only right a seller enjoys out of an action in lesion is to have the sale rescinded. It should follow that the seller is to recover the ownership of the corporeal immovable he had sold within the immediate past year. A seller cannot choose to bring an action for an "alternative" right such as the right to demand a supplement in price to bring the sale price of the immovable closer to its fair market value. Only the buyer, when sued for the return of the immovable, **"may elect either to return the immovable to the seller, or to keep the immovable by giving to the seller a supplement equal to the difference between the price paid by the buyer and the fair market value of the immovable**

determined according to the preceding Article." (La. C.C. art. 2591.) When a buyer elects to return the immovable to the seller, he triggers the occurrence of an implied resolutory condition since the sale will be retroactively rescinded and the ownership of the immovable returned to the seller.

The rights of the parties following an action in lesion will depend on whether the buyer is still in possession or not of the immovable and, should he be in possession of the immovable, on what choice the buyer decides to make.

Should the buyer still be in possession of the immovable and elect **"to return the immovable he must also return to the seller the fruits of the immovable from the time a demand for rescission was made. In such a case, the seller must return to the buyer the price with interest from the same time." (La. C.C. art. 2592.)**

A partial extinction of one obligation or the other between the two parties could result from legal "compensation"[66] or from conventional compensation. On the other hand, should the buyer elect **"to keep the immovable he must also pay to the seller interest on the supplement from the time a demand for rescission was made." (La. C.C. art. 2592.)**

A buyer who chooses to return the corporeal immovable to the seller does so as an owner himself until the rescission of the sale. It follows that **"[w]hen the buyer has granted a right on the immovable to a third person, rescission may not impair the interest of that person. The seller who receives back the immovable so encumbered is entitled to recover from the buyer any diminution in value suffered by the immovable because of the right of the third person. That recovery may not exceed the supplement the seller would have recovered if the buyer had not encumbered the immovable and had decided to keep it." (La. C.C. art. 2596.)** An attempt is made to give its full retroactive effect to this equivalent to an implied resolutory condition brought about by the seller and to return the parties to the *status quo ante*. Since the rights that good faith third parties have received from the original buyer must be protected, but because they encumber the property and, thus, bring down its value, the buyer will have to make up for any diminution in value suffered by the immovable because of the right of third parties. But the buyer, who was a legitimate owner, should not be impoverished for the benefit of the original seller; in his respect, the law will set a limit to the amount of the recovery owed the seller. That recovery may not exceed the supplement the seller would have recovered if the buyer had not encumbered the immovable and had decided to keep it. (La. C.C. art. 2596.) The amount of this supplement and its limit are the same as those referred to in article 2594 discussed below.[67]

If a buyer should have granted rights to third persons and, thereby, encumbered the property, that same buyer may have caused deteriorations to the property while it was his. On the other hand, he may have made improvements on the property and increased its value. Here again the operation of the resolutory condition combined with the principle of *Unjust Enrichment* should lead to the return of the parties to

---

[66] On Compensation, see Précis, Louisiana Law of Obligations in General, p. 158–166.

[67] *See infra*, p. 34.

the *status quo ante* so that neither one should be enriched at the expense of the other. It is the policy reflected in **article 2597: "When rescission is granted for lesion the seller must take back the immovable in the state it is at that time. The buyer is not liable to the seller for any deterioration or loss sustained by the immovable before the demand for rescission was made, unless the deterioration or loss was turned into profit for the buyer.**

The seller must reimburse the buyer for the expenses of the sale and for those incurred for the improvement of the immovable, even if the improvement was made solely for the convenience of the buyer."

In the event the buyer is no longer in possession of the immovable, should the buyer have selected the alternative to sell the immovable, **"the seller may not bring an action for lesion against a third person who bought the immovable from the original buyer." (La. C.C. art. 2594-1.)** It is worth pointing out here an important difference regarding the position of a seller with the right of redemption[68] since the latter enjoys the right to bring an action against third persons who bought the immovable from the seller's first buyer. (La. C.C. art. 2572.)

This difference in treatment between "lesion" and "redemption" can be explained (but not justified, as we will attempt to illustrate below) by the history of "lesion". The drafters of the Civil Codes of 1825 and 1870 decided not to give a vendor who sells at a lesionary price the right to go against a third party buyer of the immovable. Such a right of action — a right in rem — that the French Civil Code granted and grants expressly to the seller, was therefore not incorporated into the Louisiana Civil Codes of 1825 and 1870. It follows that a seller who is protected, to some extent, by the law of lesion, is not as well protected as a seller who, in a contract of sale, has reserved to himself the right of redemption.[69] This conflict, we believe, is difficult to rationalize.

In the situation of a buyer who has subsequently resold the immovable, the seller may recover from that original buyer "whatever profit" the latter realized from the sale to the third person. That recovery may not exceed the supplement the seller would have recovered if the original buyer had chosen to keep the immovable. (La. C.C. art. 2594-2.) One may wonder what meaning to give to "whatever profit" when the recovery may not exceed the supplement the seller would have recovered from the original buyer, which is a supplement equal to the difference between the price paid by the buyer and the fair market value of the immovable. (La. C.C. art. 2591.) We assume that the amount of "whatever profit" the first party buyer must return to the seller is the difference between the lesionary price of the original sale and the resale price received from a second party buyer, whatever it is but within the limit of "a supplement," received from the second party buyer. We presume, thus, that the first buyer, now subsequent seller to the second party buyer, should keep for himself the "surplus profit" he could have made by selling to that second party buyer at a price above the lesionary price plus a supplement equal to the difference.

---

68 On the Right of Redemption, *see infra*, p. 46.

69 *See infra*, Sale with the Right of Redemption, p. 46.

§ 2.5.3. LESION AND INDIVISION.

Article 2600 is somewhat puzzling, as it appears to conflict with some well established rules of law on lesion. It provides as follows: **"If more than one seller concurred in the sale of an immovable owned by them in indivision, or if each of them sold separately his share of the immovable, each seller may bring an action for lesion for his share.**

Likewise, if a seller died leaving more than one successor, each successor may bring an action for lesion individually for that share of the immovable corresponding to his right."[70]

One first question we have about this article is prompted by the statement in article 2589 that lesion **can be claimed only . . . in sales of corporeal immovables.** Is a share in an immovable a corporeal immovable? Aren't corporeal things, **things that have a body . . . and can be felt or touched?** (La. C.C. art. 461.) **Rights and actions that apply to immovable things are incorporeal immovables,** according to the first sentence of article 470. Isn't a "share" of an immovable property like a right to an immovable thing and, therefore, an "incorporeal immovable" and not a corporeal immovable?

A second question regarding the applicability of lesion to an indivision or a share of an immovable is the nature of the right of the seller: a seller has only one right, which is to demand the return of the corporeal immovable. (La. C.C. art. 2589.) In defense to this action, the buyer may choose to return the immovable or pay a supplement. How is the buyer, under article 2600, to exercise "his" option? Return a share? Wouldn't that make the original seller who recovers "his share" in exchange for the return of its lesionary value (which means that the buyer is "forced" to pay something of value, money, instead of returning the immovable) now an owner in indivision with the buyer himself who "owns" another share or two other shares in indivision? How should one determine the amount of the difference in value between the price paid for the share and its fair market value, as required by article 2591?

Article 6
Form

The legal nature of the "thing" sold will determine the form or the lack thereof of the sale of that thing.

The sale of movable things is a consensual contract requiring only for its validity the exchange of consent of the parties to the sale. Civil Code article 518 is further explained by articles 2439 and 2456. This latter article states that **"[o]wnership is transferred between the parties as soon as there is agreement on the thing and the price is fixed, even though the thing sold is not yet delivered nor the price**

---

[70] This article is to serve as a model for Civil Code article 2584 which states:

"If more than one seller concurred in the sale with right of redemption of an immovable, or if a seller has died leaving more than one successor, the exercise of the right of redemption is governed by the rules provided for the division of the action for lesion among multiple sellers, or among successors of the seller or of the buyer.

paid." Article 1846 is concerned only with the burden of proof and not with a writing as a requirement for the validity of a contract. These articles which do not expressly refer to movables have to be read in contrast, or *a contrario*, with other Code articles which refer to immovables specifically and, therefore, are applicable to immovables only.

Civil Code articles 517, 1832, 1839 and 2440 do require, as a general rule, a writing for the validity of a contract bearing on an immovable. **Article 2440** states very clearly that **"[a] sale or promise of sale of an immovable must be made by authentic act or by act under private signature, except as provided in Article 1839.**" The exception mentioned in this latter article is to the effect that **"an oral transfer is valid between the parties when the property has been actually delivered and the transferor recognizes the transfer when interrogated on oath."**[71]

---

[71] La. C.C. art. 1839-1. *See also* La. C.C. arts. 2620 & 2623. On Registry, see La. C.C. arts. 3338–3368.

Chapter 3

EFFECTS OF A CONTRACT OF SALE

Upon its perfection, a contract of sale will have two effects which, in turn, will create obligations on the seller and the buyer. One first and essential effect of a perfected contract of sale is to transfer the ownership of the thing sold from the seller to the buyer; the second effect of such a contract is to transfer the risk of loss of the thing from the seller to the buyer. In turn, these two effects of a contract of sale create obligations on the parties to the contract. The seller's obligations are to deliver the thing to the buyer, to warrant the buyer against eviction and to warrant the buyer against redhibitory defects in the thing sold. As regards the buyer, he is under the obligation to pay the price and to remove the thing that has been delivered by the seller.

In this Chapter 3 we will look at the two essential "Effects of the contract of sale" and in Chapter 4 we will analyze the obligations of the seller and buyer as created by the contract of sale.

ARTICLE 1
TRANSFER OF OWNERSHIP

The Louisiana Civil Code expresses, on the one hand, some basic "Principles" and, on the other hand, a variety of possible "Alterations" of these Principles.

§ 3.1.1. PRINCIPLES.

The principles on the transfer of ownership are few and are explained by the nature, movable or immovable, of the thing sold. Besides referring to the moment of the transfer of ownership of that movable or that immovable between the parties, the principles are also concerned with the timing of the transfer of ownership between seller and buyer as affecting third parties.

With respect to immovables, we find the same principles expressed in three Code articles, 517 in Book II of the Civil Code and 2440 and 2442 in Book III of the Civil Code:

Article 517 states: **"The ownership of an immovable is voluntarily transferred by a contract between the owner and the transferee that purports to transfer the ownership of the immovable. The transfer of ownership takes place between the parties by the effect of the agreement and is not effective against third persons until the contract is filed for registry in the conveyance records of the parish in which the immovable is located."**

Article 2440 states: **"A sale or promise of sale of an immovable must be made by authentic act or by act under private signature, except as provided in Article**

1839."

This article should be read in conjunction with **article 2442** so as to parallel article 517. Article 2442 reads as follows: **"The parties to an act of sale or promise of sale of immovable property are bound from the time the act is made, but such an act is not effective against third parties until it is filed for registry according to the laws of registry."**

As to the transfer of ownership of movable things, we find again two sets of articles: art. 518 in Book II and art. 2456 in Book III:

Article 518 states: **"The ownership of a movable is voluntarily transferred by a contract between the owner and the transferee that purports to transfer the ownership of the movable. Unless otherwise provided, the transfer of ownership takes place as between the parties by the effect of the agreement and against third persons when the possession of the movable is delivered to the transferee. When possession has not been delivered, a subsequent transferee to whom possession is delivered acquires ownership provided he is in good faith. Creditors of the transferor may seize the movable while it is still in his possession."**

Article 2456 states: **"Ownership is transferred between the parties as soon as there is agreement on the thing and the price is fixed, even though the thing sold is not yet delivered nor the price paid."**

A single **article, 2467,** makes up a whole Chapter, Chapter 6 "At whose risk the thing is, after the sale is completed." This article reads as follows: **"The risk of loss of the thing sold owing to a fortuitous event is transferred from the seller to the buyer at the time of delivery. That risk is so transferred even when the seller has delivered a nonconforming thing, unless the buyer acts in the manner required to dissolve the contract."**

An important change to the Louisiana law of sale as it existed under the Civil Code of 1870 did take place with Acts 1993, No. 841. Since the implementation in Jan. 1995 of the law of 1993, the transfer of ownership and the transfer of risk of loss have been dissociated, split, so that the ownership will pass first but the risk of loss will pass only with the delivery of the thing sold, meaning that the risk of loss is actually tied to the possession of the thing. One reason that can be given for this splitting of ownership and risk of loss is that the party who is in possession of the thing sold is the one more likely to have that thing insured and, therefore, it is reasonable to state as a principle, susceptible of modifications, that she ought to bear the loss of the thing she has insured. Strangely enough, the Louisiana law of 1993-95 has made an about-face and reverted to its Roman law origin.

One should add to these long-established principles a new rule of law incorporated in the Louisiana Civil Code and borrowed from international transactions. As regards the ownership of "things in transit," **article 2613** states:

"When, according to the terms of the contract, the seller sends the things to the buyer through a common carrier, the form of the bill of lading determines ownership of the things while in transit.

When the bill of lading makes the things deliverable to the buyer, or to his order, ownership of the things is thereby transferred to the buyer.

When the bill of lading makes the things deliverable to the seller, or to his agent, ownership of the things thereby remains with the seller.

When the seller or his agent remains in possession of a bill of lading that makes the things deliverable to the buyer, or to the buyer's order, the seller thereby reserves the right to retain the things against a claim of the buyer who has not performed his obligations."

With respect to the transfer of the risk of loss of these same things, **article 2616** states: **"When the contract requires the seller to ship the things through a carrier, but does not require him to deliver the things at any particular destination, the risk of loss is transferred to the buyer upon delivery of the things to the carrier, regardless of the form of the bill of lading.**

When the contract of sale requires the seller to deliver the things at a particular destination, the risk of loss is transferred to the buyer when the things, while in possession of the carrier, are duly tendered to the buyer at the place of destination.

When the parties incorporate well established commercial symbols into their contract, the risk of loss is transferred in accordance with the customary understanding of such symbols."

§ 3.1.2. MODIFICATIONS, ALTERATIONS OF THE PRINCIPLES.

If the principles are few, and rather easy to apply, there are many possible alterations or modifications that either the Code itself or the parties to a contract of sale can bring to these principles. The importance of these modifications/ alterations is that they emphasize this fundamental notion that a contract of sale, when it is perfect or complete, *does not* necessarily and always *transfer immediately* the ownership of the thing sold from the seller to the buyer. If the transfer of ownership of a thing is of the essence of a contract of sale, in this sense that it is the *raison d"être* of such a contract, that is why a buyer buys and a seller sells, this transfer does not have to occur immediately upon agreement, oral or in writing, between the parties. The Code offers some examples of sales wherein the ownership of the thing sold is transferred to the buyer some time, short or long, after the completion of the sale. These examples illustrate the fact that an immediate transfer of ownership upon perfection of a contract of sale is not a rule of public order. The Code itself provides for modifications and parties to a contract of sale are invited to devise their own kind of sale as a contractual modification of the principles formulated in the Code.

A. Codal Modifications/Alterations to the Immediate Transfer of Ownership.

1. *Thing to be Individualized.*

One first such modification is provided by Civil Code article 2457 which is, in the law of Sale, but an application of some rules applicable to conventional obligations as stated in articles 1973, 1974 and 1975.

Article 2457 states: **"When the object of a sale is a thing that must be individualized from a mass of things of the same kind, ownership is transferred when the thing is thus individualized according to the intention of the parties."** This "individualization" of the thing sold is to take place in the future, after the seller, for example, has taken the time to "individualize" what he sold. As a result, the transfer of ownership of that thing is delayed, postponed, suspended . . . until the thing has been individualized from a mass of things of the same kind. This process of individualization can consist in isolating the thing on a shelf, pasting a label on the thing, packaging the thing . . . etc . . . It follows that when a thing has to be individualized, the transfer of ownership is subject to a suspensive condition in the same manner as is the ownership of a future thing, **the coming into existence of [which] is a condition that suspends the effects of the sale.**[72] Since we are dealing, here, with a suspensive condition, upon occurrence of that condition there would be retroactivity of the ownership of the thing for the benefit of the buyer as of the date of perfection of the contract.[73] Reasoning from "the greater to the lesser" (*a majori ad minus*), from "condition" to "term," there is absolutely no obstacle of public order that would prevent parties to a sale to decide to postpone, by way of a suspensive term of a few days or weeks, the transfer of ownership of the thing sold. In this particular instance there would be no retroactivity of the transfer of ownership to the date of perfection of the contract of sale.[74]

A sale of a percentage, 25% or 40%, is not a sale of a thing to be individualized but the sale of a right, a thing immediately existing, which makes the buyer an owner in indivision, a co-owner of an incorporeal thing.

2. *Thing Sold by Weight, Tale or Measure and Sale in a Lump.*

Article 2458 states: **"When things are sold by weight, tale, or measure, ownership is transferred between the parties when the seller, with the buyer's consent, weighs, counts or measures the things.**

When things, such as goods or produce, are sold in a lump, ownership is transferred between the parties upon their consent, even though the things are not yet weighed, counted, or measured."

---

[72] La. C.C. art. 2450. On Future Things, see *supra*, p. 21.

[73] On Condition, see Précis: Louisiana Law of Obligations in General, p. 39–54.

[74] On Term, see Précis: Louisiana Law of Obligations in General, p. 28–39.

Under the first paragraph of this article, the ownership of the item to be weighed/counted will pass upon the individualization of that item following the process of weighing/counting. In this case again there exists a suspensive condition the occurrence of which will have a retroactive effect.

The second paragraph of this same article reverts to the general principle **"When things, such as goods or produce, are sold in a lump, ownership is transferred between the parties upon their consent, even though the things are not yet weighed, counted, or measured."** The ownership of the "lump" passes at the time of the agreement between the parties. Although no reference is made here to the price being a lump price or a determinable price, we believe that in a sale of a lump thing, the price itself should be a lump price. One reason is that one object in a contract of sale should be treated in the same manner, a parallel manner, as the other object; thus a lump thing should have as its parallel a lump price. Another reason can be found, by analogy, in the sale of an immovable for a lump price (La. C.C. art. 2494) and in the sale of a certain and limited body or a distinct object sold for a lump price (La. C.C. art. 2495). In these instances a lump thing is matched with a lump price.

3. *Thing Sold on View or Trial.*

"When the buyer has reserved the view or trial of the thing, ownership is not transferred from the seller to the buyer until the latter gives his approval of the thing." (La. C.C. art. 2460.) It is possible to contemplate two different kinds of sale on view or trial depending on whether the buyer is viewing or trying a "sample" of the principal thing he intends to buy eventually or whether he is "viewing or trying" that principal thing itself he wishes to buy.

In the first instance, if we assume that the potential buyer approves the "sample" he received from the seller, the sale cannot yet be complete or perfect until the principal thing can become the "object" of the seller's obligation.

Three different legal relationships now present themselves to the buyer and the seller. One relationship can be described as the sale being perfect, and the ownership transferred to the buyer, as soon as the seller has individualized the principal thing, out of a mass for example. In such a case the sale would be somewhat like the sale of a thing to be weighed or counted, thus a thing to be individualized. One should add, here, that the seller would be bound by an obligation to act in good faith in making sure that the principal thing he will deliver to the buyer matches perfectly the sample previously approved by the buyer. A breach of that obligation by the seller would be tantamount to the occurrence of a resolutory condition.[75] We can find some support for this kind of legal relationship in articles 2603 to 2606 which are presented below.[76]

A second and very different type of relationship between buyer and seller following approval of a sample by the buyer would give that buyer the choice and ultimate decision of perfecting or not the contract of sale. The sample is just that,

---

[75] On Resolutory Condition, see Précis: Louisiana Law of Obligations in General, p. 40–41.

[76] *See infra*, p. 42.

a "sample"; it is like an advertisement which is made available to a "customer" in the hope he would become a "buyer." Neither the advertisement nor the sample are the actual things that will be sold. So, it is possible to look at the buyer expressing his "agreement" that the "principal thing" he receives from the seller does fully conform to the sample previously approved as, actually, the buyer's consent to the sale itself. The sale would then be perfected at that time only, with possession of the principal thing being in the hands of the buyer before the sale is actually perfect or complete, which is not an unusual situation in business transactions, and without retroactivity to the time the principal thing had been individualized by the seller.

A third approach to the relationship between buyer and seller in a sale by sample could be to equate the buyer expressing his agreement to a suspensive condition consisting in stating his "approval" by way of "confirmation" of his prior consent given on the basis of the sample. In this situation, the occurrence of the suspensive condition would have retroactive effect to the time the buyer approved the sample.

Since the retroactive effect of conditions, whether suspensive or resolutory, creates problems and difficulties[77], particularly as regards the rights of third persons whenever movables are involved, our preference goes to the second type of relationship and, thus, to look at the "approval" of the principal thing by the buyer as the actual consent of the latter so as to "complete" the contract of sale and vest the ownership of the principal thing in the buyer as of that time only.

4. *Buyer's Right to Inspect.*[78]

Under Civil Code article 2603, **"[t]he seller must deliver to the buyer things that conform to the contract. Things do not conform to the contract when they are different from those selected by the buyer or are of a kind, quality, or quantity different from the one agreed."** This obligation imposed on the seller is balanced (or secured?) by the buyer's **"right to have a reasonable opportunity to inspect the things, even after delivery, for the purpose of ascertaining whether they conform to the contract." (La. C.C. art. 2604.)** As stated above with respect to a sale on view or trial, it is essential to determine the legal nature of this right of inspection; is it tantamount to a suspensive condition, or to a resolutory condition or, still, to the actual consent, i.e. acceptance, of the buyer? If, under article 2605, the buyer may reject nonconforming things within a reasonable time, is that buyer rejecting those noncorforming things as their "owner"? As their "possessor" after he received delivery from the seller? Does article 2606 provide some guidance where it states that, **"A buyer who, with knowledge, accepts nonconforming things may no longer reject those things on grounds of that nonconformity, unless the acceptance was made in the reasonable belief that the nonconformity would be cured?"** The verb "accepts" and the noun "acceptance," if taken literally, would suggest that the sale is not perfect or complete until then, until the buyer "accepts" the nonconforming goods and that, therefore, the ownership of those things does not pass to the buyer until that same time of acceptance. On the other hand, one could read the verb "accepts" and the noun "acceptance" as

---

[77] *See* Précis: Louisiana Law of Obligations in General, p. 51 *et seq.*

[78] *See* comments, *supra* p. 18, on the new articles 2601–2617 on Sales of Movables.

referring only to the nonconforming things which, because they are nonconforming, become "new objects, new things" different from the conforming things, and must, therefore, be "accepted" as such by the buyer. Our preference would be to look at the right of inspection as similar to the right of view or trial and, therefore, to look at the approval given by the buyer following his inspection as equivalent to "consent or acceptance". The ownership, therefore, would not pass to the buyer until he would have completed his inspection of the thing delivered by the seller. We believe that **article 2607** provides some support for this view where it refers to an acceptance by the buyer of conforming things upon delivery by the seller; acceptance or consent is expressed at that time only. This article states: **"Out of a quantity of things delivered by the seller, the buyer may accept those things that conform to the contract and form a commercial unit and may reject those that do not conform. The buyer must pay at the contract rate for any things that are accepted."**

Furthermore, where article 2610 gives the seller the right to "cure" the nonconformity, it is because the thing must be brought to the condition in which it should have been for the buyer to give his consent or acceptance. To cure a nonconformity in a thing is to make the thing fit for its ordinary use or for the particular use a buyer intended for the thing. It is not the same thing as repairing a defect, a vice, in the thing.[79] An obligation to cure is the fulfillment of a primary obligation to deliver the very thing on which the parties have agreed, subjectively or objectively, whereas an obligation of warranty is an accessory obligation resulting from a hidden defect in the principal thing. As will be discussed below in Warranty Against Defects, the distinction between noncorforming things and defective things is not always easy to make.

Article 2608[80], is somewhat parallel to article 2605 in that both articles deal with the rejection of the thing and either the reasonable notice given by the buyer or the reasonable instructions given by the seller. However, the two articles differ in this very important respect: article 2605 applies to ordinary, non-professional buyers and sellers, whereas article 2608 applies specifically to merchants. This article requires no "civil law" comment here as it is an almost verbatim transposition of article 2-603 of the UCC which provides details helpful in understanding the background of article 2608 of the Louisiana Civil Code.

---

[79] *See* Warranty Against Defects *infra*.

[80] The text of article 2608 reads as follows: **"When the seller has no agent or business office at the place of delivery, a buyer who is a merchant and has rejected the things must follow any reasonable instructions received from the seller with respect to those things. If the seller gives no such instructions, and the things rejected are perishable or susceptible of rapid decline in value, the merchant buyer must make reasonable efforts to sell those things on the seller's behalf.**

In all instances of rejection, a buyer who is a merchant must handle the rejected things as a prudent administrator."

5. *Things in Transit.*

Articles 2613, 2614, 2616 and 2617[81] were incorporated in the Civil Code in 1993 for the purpose of applying specifically to contracts of sale of things that have to be "carried," "transported," or "shipped," things therefore that are entrusted to a carrier for delivery to the buyer. Since these Code articles have been shaped and framed on the basis of the UCC and the CISG we will restrict ourselves here, for reasons of space, to providing references to these two texts: UCC § 2-703 *et seq.*; UCC § 7-301 *et seq.*; CISG, Articles 66 to 69, Art.71.

B. Conventional Alterations to the Immediate Transfer of Ownership.

Since the "Law" allows for alterations to the principle of the immediate transfer of ownership of the movable thing upon mere exchange of consent between the parties, the principles of freedom of contract and public order avail natural and legal persons of the right of adapting the timing of the transfer of ownership from the seller to the buyer as they wish. We will describe here some "conventional alterations" to the transfer of ownership.

1. *Lay Away Sale.*

In a Lay Away sale, the seller retains possession of the thing until the buyer has paid the price. But such a sale must not run afoul of the "jurisprudential prohibition" of the conditional sale, which will be addressed below.

Two types of lay away sales are conceivable. In one type, the thing which the buyer wants to buy is not individualized or singled out from a larger quantity or mass and will not be individualized until later or until a particular event occurs. In the meantime the buyer pays regularly (or not) a definite amount (or not) until the thing is individualized. Before individualization of the thing, its ownership is with the seller and so is the risk of loss. This type of lay away sale resembles the sale of a future thing that is itself tantamount to a sale under a suspensive condition, i.e. of the thing coming into existence.

In the second type of lay away sale, the seller singles out, individualizes the thing the buyer wants but the seller retains its possession until the buyer comes up with the price. In this instance, the ownership of the thing passes to the buyer upon individualization and by mere consent but the risk of loss remains with the seller as delivery has not taken place, because, essentially, the seller has possession of that thing and must take care of it for the buyer as he is in a better position to have insurance on the thing.

---

[81] Article 2615 is out of place in between these articles on Things in Transit and should be relocated as it deals with a general remedy available to both the seller and the buyer and resembles, to some extent, the contents of article 2013.

2. *Conditional Sale.*

We have seen above the contract of sale of a future thing as regulated by the Civil Code. In such a sale, the ownership of the thing does not pass to the buyer until a future event happens, i.e. the thing coming into existence. In other words, the sale is perfect but the transfer of ownership is suspended until the event happens. It is important to remember that, in such a sale, the thing sold is the object of the seller's obligation to deliver, to make available to the buyer. It would seem perfectly logical and reasonable to treat the other object in a contract of sale — the *price* — in the same manner as the *thing* is treated by the Civil Code. Yet, ever since a 1908 decision of the Louisiana Supreme Court[82] the jurisprudence has stood firm on its grounds and has ruled as being impossible and non-existent a contract of sale of a movable which makes the transfer of ownership of the movable conditional upon the payment of the price. The Court basically ruled that a sale that does not transfer ownership is an impossibility. Needless to say that such a ruling is totally unjustified and fails to understand, first, the legal nature of a suspensive condition with its retroactive effect, second, the parallelism created in the Civil Code in the treatment of a "future *thing*" and the treatment of "a future *price*" and, third, the absence in the Civil Code of any provision stating that the transfer of ownership upon mere exchange of consent of the parties was a rule of public order and could not be deviated from. As a consequence of this decision the Louisiana Legislature had to step in to "foster the leasing of movable property to individuals and businesses, thus providing economic growth and development. To this end, financed leases, which have previously been construed as conditional sales transactions, are hereby recognized as valid and enforceable in this state."[83] Furthermore, whereas the conditional sale of movables upon payment of the price was not recognized by the jurisprudence in clear violation of the Code articles, the Legislator, in a Revised Statute again, created the "Bond for Deed" which it defined as "a contract to sell real property, in which the purchase price is to be paid by the buyer to the seller in installments and in which the seller after payment of stipulated sum agrees to deliver title to the buyer."[84]

3. *Sale or Return.*

A contract of sale or return looks very much like the combination of two sales with each party changing position from one contract to the other. As the conjunction "or" suggests, such a contract falls under the broad understanding of alternative obligations.[85] Basically, the seller sells a certain number of items to the buyer with the understanding that, should the buyer having failed to sell these items to others and remain in possession of some of these items by the end of a certain period, that buyer could exercise the alternative of "returning" these remaining items to the seller. Such a contract of sale is very much like a sale with a resolutory condition. The event consisting in the resolutory condition is the decision of the buyer to

[82] *Barber Asphalt Paving Co. v. St Louis Cypress Co. Ltd.*, 121 La. 152, 46 So. 193, 1908.

[83] La. R.S. § 9:3302.

[84] La. R.S. § 9:2941.

[85] *See* Précis: Louisiana Law of Obligations in General, p. 73–77.

return the remaining items. So, as long as the buyer of all the items sold to him by the seller has not triggered the occurrence of the resolutory condition, the buyer is the owner and bears the risk of loss. When the resolutory condition occurs, the ownership of the remaining items reverts back to the original seller who will refund to the buyer the price of the items returned.

This type of contract of sale must be distinguished from a contract of *consignment*. In the latter contract one party, the consignor, entrusts to the other, the consignee, the possession of some movable items for the consignee to sell on behalf of the consignor, actual owner of the items. A consignment is somewhat similar to a contract of representation (La. C.C. art. 2985) or a contract of mandate (La. C.C. art. 2989; *see also* UCC § 2-326).

Article 2
Sale with a Right of Redemption

§ 3.2.1. CONCEPT.

The large number of Code articles devoted to this topic (La. C.C. arts. 2567–2588) is not illustrative of the use made of this type of sale in real life. There are few cases, and even less recent cases, dealing with the right of redemption. For that reason, we do not intend to elaborate on this form of sale.

Selling an item — a tract of land in most instances — with the right of redemption was a device meant to enable an owner, short on cash, to receive quickly what he was lacking, cash, by selling some land but with the definite intent, after a certain while, to get that land back, to redeem it, by "repaying" to the buyer a price in money for that same land. To that effect, the seller would expressly reserve to himself in the contract of sale the right to buy back, in the future, what was his property at one time. Considering that few buyers, of land in particular, would want to enter into this type of sale, it should not be a surprise to find very few cases on this matter. Yet, a sale with the right of redemption raises so many important issues that it deserves a selective analysis of these issues.

The Louisiana Civil Code defines this type of sale as follows: **The parties to a contract of sale may agree that the seller shall have the right of redemption, which is the right to take back the thing from the buyer. (La. C.C. art. 2567.)** A sale with the right of redemption is but a sale with a resolutory condition as regards the thing sold.[86] Since, here, it is the seller who has reserved to himself the right of redemption, the right to bring about the resolutory condition, this sale is different from a sale with an option to repurchase in which it would be the buyer who would grant to the seller that option. The legal regimes of the two types of sale differ.

---

[86] On Resolutory Condition, see Précis: Louisiana Law of Obligations in General, p. 39–54.

§ 3.2.2. LEGAL REGIME.

The distinction can be important when one looks at the time period allowed for an option in contrast with the time period allowed for a right of redemption. We have seen that in an Option bearing on an immovable the absolute time limitation for a valid Option is ten years.[87] The same time limit applies to the right of redemption which may not be reserved for more than ten years when the thing sold is an immovable. (La. C.C. art. 2568.) As regards an Option bearing on a movable, article 2620 merely requires that there be a stipulated time. On the other hand, in a sale with the right of redemption the seller must exercise his right within an absolute limit of ten or five years and **"if a longer time for redemption has been stipulated in the contract that time must be reduced to either ten or five years, depending on the nature of the thing sold." (La. C.C. art. 2568.)** If the right of redemption is not exercised within the prescribed time periods, the buyer then becomes the unconditional owner of the thing sold. (La. C.C. art. 2570.) Most importantly, the time period is not a prescriptive period that could be suspended or interrupted, but a peremptive period that runs against all persons including minors. It may not be extended by the court. (La. C.C. art. 2571.)

A. Object and Price.

The object to be "redeemed" or recovered by the seller is that very object that was sold. As article 2567 states, the right of redemption **". . . is the right to take back the thing from the buyer."** It is that same thing that the seller can recover from third parties (La. C.C. art. 2572) and that he can recover free of encumbrances (La. C.C. art. 2588). It is, therefore, that very same thing that was originally sold.

As to the price that the original seller who wants to redeem the thing he has sold will have to pay back to the original and first buyer, the Civil Code does not require that the price of redemption be the same as the price of the sale. Actually, because the nature of the sale with the right of redemption equates it, to some extent, to what a loan with the granting of a thing as a security would be, it is possible for the parties to the sale to stipulate in that contract that the price of redemption will be higher than the price of the sale just like in a loan the lender is entitled to the payment of interest over the duration of the loan. Therefore, the higher price of a redemption is justified by the right that the "buyer-lender" would have had to receive interest from the "seller-borrower" over the period opened for the exercise of the right of redemption or, its equivalent, the duration of the loan.

B. Effects of the Right of Redemption.

When a sale with the right of redemption bears on an immovable and that contract of sale has been recorded, the seller's **"right of redemption is effective against third persons only from the time the instrument that contains it is filed for registry in the parish where the immovable is located." (La. C.C. art. 2572-1.)** Third parties are put on notice by the Public Records that this particular

---

[87] On Option, see *supra*, p. 9.

sale could be "rescinded" as a result of the seller exercising his right to redeem.

It is most interesting to ask why a seller with the right of redemption is allowed to get his immovable back from a third person when the seller of an immovable at a lesionary price is denied the same right of action against the third party buyer, considering that both types of sale are recorded in the Public Records for all to see. Why is a seller who protects himself in a contract (for as long as ten years) better "protected" than a seller who, under the "Law", is presumed to have made an error or to have been forced to sell at a lesionary price, particularly when the right to bring an action for lesion is limited to only one year from the sale?

Since there is no Public Records for movables, if a sale with the right of redemption bears on a movable that the buyer has alienated to a third person before the seller does exercise his right of redemption, the seller's right to go against the third person will be effective only if, at the time of purchase, that third person had actual knowledge of the existence of that right (La. C.C. art. 2572-2). It is worth noting that article 2572 does require actual knowledge or subjective knowledge[88] on the part of the third person. Why not apply the standard of good faith of article 3481 which states, **"Good faith is presumed. . . . This presumption is rebutted on proof that the possessor knows, or should know, that he is not owner of the thing he possesses."**

The first buyer and, we believe, third party buyers, may raise the benefit of discussion when the creditors of the seller attempt to get to the thing sold to a buyer before these creditors should have attempted to go against the property of their primary debtor, i.e. the seller under the right of redemption (La. C.C. art. 2574; La. C.Civ.P. art. 5151).

Should the seller be successful in the exercise of his right of redemption against the buyer, the latter will keep the fruits and the products of the thing sold up to the time of the exercise of the right of redemption. (La. C.C. art. 2575.) The buyer is also **"entitled to all improvements he made on the thing that can be removed when the seller exercises the right of redemption. If such improvements cannot be removed, the buyer is entitled to the enhancement of the value of the thing resulting from the improvements. The buyer is also entitled to the enhancement of the value of the thing resulting from ungathered fruits and unharvested crops.**

If the thing sold under right of redemption is naturally increased by accession, alluvion, or accretion before the redeeming seller exercises the right, the increase belongs to the seller." (La. C.C. art. 2577.)

As regards the improvements that cannot be removed, it is worth pointing out that the buyer is only entitled to the enhancement of the value resulting from the improvements. This buyer, for reasons we cannot explain, is not as well treated as a possessor in good faith who, under article 496, is given the benefit of three alternatives and not just one as under article 2577. Is it that a buyer in a sale with the right of redemption is not a good faith possessor because he knows of the possibility of the sale being rescinded? Is the fact that he consented to allow the

---

[88] On Actual Knowledge, see *supra*, p. 6.

seller to reserve his right of redemption held against him when he entered the contract of sale with the intent, or subjective cause, to help to some extent the seller who, likely, needed cash? Is the buyer only a "precarious" owner?

This might be the explanation behind article 2578, which requires that the buyer administer the thing sold with the degree of care of a prudent administrator and which holds him liable for any deterioration caused by the lack of such care. But, why, then is this duty of care the same as that of a "manager" or "gestor" under article 2295 (a person who acts without authority to protect the interests of another) and not that of a party who acts under a contract, such as a mandatary (prudence and diligence) under article 3001 or that of a depositary (diligence and prudence) under article 2930?

The buyer under a right of redemption is entitled, at least, to be paid by the seller the expenses of the sale and the reimbursement of the expenses he incurred in making the necessary repairs to preserve the thing in a good condition. (La. C.C. art. 2587.)

As regards encumbrances that the buyer may have placed on the immovable while under his ownership, **article 2588** is a logical application of article 2572 where it states that **"[t]he seller who exercises the right of redemption is entitled to recover the thing free of any encumbrances placed upon it by the buyer. Nevertheless, when the thing is an immovable, the interests of third persons are governed by the laws of registry."**

Once again, it is appropriate to point out here that a seller of an immovable who has the right to bring an action in lesion[89] not only cannot bring this action against a third party purchaser to recover the immovable (La. C.C. art. 2594) but, even more, that same seller, should he be able to bring an action in lesion against his own buyer, will have to receive back the immovable from that buyer with the encumbrances created by the latter for the benefit of third persons.

Article 3
Risk of Loss

Few Code articles address the issue of the transfer of the risk of loss from the seller to the buyer. Actually, only one article, 2467, is listed under the title of Chapter 6 "At Whose Risk the Thing is, After the Sale is Completed." On the other hand, other persuasive sources of law devote more space to the treatment of that issue mainly because they are more "commercially" inspired than the Louisiana Civil Code.[90] Still, following the 1993–1995 legislative revision of the law of sale, one must add to article 2467 a few new articles on "Sales of Movables."

---

[89] On Lesion, see *supra*, p. 31.

[90] *See* the UCC: for example, § 2-303, § 2-509, § 2-510; see the CISG: for example, articles 66 to 70; see also on "Damages": articles 74 to 77.

§ 3.3.1. RISK OF LOSS AND FORTUITOUS EVENT.

"The risk of loss of the thing sold owing to a fortuitous event is transferred from the seller to the buyer at the time of delivery.

That risk is so transferred even when the seller has delivered a nonconforming thing, unless the buyer acts in the manner required to dissolve the contract." (La. C.C. art. 2467.)

The policy reason that justifies the rule stated in this article is that the party in possession of the thing is in the best position to protect it from a risk of loss in addition to being the party most likely to have insurance for the loss of the thing. A major change occurred in 1993–1995 when the new law of sale separated or split the transfer of ownership from the transfer of risk of loss. Until then, and contrary to what was the Roman law on these issues, Louisiana law was in line with most civil law jurisdictions which had adopted the policy of tying the transfer of risk of loss to the transfer of ownership. Hence the maxim "*res perit domino.*" Today, the law of sale of the Louisiana Civil Code treats separately the transfer of ownership from the transfer of risk of loss, thereby adopting the practical positions of the UCC and the CISG.

As regards the sale of movable things, delivery of the thing will trigger the shift of the risk of loss from the seller to the buyer. Delivery of a movable thing[91] being merely the handing over of the movable to the buyer (La. C.C. art. 2477-2), the risk of loss will pass to the buyer at the moment the buyer takes delivery of the thing (La. C.C. art. 2549).

As regards the transfer of the risk of loss in a sale of an immovable thing, **"delivery . . . is deemed to take place upon execution of the writing that transfers its ownership." (La. C.C. art. 2477-1.)**

In the event the loss affecting the thing sold is only partial between the time of the transfer of ownership to the buyer and the time of delivery by the seller, article 1861 states that an obligee may refuse to accept a partial performance. The buyer could refuse to accept that partial performance with, of course, a reduction in his own performance, i.e. a reduction in the price. However, under **article 2014, "A contract may not be dissolved when the obligor has rendered a substantial part of the performance and the part not rendered does not substantially impair the interest of the obligee."** In this particular instance, the Court will have to decide whether or not the seller is in a position to carry out, i.e. deliver, a substantial part of his performance. Article 2014, which aims at preserving as much as possible the integrity of contracts is supported in its aim by **article 1877** which provides that **"When a fortuitous event has made a party's performance impossible in part, the court may reduce the other party's counterperformance proportionally, or, according to the circumstances, may declare the contract dissolved."**

---

[91] See the discussion on Deliver, *infra* p. 55 *et seq.*

§ 3.3.2. RISK OF LOSS AND MOVABLES.

Article 2616 is restricted in its field of application to sales of things in transit, things that are shipped through a carrier. It provides as follows:

"When the contract requires the seller to ship the things through a carrier, but does not require him to deliver the things at any particular destination, the risk of loss is transferred to the buyer upon delivery of the things to the carrier, regardless of the form of the bill of lading.

When the contract of sale requires the seller to deliver the things at a particular destination, the risk of loss is transferred to the buyer when the things, while in possession of the carrier, are duly tendered to the buyer at the place of destination.

When the parties incorporate well established commercial symbols into their contract, the risk of loss is transferred in accordance with the customary understanding of such symbols."

The focus of attention should be either on the existence of a place of destination where delivery is to occur, or on the addition of commercial symbols in the contract. In this respect, one should look not only at the UCC (§ 2-509 *et seq.*) but, more specifically at the CISG (Arts. 66–69) and at the INCOTERMS of the International Chamber of Commerce.

Chapter 4

OBLIGATIONS OF THE SELLER AND THE BUYER

A Contract of Sale being a synallagmatic and commutatitve contract (*see* La. C.C. arts. 1908 & 1911), it imposes obligations on both parties to that contract. As the Civil Code does, we will study "The Obligations of the Seller" first (Louisiana Civil Code Book III, Title VII, Chap. 7) and "The Obligations of the Buyer" second (Louisiana Civil Code Book III, Title VII, Chap. 10). However, since the relevant Chapters 7 and 10 are not all-inclusive and self-sufficient, many Code articles from other Titles and Chapters in the Civil Code will be brought into our analysis of these two topics.

Article 1
Obligations of the Seller

The first article listed under this Title, **2474**, lays down a general rule or principle[92] which is tailored to fit the contract of sale: **"The seller must clearly express the extent of his obligations arising from the contract, and any obscurity or ambiguity in that expression must be interpreted against the seller."** Since the import of this article is more relevant to the law of Conventional Obligations than the law of Sale, it is mentioned here only as a reminder of the general rule it restates. However, because this general rule stands out as some sort of a warning to all sellers that they better express themselves clearly and unambiguously as to the extent of their obligations, sellers are hereby put on notice that a buyer, presumably the weaker of the two parties to the contract of sale, will benefit from the protection of the law. Therefore, the courts should comply with and implement that concern of the legislator whenever a seller is attempting to exonerate himself from any obligation imposed by law.[93]

Besides this general obligation imposed on a seller, more specific obligations deriving from the nature of the contract of sale are listed in **article 2475: "The seller is bound to deliver the thing sold and to warrant to the buyer ownership and peaceful possession of, and the absence of hidden defects in, that thing. The seller also warrants that the thing sold is fit for its intended use."** We can identify three obligations, of a different legal nature, to be carried out by the seller: an obligation of delivery, an obligation of warranty that the buyer will not be evicted from the ownership of the thing he bought and an obligation of warranty to the buyer against hidden defects or vices in the thing purchased.

The second sentence of article 2475 refers to a subject matter, "fitness," which is different from the previously mentioned obligation of warranty against defects

[92] A contract is to be read and interpreted against the main drafter of that contract.

[93] *See* La. C.C. arts. 2057, 2503 *in pari materia*.

referred to in the first sentence. This same second sentence of article 2475 requires that a reference be made to articles 2524 and 2603 because of the close parallel between the substance of these articles, "fitness" and "conformity," with the substance of the second sentence of article 2475, "fitness."

Article 2524 will be discussed below under "Redhibition," or defects and vices, because this is where it has been placed in the Civil Code. As we will explain later, neither article 2524 nor its companion, article 2529 belong there.

The letter of **article 2524** is self-explanatory:

"The thing sold must be reasonably fit for its ordinary use.

When the seller has reason to know the particular use the buyer intends for the thing, or the buyer's particular purpose for buying the thing, and that the buyer is relying on the seller's skill or judgment in selecting it, the thing sold must be fit for the buyer's intended use or for his particular purpose.

If the thing is not so fit, the buyer's rights are governed by the general rules of conventional obligations."

As regards **article 2603**, it deals specifically with the seller's obligation to deliver. It states that:

"The seller must deliver to the buyer things that conform to the contract.

Things do not conform to the contract when they are different from those selected by the buyer or are of a kind, quality, or quantity different from the one agreed."

Should we read "***fit***" in article 2475, "fit for its intended use," and "fit for its ordinary use" in article 2524 as meaning something different from "***conform***" in article 2603? Our reading of the Louisiana Civil Code and, particularly, of the civil law foundations of the law of "conventional obligations" on "object" and "cause" on the one hand, and "performance of obligations" and "contracts" on the other hand, leads us to say that they should be read as meaning the same thing but within two different legal contexts. The concept of "conform" includes the two concepts of "fitness" (*intended* or *subjective* and *ordinary* or *objective*). The reason is that the seller's obligation to "deliver" can only be an obligation to deliver the very thing that was agreed upon and sold, with its particular characteristics, its intended or ordinary fitness in particular, following the exchange of consent between the seller and the buyer. Both parties agreed as to the "thing sold" and as to the cause of the buyer's purchasing the thing. In other words, "fitness" of use, whether intended or ordinary, is a matter concerning that phase of the contract of sale which is that of the formation of the contract, whereas the "conformity" of the thing has to do with the obligation of the seller to deliver that thing with its "fitness," an obligation which can come into existence only after the contract of sale has been perfected. The second obligation, the obligation to deliver, is contingent upon the existence of a contract of sale that transfers the ownership of the thing to the buyer. It must be pointed out that the same words "fit," "fitness," can be found in sections 2-314 and 2-315 of the UCC, "conforming" and "nonconformng" in sections 2-501 and 2-502 of the UCC, and the words "conform" and "fit" can be found in articles 35 and 50 of the CISG.

§ 4.1.1. OBLIGATION TO DELIVER.

The obligation to deliver is governed, primarily, by articles 2477 to 2498. However, other Code articles must be consulted for a proper analysis of that obligation, particularly articles 1854 to 1863 on the performance of obligations. A survey of the general and specific rules on delivery will lead to dealing separately with the extent of the delivery of movables in contrast with the delivery of immovables.

A. Delivery: General Rules: Methods, Object, Cost, Place, Time, Breach.

Delivery is, basically, the obligation the seller has to place the thing sold at the disposal of the buyer so that the latter can **take delivery of the thing**. (La. C.C. art. 2549.) Thus, the seller "delivers" and the buyer "takes delivery." How are these obligations fulfilled?

Article 2477 gives a list of different methods available to a seller to "deliver": **"Delivery of an immovable is deemed to take place upon execution of the writing that transfers its ownership.**

Delivery of a movable takes place by handing it over to the buyer. If the parties so intend delivery may take place in another manner, such as by the seller's handing over to the buyer the key to the place where the thing is stored, or by negotiating to him a document of title to the thing, or even by the mere consent of the parties if the thing sold cannot be transported at the time of the sale or if the buyer already has the thing at that time."

As was emphasized above under transfer of ownership, as a general rule, a writing is required for the transfer of ownership of an immovable. The execution of that same writing is the fulfillment by the seller of his obligation to deliver the immovable sold. In a sense, the writing of the document is tantamount to the seller handing over that immovable to the buyer. The seller is simultaneously transferring the ownership of the immovable and actually delivering that immovable by means of the writing. Once upon a time, under Roman law, a seller would deliver the immovable to the buyer by placing a fistful of dirt into the buyer's hand.

As far as delivery of an immovable taking place and having effect vis-à-vis third parties to the sale, it is the filing of the written instrument in the public records that will put these third parties on notice that delivery has taken place.[94]

As concerns the delivery of a movable, article 2477 offers a series of alternatives which can take the form of a physical, or actual delivery, such as from hand to hand. A delivery can also be fictitious or symbolic, such as a delivery by way of a document or handing over the keys to a place where the movable is located. The

---

[94] La. C.C. art. 517: "The ownership of an immovable is voluntarily transferred by a contract between the owner and the transferee that purports to transfer the ownership of the immovable. The transfer of ownership takes place between the parties by the effect of the agreement and is not effective against third persons until the contract is filed for registry in the conveyance records of the parish in which the immovable is located."

methods of making delivery amount — in reality or fictitiously — to placing the movable in the possession and at the disposal of the buyer. But how can third parties be bound by these different methods of making delivery between seller and buyer? **Article 518** provides the answer: **"The ownership of a movable is voluntarily transferred by a contract between the owner and the transferee that purports to transfer the ownership of the movable. Unless otherwise provided, the transfer of ownership takes place as between the parties by the effect of the agreement and against third persons when the possession of the movable is delivered to the transferee. When possession has not been delivered, a subsequent transferee to whom possession is delivered acquires ownership provided he is in good faith. Creditors of the transferor may seize the movable while it is still in his possession."**

Delivery of incorporeal things may present some difficulties since the "thing" has no body, no corpus; it cannot be seen or touched. **Article 2481** addresses the problem in these words: **"Delivery of incorporeal movable things incorporated into an instrument, such as stocks and bonds, takes place by negotiating such instrument to the buyer. Delivery of other incorporeal movables, such as credit rights, takes place upon the transfer of those movables."**[95]

How is the delivery of an incorporeal thing, a non-visible thing, effective against third persons? **Article 2643** states that: **"The assignment of a right is effective against the debtor and third persons only from the time the debtor has actual knowledge, or has been given notice of the assignment. If a partial assignment unreasonably increases the burden of the debtor he may recover from either the assignor or the assignee a reasonable amount for the increased burden."**

As regards the cost of making delivery, articles 2482 and 2483 place the cost or the expenses of the delivery on the seller. He must obtain the thing which he has sold and deliver it to the buyer; if there are expenses related to placing that thing at the disposal of the buyer for the latter to remove, the seller will have to bear these expenses. This obligation is a "general obligation" of any obligor as already stated in **article 1863: "Expenses that may be required to render performance shall be borne by the obligor."**

The object of the seller's obligation to deliver is **the thing sold**. (La. C.C. art. 2475.) It is the "thing" as it existed at the time of the sale or **"the thing sold in the condition that, at the time of the sale, the parties expected, or should have expected, the thing to be in at the time of delivery, according to its nature." (La. C.C. art. 2489.)** Until delivery, the seller is under an obligation to care, as a prudent administrator, for a thing now belonging to the buyer. As "obligor" of the obligation to deliver, the seller falls under the four different instances contemplated by Civil Code article 1873 in the case of his failure to deliver as a result of a fortuitous event.

As regards the place of delivery, **article 2484** provides that **"[d]elivery must be made at the place agreed upon by the parties or intended by them. In the absence of such agreement or intent, delivery must be made at the place where the thing is located at the time of the sale."** The wording of this article should

[95] *See also* La. C.C. arts. 470, 473.

not be read narrowly to mean that delivery can take place only and exclusively as stated. Indeed, article 1862 provides for more "places" of delivery than article 2484 does and the two articles should be read as one complementing the other, *in pari materia*.

The same is true as concerns the expenses incurred by the seller in his obligation to deliver. Article 1863 is to be read in conjunction, *in pari materia*, with **article 2483: "The cost of making delivery is borne by the seller . . . in the absence of agreement to the contrary."** Once delivery by the seller has taken place, the buyer's obligation is to "remove" the thing from where it has been delivered and the cost related to the **"taking of delivery . . . is borne by the buyer . . . in the absence of agreement to the contrary." (La. C.C. art. 2483.)** When, in our daily life, we are told by a seller that "we will deliver to your house" either at no charge or for a fee, what we are actually told is that the seller will perform our obligation to "remove" the thing and that, because removing is our obligation, either the seller will do it at no charge or at "our expense" and thus for a fee.

It may happen that the seller breaches his obligation to deliver at all or to deliver on time. **"When the seller fails to deliver or to make timely delivery of the thing sold, the buyer may demand specific performance of the obligation of the seller to deliver, or may seek dissolution of the sale. In either case, and also when the seller has made a late delivery, the buyer may seek damages." (La. C.C. art. 2485.)** This specific article under the law of Sale should be read *in pari materia* with the general law of Conventional Obligations on breach of obligations as stated in Louisiana Civil Code articles 1986 and 2013. A seller may be justified in not delivering the thing sold to his buyer, therefore in not making the thing available to the buyer for the latter to remove. Under **Civil Code article 2487**, a seller may exercise a right of retention, the right to withhold physical possession of the thing until the buyer carries out his own obligations: **"The seller may refuse to deliver the thing sold until the buyer tenders payment of the price, unless the seller has granted the buyer a term for such payment."**

B. Extent of the Obligation to Deliver: Movables, Immovables.

As regards the delivery of *movables*, quite a number of new Code articles were included as a result of the legislative reforms of 1993–95. As stated previously, a new Chapter on Sales of Movables was added to the previously existing Code articles on the law of Sale. These new articles are heavily influenced by the Convention on Contracts for the International Sale of Goods, or CISG, which should be referred to for a comprehensive understanding of the Louisiana Civil Code articles on the sale of movables.

As suggested above, article 2603 deals with "delivery" of a thing that should conform to the thing agreed upon in the contract.[96] The seller must **deliver to the buyer things that conform to the contract**, and, to make sure that the things

---

[96] See the discussions on the effects of a contract to sell, transfer of ownership and sale with a right of inspection, *supra* p. 42.

which are delivered to him conform to the contract, the buyer **"has a right to have a reasonable opportunity to inspect the things." (La. C.C. art. 2604.)** Should the buyer, after inspection, come to the conclusion that the things delivered are not "conforming," the **buyer may reject nonconforming things within a reasonable time** while, at the same time, the **buyer must give reasonable notice to the seller to make the rejection effective. (La. C.C. art. 2605.) "Upon rejection of nonconforming things by the buyer, the seller may cure the nonconformity when the time for performance has not yet expired or when the seller had a reasonable belief that the nonconforming things would be acceptable to the buyer. In such a case the seller must give reasonable notice of his intention to cure to the buyer." (La. C.C. art. 2610.)**

Different rules apply if both the seller and the buyer are "merchants." (La. C.C. art. 2608.) It is important to keep in mind that the obligation of the seller, under the above articles, is to "deliver things that conform to the contract"; in other words the contract has been formed by agreement of the parties on the quality, the objective or subjective features, characteristics, fitness of the thing which is the object of the seller's obligation to deliver. Therefore, in this case, the issue is not one and cannot be one of defect or vice in the thing as **article 2520** defines "a defect" leading to redhibition when **"it renders the thing useless, or its use so inconvenient that it must be presumed that a buyer would not have bought the thing had he known of the defect . . . "**

Special consideration must be given to article 2615, a special article of the law of Sale, because of the fundamental difference it reflects in its wording with article. 2013, a general article under Conventional Obligations. **Article 2615** states that **"[i]n an action for judicial dissolution of a sale of movable things the court must grant dissolution, upon proof of the defendant's failure to perform, without allowing that party any additional time to render performance." Article 2013** reads as follows: **"When the obligor fails to perform, the obligee has a right to the judicial dissolution of the contract or, according to the circumstances, to regard the contract as dissolved. In either case, the obligee may recover damages. In an action involving judicial dissolution, the obligor who failed to perform may be granted, according to the circumstances, an additional time to perform."**

One will have noticed that under article 2615 the Court is not allowed to give the defendant (the seller in his obligation to deliver) any additional time to perform whereas, under article 2013, the **"obligor . . . may be granted an additional time to perform."**

As concerns the obligation of a seller to deliver the full extent of the *immovable* sold, that obligation will vary with the particular type of contract of sale the seller and the buyer have entered into. After laying down a general rule in article 2491, the Civil Code provides for three different types of contracts of sale in articles 2491 to 2495. Obviously, to each type of contract should be attached a particular remedy or no remedy at all.

The general rule stated in **article 2491** fits the definition of any synallagmatic and commutative contract and, therefore, should be considered as the general rule. It states that **"[t]he seller must deliver to the buyer the full extent of the**

immovable sold. That obligation may be modified in accordance with the provisions of the following Articles."

The problem is that this general rule may not find any occasion to be applied in the context of **the provisions of the following articles**. Let us consider the three types of sale described in **the following articles**.

The first type of sale of an immovable requiring the seller to deliver the extent of the immovable sold is the sale per measure as described in **article 2492: "If the sale of an immovable has been made with indication of the extent of the premises at the rate of so much per measure, but the seller is unable to deliver the full extent specified in the contract, the price must be proportionately reduced.**

If the extent delivered by the seller is greater than that specified in the contract, the buyer must pay to the seller a proportionate supplement of the price. The buyer may recede from the sale when the actual extent of the immovable sold exceeds by more than one twentieth the extent specified in the contract."

The first paragraph of the article contemplates there being a deficiency in the extent delivered; the buyer has received less than he paid for. The remedy is for the price to be reduced proportionately. What does proportionately mean? In proportion to the average price or rate of the measure of the whole extent delivered? What if the deficiency was in the front of the property which was "proportionately" much more valuable than the back of the property or its west side? Why is there is no limit to the deficiency? Is the buyer to take any deficiency, whatever its extent? What if the buyer needed a certain "measure" to make a proper use, as he intended, of the property that should have been delivered by the seller as per the act of sale? Why not allow the buyer to get out of the contract should the deficiency reach a certain proportion of the whole extent, such as one twentieth as is stated in the second paragraph of this same article 2492?

In this second paragraph, we are told that there may be excess, a greater extent in the property delivered as compared with the property bought per measure. In that situation **the buyer must pay to the seller a proportionate supplement of the price**. Up to that part in this subparagraph we have a parallel in the structure and the remedy with the structure and the remedy provided in the first paragraph of article 2492. But this parallelism is broken with the second sentence of this second paragraph; it reads as follows: **"The buyer may recede from the sale when the actual extent of the immovable sold exceeds by more than one twentieth the extent specified in the contract."** Thus, up to 1/20th more in the extent delivered than the extent sold, the buyer must pay a "proportionate" supplement in price. Beyond an excess of 1/20th the buyer may recede, or get out of, the sale. In this respect, it can be argued that the parallelism in the substance and structure of these two paragraphs of article 2492 should lead to granting the parties to the sale the same remedies (*ubi eadem ratio idem lex*; "where the reason for the law is the same, the law ought to be the same"). In other words, the buyer, under the first paragraph, should be given the right to recede from the sale if the deficiency is 1/20th of the extent as the buyer, under the second paragraph, is allowed to do. On the other hand, an *a contrario sensu* reasoning would lead one to say that the legislature intended to provide for the rescission of the sale in the case of a 5% excess, but intended to make no comparable provision in the case of a 5% deficit so as not to allow a rescission of the sale in this latter case. Why is a buyer not treated exactly like a seller? The answer may be in the extensive use made by the Courts of a *sale per aversionem*, as explained below.

The second type of sale of an immovable referred to in the Civil Code is the sale for a lump price. **Article 2494** states: **"When the sale of an immovable has been made with indication of the extent of the premises, but for a lump price, the expression of the measure does not give the seller the right to a proportionate increase of the price, nor does it give the buyer the right to a proportionate diminution of the price, unless there is a surplus, or a shortage, of more than one twentieth of the extent specified in the act of sale. When the surplus is such as to give the seller the right to an increase of the price the buyer has the option either to pay that increase or to recede from the contract."**

In this type of sale, the focus placed on the "lump price" prevails over the measurement, the expression of the measure of the immovable, in giving this type of sale its name. The first paragraph gives no remedy to either party up to 1/20th either way, in surplus or in deficiency. But, once again, the second paragraph treats the seller better than the buyer since, whereas the buyer may opt to pay any increase above 1/20th or recede from the contract, the same buyer must apparently suffer any deficiency in the measure above 1/20th without having the right to recede from the contract. One could say, in defense of the Code article, that it is much easier for a buyer to receive some money back from the seller in the event the latter cannot deliver the full extent of the immovable sold, than it can be for a buyer to pay more money, and may be still more money, to a seller who has delivered a greater extent of an immovable than he had intended to sell. It remains, nevertheless, that the cause of the contract of sale as it was communicated by the buyer to the seller may justify the rescission of the sale in favor of a buyer who receives an extent of an immovable far less than the extent he thought he had bargained for.

In considering articles 2492 and 2494, one must include consideration of article 2497, which expands on the right of the buyer to recover from the seller. Also, article 2498 warrants consideration as it deals with the prescriptive period of one year affecting the rights of action of the seller and the buyer.

A third type of sale of an immovable is described in **article 2495**. It states that **"[w]hen an immovable described as a certain and limited body or a distinct object is sold for a lump price, an expression of the extent of the immovable in the act of sale does not give the parties any right to an increase or diminution of the price in case of surplus or shortage in the actual extension of the immovable."**

This type of sale bears different names: sale per metes and bounds, sale of a certain and limited body, *sale per aversionem* . . . The lack of specificity of this article makes its strength; it makes it the preferred type of sale for the courts to have recourse to because they can give to the words "certain," "limited" and "distinct" a meaning as broad or restricted as they want . . . considering that, either way, neither the seller nor the buyer can have a remedy. No shortage whatever it is and no surplus whatever it is can give rise to a remedy. The *sale per aversionem* is an easy label to use and it makes it easy for the courts to solve any potential disagreement between the parties to that sale. We are wondering, however, if a seller in a sale *per aversionem* would not still have a right to bring an action in lesion?[97] Indeed, under article 2589 a **"seller may invoke lesion even if he has renounced the right to claim it."** In other words, the right to invoke lesion is a right of public order; it cannot be renounced before it has been vested in the seller, thus after the sale. It could be argued that since a sale per aversionem grants no right of action to either party, it is a sale which makes the seller renounce his right to lesion before the sale. Once that sale has taken place, the seller should have the right to argue lesion beyond moiety as long as we look at lesion as being a right of public order until the beneficiary of that right can confirm the sale by renouncing lesion.

§ 4.1.2. OBLIGATION OF WARRANTY AGAINST EVICTION; WARRANTY OF LAW.

The warranty of law against eviction, that is to say the warranty which the law states that the seller owes his buyer, is defined and described as follows in **Civil Code article: "The seller warrants the buyer against eviction, which is the buyer's loss of, or danger of losing, the whole or part of the thing sold because of a third person's right that existed at the time of the sale. The warranty also covers encumbrances on the thing that were not declared at the time of the sale, with the exception of apparent servitudes and natural and legal nonapparent servitudes, which need not be declared. If the right of the third person is perfected only after the sale through the negligence of the buyer, though it arises from facts that took place before, the buyer has no claim in warranty."**

On the other hand, **article 2503** states that **"[t]he warranty against eviction is implied in every sale. Nevertheless, the parties may agree to increase or to limit the warranty. They may also agree to an exclusion of the warranty, but even in that case the seller must return the price to the buyer if eviction occurs, unless it is clear that the buyer was aware of the danger of eviction, or the buyer has declared that he was buying at his peril and risk, or the seller's obligation of returning the price has been expressly excluded. In all those cases the seller is liable for an eviction that is occasioned by his own act, and any agreement to the contrary is null. The buyer is subrogated to the rights in warranty of the seller against other persons, even when the warranty is excluded."**

It follows that *warranty of eviction under the law is only* of the *nature* of the contract of sale, in the sense that all contracts of sale carry implicitly, as an effect deriving from the very nature of a sale, this obligation of warranty by the seller against the eviction of the buyer from the thing the latter bought. In other words, the buyer is entitled to receive "his money's worth" when he enters into the synallagmatic and commutative contract of sale and "warranty" is providing the buyer with the assurance he is getting exactly that, his money's worth. But this assurance, this warranty, is only an accessory obligation of a contract of sale that is

---

[97] On Lesion, see *supra*, p. 31.

usually, traditionally or typically flowing from the principal obligation which is to transfer the ownership of the thing to a buyer. But being a usual, traditional or typical obligation does not mean that it "makes" the contract of sale; it means only that it is of the nature of a sale but not of the essence of that contract. In other words, a sale is still a sale even though the seller and the buyer agree that the warranty is "limited" or even "excluded." Thus the parties to a contract of sale can work out their own warranty outside the framework of the law, the Civil Code in our case.[98]

The rights of the parties — and particularly those of the buyer — depend on the scope of application of the warranty.

A. Scope of Application of the Warranty Against Eviction: Nature of the Thing Sold.

1. *Corporeal Things.*

The wording of Civil Code article 2500 suggests that the thing sold is an immovable; it refers to encumbrances, apparent and non apparent natural and legal servitudes, which are usually associated with immovables.[99] However, there is no legal reason why this same article 2500 could not apply to a sale of a movable from which a buyer would be evicted by the true owner except that, as seen above, good faith buyers who rely on the possession of the movable thing by an apparent owner-seller have a much better chance not to be evicted from the ownership of that movable than the purchaser of an immovable.

Article 2500 contemplates both an actual loss by total eviction from the thing bought and a partial loss resulting from **"encumbrances on the thing not declared at the time of the sale"** so that the buyer does not have the full *usus* and *fructus* of the principal thing. The greater or lesser extent of a partial eviction will be determined by the court mostly on the basis of the nature and integrity of the cause that led the buyer to buy.[100]

It is important to point out also that the buyer does not have to wait until he is actually evicted from the ownership of the thing he bought to bring an action in warranty; the buyer who is threatened with eviction and who is, then, running the risk of **"losing the whole or part of the thing sold"** may bring an action in eviction. Obviously, depending on the extent of the eviction, the buyer may either demand the rescission of the sale so as to recover the purchase price, at least, in case of a total eviction,[101] or seek a diminution of the price in case of a partial eviction.[102]

---

[98] *See infra*, § 4.1.3, Conventional Warranty against Eviction, p. 70.

[99] See *supra*, p. 33 for example the Code articles on Lesion and 2596 in particular; *see also supra* p. 46, Right of Redemption and Art. 2588 in particular.

[100] *See* La. C.C. art. 2511; *see* La. C.C. arts. 1966–1970, discussing Cause.

[101] *See* La. C.C. arts. 2506 and 2511 (explaining remedies and rights of the parties).

[102] *See* La. C.C. art. 2511.

2. *Incorporeal Things.*

The object of the seller's obligation may be an incorporeal thing: a right.

Two Code articles dealing with rights are listed under the Civil Code articles on Warranty against Eviction. Article 2513 finds its source in a long civil law tradition. The other, article 2502, was added to the Civil Code with the 1993 revision and has brought some disruption to the understanding of the civil law concepts of warranty, ownership, prescription and good faith and to their cross-relationship.

Louisiana Civil Code article 2513 provides that **"[i]n a sale of a right of succession, the warranty against eviction extends only to the right to succeed the decedent, which entitles the buyer to those things that are, in fact, a part of the estate, but it does not extend to any particular thing."**

We have seen the same substantive law stated in article 2650 under Assignment of Rights.[103] These articles merely incorporate article 461-2[104] into nominate contracts: sale and assignment. In these two instances, the seller's warranty or the assignor's warranty against eviction extends only to the actual existence of the right in the seller or assignor himself, but neither the seller nor the assignor can warrant something one does not sell or the other does not assign and that is the "material content or extent," i.e. the assets which may or may not fall under the right sold or assigned.

Article 2502 incorporates into the Louisiana Civil Code the common law concept of *Quitclaim Deed.* This article reads as follows: **"A person may transfer to another whatever rights to a thing he may then have, without warranting the existence of any such rights. In such a case the transferor does not owe restitution of the price to the transferee in case of eviction, nor may that transfer be rescinded for lesion.**

Such a transfer does not give rise to a presumption of bad faith on the part of the transferee and is a just title for the purposes of acquisitive prescription.

If the transferor acquires ownership of the thing after having transferred his rights to it, the after-acquired title of the transferor does not inure to the benefit of the transferee."

An instructive comparison must be made here with the following definition taken from Black's Law Dictionary: *"Quitclaim deed. A deed that conveys a grantor's complete interest or claim in certain real property but that neither warrants nor professes that the title is valid."*

One will have noticed that the definition of a *quitclaim deed* at common law refers to the "title" itself as the thing conveyed and not to the coverage or extent of that title. There is, therefore, a fundamental difference between the concept of the sale of a right in succession in article 2513 and the concept of *quitclaim deed* as it

---

[103] For a discussion on assignment of rights, see *supra*, p. 23.

[104] La. C.C. art. 461: Corporeals are things that have a body, whether animate or inanimate, and can be felt or touched. Incorporeals are things that have no body, but are comprehended by the understanding, such as the rights of inheritance, servitudes, obligations, and right of intellectual property.

has been incorporated into article 2502. Under article 2502 the seller, *transferor* rather,[105] does not warrant anything in this "transfer," not even that he holds the proper title to "whatever right" he transfers. In the event the "transferee" of a *quitclaim deed* is evicted by a third person with a "better" title[106] the **"transferor does not owe restitution of the price to the transferee."** (La. C.C. art. 2502) And yet, we read in **article 2503**, that even when the parties to the sale agree to exclude the warranty against eviction, **"the seller must return the price to the buyer."** The same article goes on to state that **"unless it is clear that the buyer was aware of the danger of eviction . . . or the seller's obligation of returning the price has been expressly excluded."** Thus, if we were to consider that a buyer who buys under a *quitclaim deed* is a buyer who is aware of the danger that he might be evicted, or that he is a buyer who has agreed not to receive his price back under any circumstances, then we might conceivably place a sale under a *quitclaim deed* under the latter two situations contemplated by article 2503. However the problem is compounded by the fact that the Louisiana jurisprudence has taken the position that even when the seller himself, under a *quitclaim deed*, benefits from the after acquired title doctrine, he can evict his own buyer since that benefit does not filtrate through him to become a benefit to his buyer.[107] We believe that such a jurisprudence is contrary not only to a reasonable interpretation of article 2503 but, even more, that it is contrary to the law itself as it is found in the second paragraph of article 2503, which states: **"In all those cases the seller is liable for an eviction that is occasioned by his own act, and any agreement to the contrary is null."** We believe that the Civil Code lays down here a rule of public order that cannot be deviated from, even by the jurisprudence.[108]

A further argument can be added in support of the view that a *quitclaim deed* should not be read as depriving the buyer of such a deed of any warranty against eviction, particularly eviction by his own seller. In a section entitled "Warranty Against Defects," which follows below, we will be discussing the "*as is*" clause that may be included by the parties to an act of sale. This clause has been interpreted as merely qualifying the warranty the seller owes his buyer but not as waiving or excluding that warranty. In other words, the seller is still under an obligation to repair the defective thing or to restore the price received if he cannot repair the thing. Why not equate a *quitclaim deed* to a sale *as is*? Why not consider that the seller under a *quitclaim deed* is selling "whatever he thinks he owns" in the same manner as a seller sells a thing *as is* without any additional warranty beyond what he thinks the condition of the thing he sells is? If no defect occurs in the thing sold

---

[105] Notice that article 2502 does not use the words "sale" or "seller" just as the common law definition does not either; so what is this article doing here under Sale? Sure the word "price" is used but the same word "price" is used also in article 2756 in relation to a contract to build by a plot. One may wonder why this type of "transfer" described in article 2502 should not be included, possibly, under Assignment of Rights? Or maybe even under a new title, "Transfer of Whatever Rights?"

[106] Even by the transferor himself who would become the beneficiary of a subsequently-received title according to the common law doctrine of "After Acquired Title."

[107] At common law, the after acquired title doctrine would benefit the buyer who, therefore, could not be evicted by his seller.

[108] Strangely enough, the same Louisiana jurisprudence is of the view that a quitclaim deed may or may not be a proper and just title for a ten-year acquisitive prescription by the buyer should that buyer also be in good faith. *See* La. C.C. arts. 3480, 3481, 3482, 3483.

as is, the seller is released from any obligation, just as a seller under a *quitclaim deed* would owe no obligation to his buyer if "whatever right he thought he was selling" he had actually sold because he was the title holder of the right over the thing, object of the right. On the other hand, if the thing sold *as is* should be defective, the seller may have to return the price to the buyer; why not transpose the "legal reason" for that obligation of warranty against defects in a sale *as is* to the obligation of warranty against eviction in a *quitclaim deed* sale? Reasoning *a fortiori ratione a minori ad majus* makes a lot of sense in these circumstances.

B. Rights of the Parties in Case of Eviction.

The Civil Code considers two types of eviction: a total eviction and a partial eviction. In both instances the buyer is given the right to call his vendor in warranty. This risk of being evicted is of a major importance, obviously, for a buyer of an immovable; in this respect, the Public Records Doctrine should be of much concern to such buyers of immovables.

1. *The Public Records Doctrine: "PRD".*

The Public Records Doctrine (or PRD for our purpose), which has now been incorporated into the Civil Code itself,[109]

Former Louisiana Revised Statute section 9:2756 read as follows: "*All sales, contracts and judgments affecting immovable property, which shall not be so recorded, shall be utterly null and void, except between the parties thereto. The recording may be made at any time, but shall only affect third persons from the time of the recording. The recording shall have effect from the time when the act is deposited in the proper office, and indorsed by the proper officer.*"[110] Newly enacted **Code article 3338** states, in part, that "**[t]he rights and obligations established or created by the following written instruments are without effect as to a third person unless the instrument is registered by recording it in the appropriate mortgage or conveyance records pursuant to the provisions of this Title:**

(1) An instrument that transfers an immovable or establishes a real right in or over an immovable.

(2) The lease of an immovable.

(3) An option or right of first refusal, or a contract to buy, sell or lease an immovable or to establish a real right in or over an immovable.

(4) An instrument. . . . "

We read in the second paragraph of **article 1839** that "**[a] transfer of immovable property must be made by authentic act or by act under private signature. Nevertheless, an oral transfer is valid between the parties when the property has been actually delivered and the transferor recognizes the transfer when interrogated on oath.**

---

109 *See* La. C.C. arts. 3338–3368. These articles amount to a most unfortunate addition, not to say violation, of the notion and substance of a Civil Code.

110 La. R.S. §§ 9:2721(A) and 9:2756, repealed by Acts 2005, No 169, § 8, eff. July 1, 2006.

An instrument involving immovable property shall have effect against third persons only from the time it is filed for registry in the parish where the property is located.”

Since July 1, 2006, the first paragraph of **article 3340** reads as follows: **“If the law or a recorded instrument expressly makes the recordation of an act or instrument a condition to the creation, extinction, or modification of rights or obligations, such act or instrument is not effective as to a third person until it is recorded. . . . ”**

As interpreted and applied by the courts of this State, the Public Records Doctrine has for its main purpose to protect the recorded transaction itself more than the right of ownership of the immovable. Thus, third persons can ignore any transaction that has not been recorded since such a transaction has effect only between the parties . . . until recorded. It follows that a third person will be protected by the PRD whenever she acquires from a “recorded” owner even though the latter may not be the true owner. Since an unrecorded transaction cannot have effect against third persons, any knowledge, whether actual or constructive, by a third person of such a transaction outside the public records is “no knowledge” at all. Conversely, the recordation of a transaction will carry with it a “presumed” knowledge of its existence by third persons; it is as if the recordation was tantamount to some form of publicity affecting all.

2. *The Call in Warranty.*

Under **article 2517, “[a] buyer threatened with eviction must give timely notice of the threat to the seller. If a suit for eviction has been brought against the buyer, his calling in the seller to defend that suit amounts to such notice.**

A buyer who elects to bring suit against a third person who disturbs his peaceful possession of the thing sold must give timely notice of that suit to the seller.

In either case, a buyer who fails to give such notice, or who fails to give it in time for the seller to defend himself, forfeits the warranty against eviction if the seller can show that, had he been notified in time, he would have been able to prove that the third person who sued the buyer had no right.”

Since the greater or lesser right of recovery that an action in warranty may provide the buyer depends much on his attitude when faced with a threat of eviction, the requirement of a “timely notice” is of major importance. A buyer runs the double risk of being evicted by a third person and of not recovering anything from his seller when the latter, if called in on time to defend his buyer, could have defeated the action in eviction by the third person. A buyer threatened with eviction would be well advised to call his vendor in warranty as early as possible in the procedure so as to shift the burden of proof in defense on his seller as long as he is pretty sure that it is the seller’s fault if he is threatened with eviction. On the other hand, **“if the right of the third person is perfected only after the sale through the negligence of the buyer, though it arises from facts that took place before, the buyer has no claim in warranty.” (La. C.C. art. 2500.)**

3. *Rights of the Buyer in Case of Total Eviction.*

Since the contract of sale is binding between the two parties to it, a seller should not have any right to resort to any legal action to evict his buyer.[111] A seller should not either be allowed to engage in what could be called a "de facto" eviction of his buyer in the sense that he should not have the right to carry out acts and actions which could amount to such disturbances of "fact" that the buyer of the immovable would not be in a position to enjoy his rights of *usus* and *fructus* which he acquired with the *abusus* of the immovable. Should the buyer have to bring an action against his former seller, the action would not be in warranty but, most likely, in tort.

A seller cannot "warrant" his buyer against disturbances of fact caused by third parties. A seller cannot be responsible for persons over whom he has no control. Again, should the buyer have to bring an action to put an end to such disturbances of fact, the action would be in tort, very likely, and against the third party.[112]

On the other hand, as seen above, the seller owes his buyer a warranty of eviction against disturbances of law for which he, the seller, is responsible. Should the buyer, with the assistance of his seller, be unable to defeat an action in eviction brought by a third person, the **"buyer who avails himself of the warranty against eviction may recover from the seller the price he paid, the value of any fruits he had to return to the third person who evicted him, and also other damages sustained because of the eviction with the exception of any increase in value of the thing lost." (La. C.C. art. 2506.)** The price to be paid by the seller to the buyer is the "full" price of the sale **"even if, at the time of the eviction, the value of the thing has been diminished due to any cause including the buyer's neglect."** On the other hand, to avoid a possible unjust enrichment of the buyer at the expense of the seller, **"if the buyer has benefitted from a diminution in value caused by his own act, the amount of his benefit must be deducted from the total owed to him by the seller because of the eviction." (La. C.C. art. 2507.)** This same Code article 2507 does not say anything about the payment of "interest" by the seller on the price he received from his buyer. We believe that, by analogy with article 2545 on warranty against defects, the seller should have known of the "defects" in the title he was transferring to the buyer and, for that reason, he should have to pay interest to his buyer on the price he received and may have used until the buyer's eviction. The same reasoning should be made, on the basis of the same analogy, as regards the reimbursement to the buyer of the reasonable expenses of the sale, assuming that the buyer incurred these expenses. Furthermore, if the buyer incurred expenses because of the lawsuit, if lawsuit there was, he should be reimbursed these expenses as long as the seller had been called in warranty to defend in the action in eviction.

In the event the thing from which the buyer has been evicted has increased in value as a result of natural events, events outside the control of the buyer, the latter is not entitled to receive from his seller **"any increase in value of the thing lost." (La. C.C. art. 2506.)** On the other hand, **"[a] seller liable for eviction must reimburse the buyer for the cost of useful improvements to the thing made by the buyer. If the seller knew at the time of the sale that the thing belonged to**

---

[111] Except possibly, as stated above, under the Quitclaim Deed and the After Acquired Title Doctrine.

[112] See, by contrast, the discussion of Lease *infra*, p. 145. *See also* La. C.C. art. 2700.

a third person, he must reimburse the buyer for the cost of all improvements." (La. C.C. art. 2509.) Improvements must be distinguished from repairs; in the latter case the buyer should assume these expenses for repairs since he is likely to have enjoyed the use of the repairs made and these repairs do not add to the value of the thing.

An item of recovery that a buyer may be granted by a court is listed in **article 2506** as **"other damages sustained because of the eviction with the exception of any increase in value of the thing lost."** The question raised here is that of the meaning of "other damages." Based on the wording of this sentence, a legitimate assumption to be made is that the "damages" are "other" than those listed before in the article. If that is so, we might include the expenses of the sale, as suggested above, the interest on the price, as suggested above, but beyond these two items there is one of great interest that could be suggested and it is the "attorney's fees" that the buyer may have had to incur to defend in the lawsuit. We believe that a seller, of an immovable in particular because of the public records, ought to know whether or not he is the owner of the thing he sells to a buyer who purchased in good faith and in trust of the seller's ownership of the thing. Since the seller is the one who did set things in motion he ought to be held responsible for the "other damages" suffered by the buyer and attorney's fees ought to be added to these "other damages." This would be particularly true of a seller who **"knew at the time of the sale that the thing belonged to a third person." (La. C.C. art. 2509.)**

4. *Rights of the Buyer in Case of Partial Eviction.*

There is partial eviction **"when the buyer is evicted from only a part of the thing sold, he may obtain rescission of the sale if he would not have bought the thing without that part. If the sale is not rescinded, the buyer is entitled to a diminution of the price in the proportion that the value of the part lost bears to the value of the whole at the time of the sale." (La. C.C. art. 2511.)** Another instance of a partial eviction can occur when the buyer is evicted from **"those things that proceed from the thing sold." (La. C.C. art. 2512.)** There occurs, in most of these instances, a failure of cause or an error as regards the cause of the contract of sale. **"Cause is the reason why a party obligates himself" (La. C.C. art. 1967-1)** and a party to the contract of sale may make an error as to the cause when the error **"bears on the . . . thing that is the contractual object or a substantial quality of that thing . . . or any circumstance that the parties regarded, or should in good faith have regarded, as a cause of the obligation." (La. C.C. art. 1950.)**

Some Civil Code articles listed under Redhibition[113] illustrate the same approach as the approach described above as concerns warranty against eviction. For example, **article 2524** states, in part, that **"the thing sold must be reasonably fit for its ordinary use** and **if the thing is not so fit, the buyer's rights are governed by the general rules of conventional obligations."** We read also in **article 2605** that **"a buyer may reject nonconforming things within a reasonable time"** and **article 2603** states that **"Things do not conform to the contract when they are**

[113] *See* Redhibition, *infra*, p. 74. For a discussion of articles 2524, 2603 and 2604, see *supra*, p. 54.

different from those selected by the buyer or are of a kind, quality, or quantity different from the one agreed."

The policy or legal foundation of the above articles on warranty against partial eviction or warranty for lack of fitness or conformity of the thing is, obviously, the same: in both instances the buyer would have bought the thing, but not at the price he paid for it. The courts will have to weigh the degree of influence that the partial failure of cause, as regards the fitness of the thing, for example, or the error as to a substantial quality of the thing had among the many reasons that motivated the buyer to buy that particular thing.

The remedies available to a buyer under warranty against partial eviction are either the rescission of the sale or **"a diminution of the price in the proportion that the value of the part lost bears to the value of the whole at the time of the sale." (La. C.C. art. 2511.)**

Obviously, a buyer does not enjoy an absolute choice in selecting one remedy over the other. The courts will exercise their discretionary powers in granting one remedy or the other to the buyer who claims to have been partially evicted. Should a court consider that a diminution of the price is the proper remedy to grant the buyer, how is the court to compute that diminution of the price **"in the proportion that the value of the part lost bears to the value of the whole at the time of the sale?"** These words of article 2511 suggest taking into consideration the particular *relative* value, and not the average value, that the part from which the buyer has been evicted bears to the whole. It is likely that a buyer of a tract of land who believes he is buying a tract 100 yards wide in the front and who is evicted from 5 yards in the front will believe that the relative value of the 5 yards in the front is far superior to the relative value, or the average value, of 5 yards in the back of the same tract.[114] One word, an adjective, used in the Code articles is "proportionate;" it is used without any qualification such as "average proportionate" or "relative proportionate."

According to article 2511, the diminution of the price is calculated in relation to the value of the whole thing **"at the time of the sale,"** and not the value at the time the court meets, months or years after the sale, to decide on the right of action of the buyer. This approach is consistent with article 2506 which denies to the buyer any "natural" increase in the value of the thing lost.

§ 4.1.3. CONVENTIONAL WARRANTY AGAINST EVICTION.

"The parties" to a contract of sale **"may agree to increase or to limit the warranty. They may also agree to an exclusion of the warranty, but even in that case the seller must return the price to the buyer if eviction occurs, unless it is clear that the buyer was aware of the danger of eviction, or the buyer has declared that he was buying at his peril and risk, or the seller's obligation of returning the price has been expressly excluded.**

---

[114] See the discussion above of Civil Code articles 2492 and 2494, p. 59–60.

In all those cases the seller is liable for an eviction that is occasioned by his own act, and any agreement to the contrary is null.

The buyer is subrogated to the rights in warranty of the seller against other persons, even when the warranty is excluded." (La. C.C. art. 2503.) As the text of this article suggests, a conventional warranty may either extend or increase the "legal" warranty imposed by law on the seller or limit and even exclude that same legal warranty.

A. Conventional Extension of the Warranty.

It is not common for a seller to agree to be bound beyond the scope of application of the legal warranty, particularly in light of the courts' broad interpretation of the law in favor of a lay person and against the professional seller. Still, a seller may agree to a non-competition clause either, or both, with respect to a time period or a geographic area. In the absence of such a contractual provision, a seller might compete with his buyer and, possibly, draw to him an amount of business such as to partially or totally evict his buyer from the market.

We have seen that under **article 2506**, the buyer is not entitled to **"any increase in value of the thing lost."** We do not believe that this provision is of public order and that, therefore, it could not be waived by contract; there is no legal reason to deny a seller the right to stipulate in the contract of sale of an immovable, in particular, that he will pay back to the evicted buyer not only the price the latter paid but also the natural increase in value gained by the immovable between the sale and the eviction of the buyer.

A seller could also provide in the contract of sale for an alternative obligation[115] such that, should the buyer be evicted from the first thing he bought, that same buyer would automatically be given the ownership of the other thing listed as an alternative thing in the contract of sale.

By and large, there is no legal obstacle to a seller agreeing to warrant his buyer against wrongful acts by third parties such as competitors, neighbors, . . .

B. Conventional Limitation or Exclusion of the Legal Warranty.

There is one exclusion or limitation of warranty against eviction that the seller cannot have included in the contract of sale: it is his liability for his own acts. **Article 2503-2** lays down a rule of public order where it states that **"in all those cases the seller is liable for an eviction that is occasioned by his own act, and any agreement to the contrary is null."** It is on the basis of this provision of the law that we expressed our objections to the *quitclaim deed* and the *after acquired title doctrine*.[116]

But what the seller cannot do with respect to his own wrongful acts, he can do as regards wrongful acts by third parties. As long as the seller is in good faith, and

---

[115] On Alternative Obligations, see Précis: Louisiana Law of Obligations in General, p. 73–77.

[116] *See supra*, p. 64.

that is a condition *sine qua non*, the parties to the sale **"may agree to an exclusion of the warranty." (La. C.C. art. 2503.)** Such an agreement on a "no-warranty clause" does not amount to the buyer assuming the risk of eviction, unless the buyer was aware of the risk or assumed that risk. The effect of such an exclusion of warranty is only to exonerate the seller from the payment of damages. Indeed, the sale being a commutative and synallagmatic contract, the seller **"must return the price to the buyer if the eviction occurs."** Such is the obligation of the seller unless **"the buyer was aware of the danger of eviction, or the buyer has declared that he was buying at his peril and risk, or the seller's obligation of returning the price has been expressly excluded." (La. C.C. art. 2503.)**

C. Regardless, Subrogation is Available.

Whether warranty against eviction has been excluded or not, and assuming that the buyer did not agree to buy in full awareness of the risk he was running, **"the buyer is subrogated to the rights in warranty of the seller against other persons, even when the warranty is excluded." (La. C.C. art. 2503-3.)** Such "other persons" could be the seller's own seller, a contractor with whom the seller had a contract of services when that contractor failed to carry out his services in a workmanlike manner. Such a subrogation takes place by operation of law as is stated in article 1829 and, therefore, does not have to be stipulated in the contract of sale.[117]

§ 4.1.4. WARRANTY OF FITNESS AND WARRANTY AGAINST DEFECTS.

In classical Roman law, the contract of sale did not carry with it any warranty against vices. It had to be expressly stipulated. An obligation of legal warranty came about when the officers in charge of regulating the markets and solving the conflicts between buyers-consumers and sellers, who were mostly foreigners, created the presumption that the sellers knew of the hidden vices in the things they were selling. Two different rights of action were available to buyers: an action for a reduction in the price (action *aestimatoria*) and an action for the rescission of the sale (action *redhibitoria*). This Roman law background on the law of warranty is reflected in the Louisiana Civil Code, which creates a legal obligation of warranty on the part of a seller but allows the parties to the sale to modify and even waive the legal warranty. Again, this particular form of warranty is of the nature of the contract of sale but not of its essence. Since warranty against defects can be waived, under certain conditions, it is evidence of the fact that a sale can exist without a warranty against defects. We shall see, however, that a waiver does not always bar a buyer of all and every right of action against his seller whenever the parties did intend to preserve the commutative feature of a contract of sale.

In addition to the co-obligations of the seller to deliver the thing to the buyer and to warrant the ownership and peaceful possession of the thing to the buyer, **article 2475** imposes on the seller a third obligation in these words: **"the seller is bound**

[117] On Subrogation, see Précis: Louisiana Law of Obligations in General, p. 103–116.

to deliver the thing sold and to warrant to the buyer ownership and peaceful possession of, and the absence of hidden defects" in the thing as well as to warrant **"that the thing sold is fit for its intended use."** Such is the warranty of law, or legal warranty, as regards the fitness of the thing (A) and the warranty of law as regards hidden defects in the thing sold (B). Besides this legal warranty, **article 2548** stipulates, in part, **"that the parties may agree to an exclusion or limitation of the warranty against redhibitory defects. . . . "** Thus, in their contract, the parties to the sale can provide for a contractual form of "their" warranty against defects (D). In addition, either on account of the nature of the thing sold or because of the kind of sale involved, the legislator has provided for special regimes of warranty against defects (C).

A. Warranty of Fitness or Conformity.

1. *Fitness.*

Somewhere intermingled with the Code articles on "defects" and "redhibition" are two articles — articles 2524 and 2529 — which deal not with things *free of defects* but with things either not fit for ordinary use or things of a kind and/or quality other than the kind or quality specified in the contract.[118] Since *those things are not defective*, **"the buyer's rights are governed by the general rules of conventional obligations** or **by other rules of sale and conventional obligations." (La. C.C. arts. 2524, 2529.)** In other words, the Code articles on "redhibition," strictly speaking, do not apply in these two instances.

Article 2524 reads as follows: **"The thing sold must be reasonably fit for its ordinary use. When the seller has reason to know the particular use the buyer intends for the thing, or the buyer's particular purpose for buying the thing, and that the buyer is relying on the seller's skill or judgment in selecting it, the thing sold must be fit for the buyer's intended use or for his particular purpose. If the thing is not so fit, the buyer's rights are governed by the general rules of conventional obligations."**

One first question to address is the following: whereas article 2475, a *general* article, uses the expression **"fit for its intended use,"** article 2524, a *specific* article, uses the expression **"fit for its ordinary use."** Hence the question: are **intended** and **ordinary** meant to convey different or identical meanings? As suggested above, we are tempted to read in these words two different but complementary meanings of one and the same concept: *cause. Cause* is defined as **"the reason why a party obligates himself." (La. C.C. art. 1967-1.)** That reason or cause (objective cause) may be shared by all as in the case of the ordinary use that anyone can make of a thing (a car is to be driven; a horse to be ridden; a house to live in) as opposed to the intended use that someone may wish to do of a thing which, although ordinary, could be used for many different subjective reasons (subjective cause) (a car because it is a vintage model or a special edition; a horse because it won a race or two; a house because of the special trees in the front yard). Whereas the first paragraph of **article 2524** incorporates the concept of objective cause, the second

[118] On Fitness and Conformity, see *supra*, p. 54.

paragraph of the same article incorporates the concept of subjective cause under the form of the intended use or particular purpose the buyer wished to make of the thing bought. Thus the statement that the remedies available are to be found in the law of conventional obligations makes perfect sense. We are not dealing with a defect in the thing, which is a matter for the law of sale to regulate. One consequence we can mention here is that the prescriptive period applicable to an action for nullity of the sale of a "thing not fit" would be the five-year prescription of article 2032 and not the prescription of article 2534.[119]

2. *Not of the Kind, Not of the Quality; Not Conforming.*

Both articles 2529 and 2603 put the blame on a seller who fails to carry out his obligation **"to deliver the thing sold." (La. C.C. art. 2475.)** As stated above, this obligation to deliver assumes the existence of a binding contract of sale and is created by the effect of the sale transferring ownership of the thing sold from the seller to the buyer.

Article 2529 states that **"[w]hen the thing the seller has delivered, though in itself free from redhibitory defects, is not of the kind or quality specified in the contract or represented by the seller, the rights of the buyer are governed by other rules of sale and conventional obligations."** Along the same line, and looking very much like articles 35 & 50 of the CISG, **article 2603** states that **"[t]he seller must deliver to the buyer things that conform to the contract. Things do not conform to the contract when they are different from those selected by the buyer or are of a kind, quality, or quantity different from the one agreed."**[120]

In the case of **article 2529,** we are told specifically that **"the rights of the buyer are governed by other rules of sale and conventional obligations."** As regards the possible application of other rules of sale, we believe that such rules could be found in the Code articles on "Sales of Movables," particularly article 2603, as stated below. Whenever some rules on conventional obligations would apply, the legal regime would be the same as described above under Code article 2524.

As regards "non conforming" things, the remedies available to a buyer are laid out in articles 2603 *et seq.* Since these articles have already been presented and analyzed under the title "Transfer of Ownership and Risk of Loss,"[121] we will refer the reader to the above title.

B. Warranty of Law Against Defects/Vices.

1. *Scope of Application of the Warranty of Law: Vice and Timing.*

Not every defect in the thing sold can trigger the seller's obligation of warranty. Some conditions or requirements must be met by a defect before the buyer may have a right of action against his seller. In addition, a buyer must act as a reasonable

---

[119] *See supra,* p. 79.

[120] *See supra,* Obligations of the Seller, p. 53 *et seq.*

[121] *See also* CISG articles 50 *et seq.*; *see also* UCC articles § 2-508 *et seq.*

person when buying so that the buyer's behavior might have to be taken into account in an action against the seller. It is obvious that the seller's behavior should, *a fortiori ratione*, be looked at carefully since he is the party in the best position to know something about the thing he sells.

a1 — As regards the conditions that must be met by a "defect or a vice" for an action to be available to a buyer against his seller, **article 2520** states a first condition under the form of a general principle: **"The seller warrants the buyer against redhibitory defects, or vices, in the thing sold.**

A defect is redhibitory when it renders the thing useless, or its use so inconvenient that it must be presumed that a buyer would not have bought the thing had he known of the defect. The existence of such a defect gives a buyer the right to obtain rescission of the sale.

A defect is redhibitory also when, without rendering the thing totally useless, it diminishes its usefulness or its value so that it must be presumed that a buyer would still have bought it but for a lesser price. The existence of such a defect limits the right of a buyer to a reduction of the price."

Both the second and the third paragraphs of article 2520 require that the defect render the thing "useless, or its use so inconvenient" or that it "diminishes its usefulness or its value." However, under the second paragraph the uselessness of the thing will lead to the rescission of the sale, whereas under the third paragraph the remedy available to the buyer is one for the reduction in the price but the sale is preserved. Since the remedy available to the buyer under the second paragraph is the more drastic of the two, we ought to read "useless," in that paragraph, with the adjective "totally" which appears in the third paragraph but in reference, obviously, to the second paragraph. Such a "re-writing" of the two paragraphs would explain clearly the difference between the two remedies.

In their evaluation of either the "total uselessness" of the thing or "its diminished usefulness or value," the courts should take the same approach they would take to the concepts of "use" and "purpose" as these concepts are referred to in Civil Code articles 2524 and 2529 and as they were described above under the title "Warranty of Fitness."[122] All in all, for a defect to exist the buyer must be able to relate his dissatisfaction with the thing bought to an inherent or intrinsic ground pertaining to the manufacturing, the composition, and the structure of the thing itself. It is not because a thing is "incompatible" with another thing (a color with another color; a medication with another medication) or with a certain purpose (too "weak" an air conditioning unit, to cool a house to the "satisfaction" of the buyer; too "small" a ladder to reach a certain height) that the thing is defective. It is most important, therefore, to make the distinction between a "defect" and a "lack of fitness or conformity" because the remedies available to a buyer will be different.

a2 — A second condition required for a defect to exist and become a cause of action is that it must have been hidden. **Article 2521** lays down this condition as follows: **"The seller owes no warranty for defects in the thing that were known to the buyer at the time of the sale, or for defects that should have been**

[122] *See supra*, p. 71.

discovered by a reasonably prudent buyer of such things." Thus, a defect is not hidden either when the defect was known to the buyer or when the buyer should have discovered the defect.

Let us take the second situation first. What does it mean that the buyer "should" have discovered the defect? The principle that should govern here is that of the "average reasonable man" standard, the standard around which most of the Code articles are built. It is "reasonable" to expect from a buyer that, before he carries his obligation "to give" money to the seller, he should carry an obligation "to do," i.e. attempt to discover a defect, that will provide support to the "cause" of the obligation to give money, the price, to the seller. That "cause," it will be recalled, is the reason why the buyer wants to buy a particular thing in a condition such that he can make an ordinary or intended use of it. We read, for example, in **article 2604** that the **"buyer has a right to have a reasonable opportunity to inspect the things, even after delivery, for the purpose of ascertaining whether they conform to the contract."**[123] That obligation to do should be evaluated by the courts in light of the particular status of the buyer. An average reasonable man buyer should be held to a "reasonable obligation to do," which should be an obligation expected of this "abstract or ideal" person who is "the average reasonable man" (evaluation *in asbracto*). Such an average reasonable buyer should make a "prudent inspection" to be considered a "reasonably prudent buyer." He should inspect the thing he wants to buy so as to discover those defects inherent and intrinsic to the thing that a reasonable person would discover. Such would be the case of apparent defects easily discoverable by a reasonable person following a simple inspection of the thing. A reasonable buyer should not be held to a higher standard of inspection, that standard expected of a professional or an expert such as a mechanic or a dealer buying a car, an architect or a contractor buying a house, a collector of stamps . . . In those instances the courts should apply a higher, more personal standard of inspection or obligation to discover (an *in concreto* standard).

The second situation contemplated by article 2521 is that of a defect known to the buyer at the time of the sale. If a defect is discovered by the buyer following his inspecting the thing to be bought, it is obviously a defect known to the buyer.

There is a duty on the part of all parties to a contract to act in good faith. As **article 1759** states: **"Good faith shall govern the conduct of the obligor and the obligee in whatever pertains to the obligation."**[124] One must stress that article 1759 uses the **shall** form of the verb, thereby imposing a command or imposing an obligation on all parties to a contract. There should exist, therefore, a "duty" of the part of any seller to disclose any defect he knows the thing to have that might lead the buyer to change his mind before attempting to buy.[125] Suffice it to say here that **article 2522** does incorporate, even under some disguise, this duty of the vendor to disclose defects in the thing to the buyer. This article states: **"The buyer must give the seller notice of the existence of a redhibitory defect in the thing sold. That**

---

[123] *See also* La. C.C. arts. 1949, 1950, 1954, 2460.

[124] *See* Précis: Louisiana Law of Obligations in General, p. 19 and 20.

[125] The Civil Code, and the courts, make an application of this "duty" wherever a distinction is made between a good faith seller and a bad faith seller as we shall see in details below under the Effects of the Legal Warranty.

notice must be sufficiently timely as to allow the seller the opportunity to make the required repairs. A buyer who fails to give that notice suffers diminution of the warranty to the extent the seller can show that the defect could have been repaired or that the repairs would have been less burdensome, had he received timely notice.

Such notice is not required when the seller has actual knowledge of the existence of a redhibitory defect in the thing sold."

Indeed, if a seller wishes to be well treated by the law as any party acting in "good faith" is, if he wishes to be held to as low as possible, if at all, an obligation to suffer a reduction in the price or to have the right to recover some credit for the use the buyer made of a defective thing, such a seller will disclose the defects he knows the thing to have. As the first paragraph of article 2522 states, such a seller is entitled to be notified by the buyer that a defect in the thing renders its use inconvenient, for example, so that the seller, in good faith, is given an opportunity to repair the thing and make the buyer whole as is required by the commutative nature of the contract of sale. Conversely, if the buyer fails to act in good faith, should he fail to notify the seller of the defect so that, acting in bad faith, he denies his seller an opportunity to repair, as the law of warranty so requires of the buyer to do, it is quite reasonable to state that such a buyer should suffer a diminution of the warranty equal to the cost of the repairs that the seller was denied the right to make.

The second paragraph of the same article contemplates the situation of a seller who has actual knowledge of a defect and does not make it known to the buyer. In such a case, the buyer is under no obligation to give notice of the redhibitory defect to the seller since the latter knows of the defect. Because the burden of proving that a seller knows of a defect in the thing he sells is a difficult burden for the "average buyer" to carry, and because that buyer is usually in a weaker bargaining position than his seller, the law has instituted the very important presumption that **"a seller is deemed to know that the thing he sells has a redhibitory defect when he is a manufacturer of that thing." (La. C.C. art. 2545-2.)** The reason or foundation for creating this presumption of knowledge on the part of a manufacturer is helpful in explaining why the rule should be interpreted broadly, *a pari ratione* therefore, to include a seller who, although not the manufacturer per se, is nevertheless knowledgeable because he is a professional and is in the business of selling those "defective things" for the manufacturer. This broad extension of the presumption of bad faith seller to others than the manufacturer makes even more sense when we take into consideration the statement made in the second paragraph of **article 2531: "A seller who is held liable for a redhibitory defect has an action against the manufacturer of the defective thing, if the defect existed at the time the thing was delivered by the manufacturer to the seller, for any loss the seller sustained because of the redhibition. Any contractual provision that attempts to limit, diminish or prevent such recovery by a seller against the manufacturer shall have no effect."**

Since this right of the seller to bring an action against the manufacturer is of public order, why not bring to the forefront that manufacturer who, in the long or short run, cannot escape his liability, by holding professional sellers to the same presumption of knowledge of the defect? The buyer should not care whether the immediate seller or some far remote manufacturer will be ultimately liable as long as the buyer receives his fair share of the deal he entered into with the seller. The jurisprudence has taken this approach by adopting a broad interpretation of the concept of manufacturer in the sense of a **"seller who has actual knowledge."**[126]

a3 — The third condition which must exist for a buyer to have an action in redhibition against his seller is that of the existence of the defect at the time of delivery. **Article 2530** states: **"The warranty against redhibitory defects covers only defects that exist at the time of delivery. The defect shall be presumed to have existed at the time of delivery if it appears within three days from that time."**

A seller can be held liable only with respect to things over which he has control and that control he exercises until possession of the thing has been transferred to the buyer. From then on, the buyer may become the cause of the total or partial destruction of the thing and should bear full responsibility for that destruction. However the cut off point in the shift in the responsibility from one party to the other can be arbitrary and irrational and result in the buyer being denied a right of action against his seller simply because an hour has gone by since the time of delivery and his taking possession of the thing. So, the Civil Code resorts to a presumption to extend the liability of the seller some time beyond the moment of delivery of the thing: **"the defect shall be presumed to have existed at the time of delivery if it appears within three days from that time." (La. C.C. art. 2530.)** This presumption is obviously meant to protect the buyer who may not have been able to make an immediate use of the thing he bought and discover it was defective. During this three-day period, no prescription can run against the buyer.[127] Considering the foundation of this presumption and its reasonableness, protect the buyer, it is understandable that the jurisprudence has extended, in light of the circumstances of each case, the three day presumption to a few more days than these three days of article 2530. Beyond the presumptive period, it will be the responsibility of the buyer, as plaintiff, to prove that the defect existed before the sale. The time available to a buyer to bring an action in redhibition will vary with the good or bad faith of the seller, as will be discussed below.[128]

2. *Effects of Legal Warranty.*

A redhibitory defect, when it meets the conditions outlined above, may give rise to one of two rights of action: an action in reduction of the price (*actio aestimatoria* or *quanti minoris*) or an action for rescission of the sale, properly speaking, or action in redhibition (*actio redhibitoria*) as this type of action is commonly referred to. Yet, the adjective "redhibitory" refers to the defect itself as a ground for either one of the two actions. Should one action or the other be successful, the rights of recovery of the buyer and the seller will depend to a large extent on the good or bad

---

[126] La. C.C. art. 2522 2nd ¶; more about bad faith sellers and manufacturers *infra*, p. 83 *et seq.*

[127] The doctrine disallowing the running of prescription is called *contra non valentem agere non currit praescriptio* (literally translated "prescription does not run against one who is unable to act").

[128] *See infra*, p. 82.

faith of the parties. In addition, third parties may have rights that will need to be protected.

b1 — The two rights of action: notice, actions, prescriptive periods.

Louisiana Civil Code article 2520 provides for the two actions in its second and third paragraphs. On the one hand, **"the existence of such a defect gives a buyer the right to obtain rescission of the sale,"** and, on the other hand when the buyer would still have bought despite the defect, **"the existence of such a defect limits the right of a buyer to a reduction of the price."** Then, **article 2541** gives the buyer a choice between the two remedies: **"A buyer may choose to seek only reduction of the price even when the redhibitory defect is such as to give him the right to obtain rescission of the sale.**

In an action for rescission because of a redhibitory defect the court may limit the remedy of the buyer to a reduction of the price." However, before a buyer can bring one action or the other against his seller, he may have to give that **"seller a notice of the existence of a redhibitory defect in the thing sold"** so that the seller may be given **"the opportunity to make the required repairs." (La. C.C. art. 2522.)**

The giving of a notice to the seller is not an absolute right of all sellers. As is pervasive all through the Civil Code, the good faith or the bad faith of a party to a contract[129] will dictate the existence or not and the greater or lesser extent of that party's rights and obligations. Article 2522 is a good illustration of the application of article 1759 to a contract of sale. As seen above,[130] article 2522 gives a good faith seller the right to be notified of the existence of a redhibitory defect so that he can attempt to repair that defect and, thereby, give the buyer the fullness of the performance that buyer has the right to demand out of a synallagmatic and commutative contract as the contract of sale is. Thus the "legal warranty" provided by any seller is an accessory obligation flowing from the principal obligation **"to deliver the thing sold in the condition that, at the time of the sale, the parties expected, or should have expected, the thing to be in at the time of delivery, according to its nature." (La. C.C. art. 2489.)**

Where the requirement of giving notice of a defect to a good faith seller is justified by that good faith, *a contrario*, where a seller is in bad faith he should be denied that right to a notice: **"such notice is not required when the seller has actual knowledge of the existence of a redhibitory defect in the thing sold."**[131] As seen above, the Civil Code takes a broader approach to the concept of "bad faith" seller, to wit a seller who knows of a defect in the thing and fails to disclose it, than is suggested by the adjective "actual" in article 2522, since **"a seller is deemed to know that the thing he sells has a redhibitory defect when he is a manufacturer of that thing."**[132] As mentioned above,[133] the broader the courts read

---

[129] *See* Précis: Louisiana Law of Obligations in General, p. 19, 20; *see also supra*, p. 76.

[130] *See supra*, p. 76.

[131] La. C.C. art. 2522.

[132] La. C.C. art. 2545; *see also supra*, p. 76, *infra*, p. 85.

[133] *Id.*

"actual" and "deemed," the more buyers will be protected in their legitimate rights and, hopefully, the more sellers will stand behind the things they sell (or else they will be held liable!) so that there will result more trust in the relationships between sellers, whether manufacturers or not, and their buyers.

If **article 2541** gives the buyer the right to choose only a reduction of the price even when the redhibitory defect is such as to give him the right to obtain rescission of the sale, that right is not absolute in the sense that it does not, and should not, bind a court. Indeed, the same article states that **"in an action for rescission because of a redhibitory defect the court may limit the remedy of the buyer to a reduction of the price."** A court will exercise its discretion in this case as a court can do, as a general principle of the law of contracts, under article 2013.[134] It is a general principle of the civil law that when parties have entered into a contract, that contract should be upheld as much as possible since it is an expression of the wills of the parties. The courts should enforce the rights and obligations of both parties as those rights and obligations were devised by these parties when entering into their contract and as supplemented by the law of the Civil Code in particular. For example, the rationale of article 2014[135] on the greater or lesser importance of a failure to perform an obligation should be applied, *a fortiori ratione*, to the obligations proper to a contract of sale so as to give to a good faith seller an opportunity to fully fulfill his obligation to deliver a thing in its best condition. To the extent a buyer has received a "substantial performance" from his seller he should be compelled to allow the seller to "perform that part not rendered" if the buyer's interest was not substantially impaired. The court is then entrusted with deciding which one of two remedies should be given the buyer.

Whatever action is open to the buyer, the same prescriptive period will apply. As **article 2534** states:

"A. (1) The action for redhibition against a seller who did not know of the existence of a defect in the thing sold prescribes in four years from the day delivery of such thing was made to the buyer or one year from the day the defect was discovered by the buyer, whichever occurs first.

(2) However, when the defect is of residential or commercial immovable property, an action for redhibition against a seller who did not know of the existence of the defect prescribes in one year from the day delivery of the property was made to the buyer.

B. The action for redhibition against a seller who knew, or is presumed to have known, of the existence of a defect in the thing sold prescribes in one year from the day the defect was discovered by the buyer.

C. In any case prescription is interrupted when the seller accepts the thing for

---

[134] La. C.C. art. 2013: "When the obligor fails to perform, the obligee has a right to the judicial dissolution of the contract or, according to the circumstances, to regard the contract as dissolved. In either case, the obligee may recover damages. In an action involving judicial dissolution, the obligor who failed to perform may be granted, according to the circumstances, an additional time to perform."

[135] La. C.C. art. 2014: "A contract may not be dissolved when the obligor has rendered a substantial part of the performance and the part not rendered does not substantially impair the interest of the obligee."

repairs and commences anew from the day he tenders it back to the buyer or notifies the buyer of his refusal or inability to make the required repairs."

2534(A)(1) deals with the good faith seller. We see here, again, that the good faith seller, when compared with the bad faith seller in paragraph 2534(B) is better treated than his bad faith counterpart. The absolute limit of the prescriptive period of an action against a good faith seller is four years from the day of delivery or one year from the day the buyer discovered the defect. Since the buyer of a good faith seller must give the latter notice of the existence of a redhibitory defect (La. C.C. art. 2522) so that the seller can make the necessary repairs, the prescriptive period will be **"interrupted when the seller accepts the thing for repairs and commences anew from the day he tenders it back to the buyer or notifies the buyer of his refusal or inability to make the required repairs." (La. C.C. art. 2534(C).)** When the seller tenders the repaired thing back to the buyer a new prescriptive period of one year begins.[136]

2534(A)(2) provides for a special and limitative prescriptive period of one year from the day of delivery in a sale of residential or commercial immovable property by a seller who did not know of the existence of the defect.

2534(B) focuses on the "bad faith seller" who is **"a seller who knew or is presumed to have known of the existence of a defect in the thing he sold."** One should add to these bad faith sellers, a seller who is "deemed" to know such as a manufacturer under article 2545. As is to be expected, this "bad faith" seller will be treated harshly in this sense that **"the action for redhibition . . . prescribes in one year from the day the defect was discovered by the buyer."** The postponement of the beginning of the prescriptive period from the day of delivery, in the case of the good faith seller, to the day of discovery of the defect in the case of a bad faith seller will protect the buyer for a long period of time within the ten year prescriptive period of a personal action beginning at the time of perfection of the contract of sale.[137] But as 2534(C) states, **"in any case prescription is interrupted when the seller (even the bad faith seller) accepts the thing for repairs and commences anew from the day he tenders it back to the buyer. . . . "**

As regards this issue of the beginning and interruption of the prescriptive period of an action in redhibition, one must consider the situations raised in the second, third, and fourth paragraphs of article 2532.

The first paragraph of this article assumes that the buyer has been successful in his action in redhibition against his seller. If such is the case, then the **"buyer is bound to return the thing to the seller, for which purpose he must take care of the thing as a prudent administrator, but is not bound to deliver it back until all his claims, or judgments, arising from the defect are satisfied."** The buyer is entitled to exercise a right that the law makes available to creditors who are in possession of things belonging to their debtor, the right of retention.[138]

---

[136] La. C.C. art. 3466.

[137] La. C.C. art. 3499.

[138] For an illustration, consider Louisiana Civil Code article 2487: "The seller may refuse to deliver

Paragraphs 2, 3 and 4 of article 2532 are somewhat out of place in this article because they contemplate situations totally different from the situation dealt with in the 1st paragraph as seen above. Indeed, in paragraphs 2, 3 and 4 we have a buyer who is in possession of the defective thing and who has not yet brought an action in redhibition before the defective thing is destroyed.

Under paragraph 2, **"if the redhibitory defect has caused the destruction of the thing the loss is borne by the seller, and the buyer may bring his action even after the destruction has occurred."** Before the buyer has had time to notify the seller of the defect in the thing, the latter is destroyed because of its own defect. The buyer is still entitled to bring an action in redhibition although it will his burden to prove that the thing was destroyed on account of its own defect. This burden should be easier the closer the seller can be assimilated to a manufacturer.

Under paragraph 3, the buyer appears to be in a predicament if the letter of this paragraph is to be taken as a definite and final statement of the law. It reads as follows: **"If the thing is destroyed by a fortuitous event before the buyer gives the seller notice of the existence of a redhibitory defect that would have given rise to a rescission of the sale, the loss is borne by the buyer."** One can understand why a buyer who fails to notify his seller of the existence of a defect in the thing when that buyer had the time and opportunity to do so and give, thereby, his seller the right to repair the defective thing, should bear the loss if a fortuitous event should destroy the thing after the buyer failed to notify his seller when he could have done so. But what if, before the buyer had the time to notify his seller of the defect, the thing was to be destroyed by a fortuitous event? Why should the fortuitous event "punish" the buyer and "reward" the seller by protecting the latter from an action in redhibition that, under normal circumstances, the buyer could have brought and, possibly, won? We are told in the fourth paragraph of this article that if the buyer had an opportunity to notify the seller before the destruction by fortuitous event, **"the loss is borne by the seller, except to the extent the buyer has insured that loss."** Again, what about the in-between situation? It is our opinion that, despite the wording of this third paragraph, a buyer should have the right to bring an action in redhibition although the burden of proof of the defect will be made difficult by the destruction resulting from the fortuitous event. One could make the argument that the buyer's insurance would likely pay for his loss, as the fourth paragraph of article 2532 indicates. That may be so, but should we not then subrogate the insurance company into the rights of its insured against the seller? Yet, subrogation presupposes that the buyer has a right of action against the seller.[139] Is it not likely that the buyer who calls on his insurance company to pay for his loss might see his premium go up, thereby "penalizing" him for having been deprived of an action against his seller despite the obstacles to overcome?

The second part of paragraph 4 of article 2532 is a mere application of the rules of subrogation. A seller, who is subrogated into the rights of his buyer, may attempt to recover whatever price he had to return to his buyer from the third party who was the cause of the loss of the defective thing as, for example, under the situation

the thing sold until the buyer tenders payment of the price, unless the seller has granted the buyer a term for such payment."

139 On Subrogation, see Précis: Louisiana Law of Obligations in General, p. 103–116.

contemplated in the first paragraph of article 2531.[140]

b2 — The rights and obligations of the seller and buyer in a redhibitory action.

The rights and obligations of the parties to the sale will vary depending, once again, on whether they are in good or in bad faith. Special problems arise when there are multiple sellers or multiple buyers.

A good faith seller being one **"who did not know that the thing he sold had a defect is only bound to repair, remedy, or correct the defect. If he is unable or fails so to do, he is then bound to return the price to the buyer with interest from the time it was paid, and to reimburse him for the reasonable expenses occasioned by the sale, as well as those incurred for the preservation of the thing, less the credit to which the seller is entitled if the use made of the thing, or the fruits it has yielded, were of some value to the buyer." (La. C.C. art. 2531,** first paragraph.) A good faith seller is also one who is neither "deemed" nor "presumed" to know of any defect in the thing he sells. Such a good faith seller is given the right to attempt to repair, correct or remedy the defect. Since he is merely required to attempt to repair, the seller is under an obligation of means that is to say to do his best in his attempt to repair the defective thing.[141] Thus, if the seller cannot repair the defective thing, but because he is a good faith seller, he will have to "place his buyer back in the situation in which he was in before the contract." As the first step towards that end, the seller must return the price he received for the thing he sold; the seller must, in addition, pay an interest on the price from the day he received that price. The assumption is that the sale was either a cash sale with payment in money to the seller, or a credit sale such that the seller received the price in money from a third party so that the seller made use of that price and, thereby, derived some benefit from it. Conversely, and in the meantime, the buyer was deprived of the use of the money of the price if he paid cash, or he had to pay interest on the price which he borrowed from a third party; either way, the buyer is out of pocket in the amount of the interest that the price could have brought him had he been able to invest it. Hence the buyer's right to claim the interest from the seller. Besides the price and the interest, the seller may owe the buyer the reasonable expenses of the sale (which may be the shipping expenses or delivery expenses) as well as the expenses the buyer may have incurred in his efforts to protect and preserve the thing until it could be returned to the seller. We find the same obligation of a seller under article 2532-1 whenever the buyer took care, as a prudent administrator, of the thing to be returned to the seller following the buyer having obtained rescission of the sale. In this capacity of a prudent administrator, the buyer should be entitled to the expenses he incurred to preserve the thing for the benefit of the seller. The impoverishment of the buyer for the benefit of the seller should be compensated by the latter.

As a counterpart to these obligations of the seller, article 2531-1 gives that seller a right to a credit if the use made of the thing, or the fruits the thing has yielded, were of some value to the buyer. The outcome is that each party acting in good faith

---

[140] *See infra.*

[141] On Obligations of Means versus Obligations of Result, see Précis: Louisiana Law of Obligations in General, p. 9–11.

will be placed back in as fair and even a situation as possible so as not to suffer any loss or impoverishment. The monetary evaluation of the credit owed the seller for the use of the defective thing will have to be made by the court according to the factual circumstances of each case and, in particular, according to the greater or lesser use the buyer made or could have made of the defective thing.

A second and most important right given to the seller is a right of action against the manufacturer of the defective thing. Under **article 2531-2, "a seller who is held liable for a redhibitory defect has an action against the manufacturer of the defective thing, if the defect existed at the time the thing was delivered by the manufacturer to the seller, for any loss the seller sustained because of the redhibition. Any contractual provision that attempts to limit, diminish or prevent such recovery by a seller against the manufacturer shall have no effect."**

This direct right of action given to a good faith seller is equivalent to a security device granted by law, as it is a right of public order in the sense that it cannot be waived by any contractual provision between the seller and his manufacturer. Again, the good faith of the seller will be his full protection against a manufacturer who is, himself, deemed to know of the defect and is, therefore, a bad faith seller.[142] Because of this direct right of action against the manufacturer and because the manufacturer is in bad faith, the manufacturer should be held solidarily liable with the seller at least for the payment of the price back to the buyer. Since the manufacturer is deemed to know of the defect, its bad faith should make him liable to the seller, under article 2545, for all the expenses the seller may have to pay back to the buyer. The seller's good faith should exonerate him from any liability and he should be made whole.[143] Since the warranty between the seller and the manufacturer cannot be waived, it would be wise for the good faith seller to call the manufacturer in warranty in any action brought under this article 2531.

One will note that the second sentence of this second paragraph of article 2531 does not tie this right of action to the exclusive existence of a contract of sale between the seller of the defective thing and the manufacturer. Therefore, reasoning *a fortiori ratione* or *a pari ratione*, the right of a seller of a defective thing to bring an action against the manufacturer should be extended to any contract, consignment, franchising, representation, etc., entered into between a manufacturer and the ultimate seller of the defective thing.

A bad faith seller, under **article 2545**, is one **"who knows that the thing he sells has a defect but omits to declare it, or a seller who declares that the thing has a quality that he knows it does not have."** Such a bad faith seller, besides not being given an opportunity to repair (but who is the buyer who will take a chance and not give his seller, in good or bad faith, an opportunity to repair?) will be **"liable to the buyer for the return of the price with interest from the time it was paid, for the reimbursement of the reasonable expenses occasioned by the sale and those incurred for the preservation of the thing, and also for damages and reasonable attorney fees. If the use made of the thing, or the fruits it might**

---

[142] *See* La. C.C. art. 2545.

[143] On Solidarity, see Précis: Louisiana Law of Obligations in General, p. 59–69.

have yielded, were of some value to the buyer, such a seller may be allowed credit for such use or fruits." One will have noticed both a resemblance and a difference between article 2531 on the good faith seller and article 2545 on the bad faith seller.

As regards the resemblance, the bad faith seller owes to the buyer the return of the purchase price, the interest on that price from the time it was paid, the reimbursement of the reasonable expenses of the sale and those incurred for the preservation of the thing, should the buyer have incurred these expenses. Again, the reason for such obligations is to return the buyer to a situation where he would not be impoverished as a result of his purchase of a defective thing. Another point of resemblance lies in the fact that **"if the use made of the thing, or the fruits it might have yielded, were of some value to the buyer, such a seller may be allowed credit for such use or fruits."** Was this "allowing a credit" to the *bad faith seller* an afterthought? A "lobbied" and forced addition included under the form of a second sentence to follow the first sentence? Why should the bad faith seller be placed on the same level as the good faith seller whose right flows naturally from his being in good faith? The use of the verb "may," in **"a seller may be allowed credit,"** appears to suggest both, first, some reticence on the part of the legislator to allow a credit to a bad faith seller and, second, some delegation of that responsibility to the courts. Since, as discussed below, a bad faith seller **"is liable for damages,"** it is somewhat difficult to reconcile allowing a credit to the bad faith seller and, at the same time, to impose on him the payment of damages.

Where article 2545 differs from article 2531, the differences are justified by the fact that the seller is in bad faith and, for that reason, should be accountable to the buyer for something more than what the good faith seller owes that buyer. The first additional item the bad faith seller owes his buyer is "damages." The granting of damages by a court is one way for that court to enforce the principle of good faith in contracts, to be involved in policing the commercial, financial . . . transactions between consumers and sellers/manufacturers, to enforce fair and even relationships between the "weak" party-buyer and the "strong" party-seller.

The great novelty of article 2545 is the statement that the bad faith seller **"is liable . . . for . . . reasonable attorney fees."** This creates quite an enticement for buyers to bring an action against a so-called *bad faith seller* since the payment of an attorney's fees can be quite a deterrent for many buyers considering bringing an action against their seller.

Since we are dealing with two parties in bad faith, the seller and the manufacturer, who owe the same "things" to the buyer, they should be held either indivisibly bound or solidarily liable vis-à-vis the buyer.[144] Between them, they should be held liable in proportion to their degree of fault and/or bad faith.[145]

b3 — *Special problems* arise when there *are multiple sellers or multiple buyers* as contemplated by **article 2538: "The warranty against redhibitory vices is owed by each of multiple sellers in proportion to his interest. Multiple buyers must**

---

[144] On Indivisibility and Solidarity, see Précis: Louisiana Law of Obligations in General, p. 59–69, 80–90.

[145] *Id.*

concur in an action for rescission because of a redhibitory defect. An action for reduction of the price may be brought by one of multiple buyers in proportion to his interest. The same rules apply if a thing with a redhibitory defect is transferred, inter vivos or mortis causa, to multiple successors."

Considering that "warranty" is an indivisible concept or entity[146] in the sense that either it exists or it does not and that, if it exists, it is most difficult to understand how two or three sellers can be *"divisibly"* **"bound to repair, remedy or correct the defect."**[147] Likewise, as article 2538 states, when warranty against a redhibitory defect is owed by **"each of multiple sellers,"** how is one to repair **"in proportion to his interest?"** How can a defect be divided in proportion to the individual interest of each one of multiple sellers? How can one seller repair his proportion of the defect without interfering with the other sellers" interests in repairing their own proportions? How should one apply this article to the situation where one of multiple sellers is in good faith and the other sellers are in bad faith? Under the law of sale as it existed before the 1993-95 revision, the obligation of warranty owed by multiple sellers was *indivisible* which, from the point of view of the right of good faith sellers to repair, made a lot of sense. On the other hand, when one is looking at the obligation of good faith sellers to return the price, with interest, to the buyer and to reimburse him the reasonable expenses of the sale,[148] it makes sense to divide these obligations to pay sums of money between the sellers because these obligations are *divisible*, money being an object which can be divided.[149] As regards bad faith sellers, as per article 2545, they owe obligations of money to the buyer and these obligations can be divided among the bad faith sellers in proportion to their degree of bad faith.

Had the first paragraph of article 2538 not been as broadly phrased but, on the contrary, had it referred specifically to the outcome of an action for rescission, as does the second paragraph of the article, and thus dealt with the sellers" obligations to reimburse the buyer and pay the expenses, that first paragraph would have been consistent with the legal effects of divisible obligations and, thus, with the second paragraph of the same article.

Indeed, the outcome of an action in rescission, to which the buyers must concur to avoid a multiplicity of actions for the same indivisible obligation to repair, amounting to the reimbursement of the price, interest, and expenses, all these obligations have for their object the payment of money and, thus, can be divided, more or less easily, among multiple buyers in proportion to each buyer's interest.

As regards the third paragraph of article 2538, the word **successors** should be interpreted broadly to include creditors of the buyers, as the same word has been interpreted broadly in relation to "lesion."[150] In addition, the use of the verb "transferred" should not be a bar to creditors of one buyer or another who may be

---

[146] On Indivisible Obligations, see Precis: Louisiana Law of Obligations in General, p. 80.

[147] La. C.C. art. 2531.

[148] *See supra*, p. 82.

[149] On Indivisible and Divisible Obligations, see note 146 *supra*.

[150] On Lesion, see *supra*, p. 31.

entitled to bring a revocatory (or Pauliana) action or an oblique action.[151]

C. Warranty of Law and Special Contracts of Sale.

Article 2537 states that **"judicial sales resulting from a seizure are not subject to the rules on redhibition."** This Code article is further supplemented by Louisiana Revised Statutes section 9:3169. On the other hand, Section 9:3174 states that all the warranties that apply to private sales apply just as much **in judicial sales of the property of successions.**

There are additional statutes that formulate special rules of warranty according to the nature of the thing sold. We can cite only a selected few here as they are special statutes outside the main structure of the Civil Code: 1) R.S. 3:1431 and 1443 et seq. on the sale of seeds; 2) R.S. 9:2774 on guarantees and warranties in construction specifications; 3) R.S. 9:3141 and 3144 et seq. on New Home Warranty Act and Exclusions of Warranties; 4) R.S. 37:1920 et seq. on Itinerant Vendors; 5) R.S. 51:911.21 and 911.23 et seq. on Manufactured Housing; 6) R.S. 51:1941, 1942, 1943 et seq. on Motor Vehicle Warranties, the so-called Louisiana Auto Lemon Law; 7) Federal Trade Commission Trade Regulation Rule, Title 16, Code of Federal Regulations Part 433 Preservation of Consumers" Claims and Defenses; 8) Truth in Lending Regulations, Title 12 Banks and Banking, or Regulation Z, 12 CFR Part 26; 9) Magnuson-Moss Warranty Act, 15 USC § 2301 *et seq.*

D. Conventional Warranty against Defects.

Since warranty against defects is not of the "essence" of a contract of sale in the sense that an absence of warranty does not negate the existence of a sale, the Civil Code states that **"[t]he parties may agree to an exclusion or limitation of the warranty against redhibitory defects. The terms of the exclusion or limitation must be clear and unambiguous and must be brought to the attention of the buyer.**

A buyer is not bound by an otherwise effective exclusion or limitation of the warranty when the seller has declared that the thing has a quality that he knew it did not have. The buyer is subrogated to the rights in warranty of the seller against other persons, even when the warranty is excluded." (La. C.C. art. 2548.) This article is the only one governing the parties' ability to devise their own conventional warranty in lieu of the legal warranty.

Although article 2548 mentions only "exclusion" and "limitation" of the warranty by law, it is obvious that, at the initiative of the seller, the contract of sale may include provisions which "increase, improve" the rights of the buyer beyond the legal warranty. A seller could grant his buyer a longer prescriptive period, five years for example, than the one or four year period from the day of delivery or the day of discovery of the defect of article 2534; a seller may offer his buyer a warranty for any defect, minor or major, coming into existence at any time for a two year period regardless of the day of delivery; a seller could offer an immediate

---

[151] La. C.C. arts. 2036, 2044.

trade-in for a thing of the same model and year instead of repairing the defective thing.

More common in practice, particularly in consumer transactions, are clauses that, in a contract of sale, limit or even exclude the seller's warranty against redhibitory defects. Such clauses must be, first of all, expressly stipulated otherwise the legal warranty would come into play, and, in second place, they **"must be clear and unambiguous and must be brought to the attention of the buyer,"** in the words of **article 2548**. A common contractual provision meant, in the mind of the seller at least, to exclude or limit the legal warranty is the *"as is"* clause. Such a clause should be interpreted against its drafter,[152] the seller very likely, and, as the courts of this State have required, it should be clear, unambiguous and brought to the attention of the buyer which means, very often, explained to the buyer. It follows that such a clause cannot bind at all a buyer **"when the seller has declared that the thing has a quality that he knew it did not have." (La. C.C. art. 2548-2.)** In this last instance, article 2545 must control and preempt the contractual exclusion of warranty against defects, just like in the case of warranty against eviction according to which a **"seller is liable for an eviction that is occasioned by his own act and any agreement to the contrary is null." (La. C.C. art. 2503-2.)**[153] The parallelism, in both form and substance, between articles 2548 and 2503 extends to the third paragraph of both of these articles where they use exactly the same terms: **"the buyer is subrogated to the rights in warranty of the seller against other persons, even when the warranty is excluded."**[154]

Article 2
Obligations of the Buyer

The buyer's obligations are few and they are the counterparts of the seller's obligations since the obligations of one party are correlative to the obligations of the other. Where the seller must transfer the ownership of the thing sold to the buyer, the latter must transfer to the seller the ownership of the price of that thing, and where the seller must deliver the thing to the buyer, the latter must take delivery of that same thing. Such are the features of the synallagmatic and commutative nature of the contract of sale.

Article 2549 refers to the two obligations of the buyer as follows: **"the buyer is bound to pay the price and to take delivery of the thing."**

§ 4.2.1. OBLIGATION TO PAY THE PRICE.

Most of the articles listed under the "Obligations of the buyer" deal with the buyer's obligation to pay the price. That obligation has, as its principal object, the price agreed upon with the seller and, as its accessory objects, any interest on the price and some expenses of the sale should it be the case.

---

[152] La. C.C. arts. 2056, 2057.

[153] *See supra*, p. 70.

[154] See *supra*, p. 71, discussing Louisiana Civil Code article 2503-3.

As regards the price, **article 2550** states that **"[p]ayment of the price is due at the time and place stipulated in the contract, or at the time and place of delivery if the contract contains no such stipulation."**

If the buyer fails to pay on time, the occurrence of the term will automatically put that buyer in default.[155] Because the buyer's obligation is to pay a sum of money, the **"damages for delay in performance are measured by the interest on that sum from the time it is due, at the rate agreed by the parties or, in absence of agreement, at the rate of legal interest . . . " (La. C.C. art. 2000.) Article 2553** does indeed provide that **"[t]he buyer owes interest on the price from the time it is due."**

Should there be any cost or expense related to the taking of delivery, **article 2483** states that **"the cost of . . . taking delivery is borne by the buyer, in the absence of agreement to the contrary."**

In the event the buyer fails to perform his principal obligation to pay the price after the ownership of the thing sold has passed to him from the seller, one remedy available to the seller is the dissolution of the sale and the return of the parties to the situation they were in before the sale. As **article 2561** states in its first sentence: **"If the buyer fails to pay the price, the seller may sue for dissolution of the sale. . . . "**

However, the circumstances may be such that there is no real risk that the seller may not receive payment of the price from the buyer because all the buyer really needs is a little more time to make his payment. In this situation, as is the case **"In an action involving judicial dissolution, the obligor . . . may be granted, according to the circumstances, an additional time to perform." (La. C.C. art. 2013.)** This rule is applied in these terms to a contract of sale of an immovable: **"When an action is brought for the dissolution of the sale an immovable and there is no danger that the seller may lose the price and the thing, the court, according to the circumstances, may grant the buyer an extension of time, not in excess of sixty days, to make payment, and shall pronounce the sale dissolved if the buyer fails to pay within that time. When there is such a danger, the court may not grant the buyer an extension of time for payment." (La. C.C. art. 2562.)**

Nevertheless, the need to preserve the stability of transactions bearing on immovables has led to the formulation of a form of exception to the automatic effect of a putting in default consisting in an express clause of dissolution of the contract of sale. As **article 2563** states: **"When the contract of sale of an immovable expressly provides for dissolution in case of failure to pay the price, the buyer still has the right to pay, in spite of the express dissolution clause, for as long as the seller has not given the buyer notice that he avails himself of that clause or has not filed suit for dissolution."** The buyer may thus prevent the dissolution of the sale by paying the price after the term has expired but before an express putting in default by the seller and the claim by the latter that he is availing himself of that dissolution clause.

---

[155] On Term, see Précis: Louisiana Law of Obligations in General, p. 28–39.

This right of the seller to seek the dissolution of the sale is not the only one available to the seller. As seen above, the seller can sue for payment of the price.[156] He can also exercise his privilege under the conditions laid down in article 3227 *et seq.* on the privilege of the vendor of movables, or article 3249 *et seq.* on the privilege of the vendor of an immovable.

When the contract of sale is perfect and the ownership of the thing is with the buyer, the seller owes an obligation of warranty against eviction whether the buyer has paid the price or not.[157] If the buyer has paid the price, as expected, and is threatened with eviction subsequently to his payment, the buyer's right is restricted to an action in eviction. As **article 2560** states: **"A buyer who paid the price before being evicted of the thing may not demand that the seller return the price or give security for it."** On the other hand, **a buyer** who has not paid the price or paid only a part of it, should he be evicted or threatened with eviction by the claim of a third person, **"may withhold payment of the price until he is restored to possession, unless the seller gives security for any loss the buyer may sustain as a result of the eviction." (La. C.C. art. 2557,** first section.)

§ 4.2.2. OBLIGATION TO TAKE DELIVERY OF THE THING.

The buyer must take delivery of the thing where the seller is required to make that delivery according to the nature of the thing to be delivered. As **article 2477** states: **"Delivery of an immovable is deemed to take place upon execution of the writing that transfers its ownership.**

Delivery of a movable takes place by handing it over to the buyer. If the parties so intend delivery may take place in another manner, such as by the seller's handing over to the buyer the key to the place where the thing is stored, or by negotiating to him a document of title to the thing, or even by the mere consent of the parties if the thing sold cannot be transported at the time of the sale or if the buyer already has the thing at that time." Should the "taking of delivery" require the payment of some expenses, such as shipping or transportation expenses, these expenses are borne by the buyer. (La. C.C. art. 2483.)

In the event the buyer fails to take delivery of the thing at the time and place where the seller is to make the delivery, that **"buyer who fails to take delivery of the thing after a tender of such delivery, or who fails to pay the price, is liable for expenses incurred by the seller in preservation of the thing and for other damages sustained by the seller." (La. C.C. art. 2555.)** Should the seller be greatly inconvenienced by the buyer's failure to take delivery, the seller, as obligee of the buyer's obligation to take delivery, **"has a right to the judicial dissolution of the contract or, according to the circumstances, to regard the contract as dissolved." (La. C.C. art. 2013.)**

When the object of the contract of sale is a movable, **"if . . . the seller chooses to seek dissolution of the sale because of the failure of the buyer to perform,**

[156] *See supra*, p. 88.

[157] See *supra*, p. 61, for a discussion on warranty against eviction.

the court may not grant to the buyer any extension of time to perform." (La. **C.C. art. 2564.**) In this same particular instance where **"the buyer fails to perform a contract of sale of movable things, the seller, within a reasonable time and in good faith, may resell those things that are still in his possession. In such a case the seller is entitled to recover the difference between the contract price and the resale price. The seller may recover also other damages, less the expenses saved as a result of the buyer's failure to perform.**

Unless the things are perishable or subject to rapid decline in value, the seller must give the buyer reasonable notice of the public sale at which the things will be resold, or of his intention to resell the things at a private sale." (La. C.C. art. 2611.)[158]

[158] In the event a buyer is unable to pay the "price" in money, he could, with the consent of the seller, "give" the latter "a thing to the obligee (seller) who accepts it in payment of a debt." La. C.C. art. 2655. On "Giving in Payment," see Précis on Conventional Obligations.

APPENDIX I

LOUISIANA CIVIL CODE 2015

Art. 2438. Rules of Other Titles

In all matters for which no special provision is made in this title, the contract of sale is governed by the rules of the titles on Obligations in General and Conventional Obligations or Contracts.

Art. 2439. Definition

Sale is a contract whereby a person transfers ownership of a thing to another for a price in money. The thing, the price, and the consent of the parties are requirements for the perfection of a sale.

Art. 2440. Sale of Immovable, Method of Making

A sale or promise of sale of an immovable must be made by authentic act or by act under private signature, except as provided in Article 1839.

Art. 2441. [Reserved]

Art. 2442. Recordation of Sale of Immovable to Affect Third Parties

The parties to an act of sale or promise of sale of immovable property are bound from the time the act is made, but such an act is not effective against third parties until it is filed for registry according to the laws of registry.

Art. 2443. Purchase of a Thing Already Owned

A person cannot purchase a thing he already owns. Nevertheless, the owner of a thing may purchase the rights of a person who has, or may have, an adverse claim to the thing.

Art. 2444 to 2446 [Reserved]

Art. 2447. Sale of Litigious Rights, Prohibitions

Officers of a court, such as judges, attorneys, clerks, and law enforcement agents, cannot purchase litigious rights under contestation in the jurisdiction of that court. The purchase of a litigious right by such an officer is null and makes the purchaser liable for all costs, interest, and damages.

Art. 2448. Things that May be Sold

All things corporeal or incorporeal, susceptible of ownership, may be the object of a contract of sale, unless the sale of a particular thing is prohibited by law.

Art. 2449. [Reserved]

Art. 2450. Sale of Future Things

A future thing may be the object of a contract of sale. In such a case the coming into existence of the thing is a condition that suspends the effects of the sale. A party who, through his fault, prevents the coming into existence of the thing is liable for damages.

Art. 2451. Sale of a Hope

A hope may be the object of a contract of sale. Thus, a fisherman may sell a haul of his net before he throws it. In that case the buyer is entitled to whatever is caught in the net, according to the parties" expectations, and even if nothing is caught the sale is valid.

Art. 2452. Sale of the Thing of Another

The sale of a thing belonging to another does not convey ownership.

Art. 2453. Sale of a Thing Pending Litigation of Ownership

When the ownership of a thing is the subject of litigation, the sale of that thing during the pendency of the suit does not affect the claimant's rights. Where the thing is immovable, the rights of third persons are governed by the laws of registry.

Art. 2454 to 2455 [Reserved]

Art. 2456. Transfer of Ownership

Ownership is transferred between the parties as soon as there is agreement on the thing and the price is fixed, even though the thing sold is not yet delivered nor the price paid.

Art. 2457. Transfer of Ownership; Things Not Individualized

When the object of a sale is a thing that must be individualized from a mass of things of the same kind, ownership is transferred when the thing is thus individualized according to the intention of the parties.

Art. 2458. Sale by Weight, Tale of Measure; Lump Sales

When things are sold by weight, tale, or measure, ownership is transferred between the parties when the seller, with the buyer's consent, weighs, counts or measures the things.

When things, such as goods or produce, are sold in a lump, ownership is transferred between the parties upon their consent, even though the things are not yet weighed, counted, or measured.

Art. 2459. [Reserved]

Art. 2460. Sale on View or Trial

When the buyer has reserved the view or trial of the thing, ownership is not transferred from the seller to the buyer until the latter gives his approval of the thing.

Art. 2461. Inclusion of Accessories

The sale of a thing includes all accessories intended for its use in accordance with the law of property.

Art. 2462. [Reserved]

Art. 2463. Expenses

The expenses of the act and other expenses incidental to the sale must be borne by the buyer.

Art. 2464. Price, Essential Elements

The price must be fixed by the parties in a sum either certain or determinable through a method agreed by them. There is no sale unless the parties intended that a price be paid.

The price must not be out of all proportion with the value of the thing sold. Thus, the sale of a plantation for a dollar is not a sale, though it may be a donation in disguise.

Art. 2465. Price Left to Determination by Third Person

The price may be left to the determination of a third person. If the parties fail to agree on or to appoint such a person, or if the one appointed is unable or unwilling to make a determination, the price may be determined by the court.

Art. 2466. No Price Fixed by the Parties

When the thing sold is a movable of the kind that the seller habitually sells and the parties said nothing about the price, or left it to be agreed later and they fail to agree, the price is a reasonable price at the time and place of delivery. If there is an exchange or market for such things, the quotations or price lists of the place of delivery or, in their absence, those of the nearest market, are a basis for the determination of a reasonable price.

Nevertheless, if the parties intend not to be bound unless a price be agreed on, there is no contract without such an agreement.

Art. 2467. Transfer of Risk

The risk of loss of the thing sold owing to a fortuitous event is transferred from the seller to the buyer at the time of delivery.

That risk is so transferred even when the seller has delivered a nonconforming thing, unless the buyer acts in the manner required to dissolve the contract.

Art. 2468 to 2473. [Reserved]

Art. 2474. Construction of Ambiguities Respecting Obligations of Seller

The seller must clearly express the extent of his obligations arising from the contract, and any obscurity or ambiguity in that expression must be interpreted against the seller.

Art. 2475. Seller's Obligations of Delivery and Warranty

The seller is bound to deliver the thing sold and to warrant to the buyer ownership and peaceful possession of, and the absence of hidden defects in, that thing. The seller also warrants that the thing sold is fit for its intended use.

Art. 2476. [Reserved]

Art. 2477. Methods of Making Delivery

Delivery of an immovable is deemed to take place upon execution of the writing that transfers its ownership.

Delivery of a movable takes place by handing it over to the buyer. If the parties so intend delivery may take place in another manner, such as by the seller's handing over to the buyer the key to the place where the thing is stored, or by negotiating to him a document of title to the thing, or even by the mere consent of the parties if the thing sold cannot be transported at the time of the sale or if the buyer already has the thing at that time.

Art. 2478. to 2479. [Reserved]

Art. 2480. Retention of Possession by Seller, Presumption of Simulation

When the thing sold remains in the corporeal possession of the seller the sale is presumed to be a simulation, and, where the interest of heirs and creditors of the seller is concerned, the parties must show that their contract is not a simulation.

Art. 2481. Incorporeals, Method of Making Delivery

Delivery of incorporeal movable things incorporated into an instrument, such as stocks and bonds, takes place by negotiating such instrument to the buyer. Delivery of other incorporeal movables, such as credit rights, takes place upon the transfer of those movables.

Art. 2482. Things Not in Possession of Seller

When at the time of the sale the seller is not in possession of the thing sold he must obtain possession at his cost and deliver the thing to the buyer.

Art. 2483. Costs of Delivery and of Removal

The cost of making delivery is borne by the seller and that of taking delivery by the buyer, in the absence of agreement to the contrary.

Art. 2484. Place of Delivery

Delivery must be made at the place agreed upon by the parties or intended by them. In the absence of such agreement or intent, delivery must be made at the place where the thing is located at the time of the sale.

Art. 2485. Buyer's Rights upon Default, Damages

When the seller fails to deliver or to make timely delivery of the thing sold, the buyer may demand specific performance of the obligation of the seller to deliver, or may seek dissolution of the sale.

In either case, and also when the seller has made a late delivery, the buyer may seek damages.

Art. 2486. [Reserved]

Art. 2487. Delivery Excused Until Payment of Price and for Insolvency

The seller may refuse to deliver the thing sold until the buyer tenders payment of the price, unless the seller has granted the buyer a term for such payment.

Art. 2488. [Reserved]

Art. 2489. Condition of Thing at Time of Delivery

The seller must deliver the thing sold in the condition that, at the time of the sale, the parties expected, or should have expected, the thing to be in at the time of delivery, according to its nature.

Art. 2490. [Reserved]

Art. 2491. Immovables, Extent of Delivery

The seller must deliver to the buyer the full extent of the immovable sold. That obligation may be modified in accordance with the provisions of the following Articles.

Art. 2492. Sale of Immovables at a Price Per Measure

If the sale of an immovable has been made with indication of the extent of the premises at the rate of so much per measure, but the seller is unable to deliver the full extent specified in the contract, the price must be proportionately reduced.

If the extent delivered by the seller is greater than that specified in the contract, the buyer must pay to the seller a proportionate supplement of the price. The buyer may recede from the sale when the actual extent of the immovable sold exceeds by more than one twentieth the extent specified in the contract.

Art. 2493. [Reserved]

Art. 2494. Sale of Immovable for Lump Price

When the sale of an immovable has been made with indication of the extent of the premises, but for a lump price, the expression of the measure does not give the seller the right to a proportionate increase of the price, nor does it give the buyer the right to a proportionate diminution of the price, unless there is a surplus, or a shortage, of more than one twentieth of the extent specified in the act of sale.

When the surplus is such as to give the seller the right to an increase of the price the buyer has the option either to pay that increase or to recede from the contract.

Art. 2495. Sale of a Certain and Limited Body or of a Distinct Object for a Lump Price

When an immovable described as a certain and limited body or a distinct object is sold for a lump price, an expression of the extent of the immovable in the act of sale does not give the parties any right to an increase or diminution of the price in case of surplus or shortage in the actual extension of the immovable.

Art. 2496. [Reserved]

Art. 2497. Restitution of Price and Expenses in Case of Rescission

When the buyer has the right to recede from the contract the seller must return the price, if he has already received it, and also reimburse the buyer for the expenses of the sale.

Art. 2498. Prescription of Actions for Supplement or Diminution of Price or for Dissolution

The seller's action for an increase of the price and the buyer's actions for diminution of the price or dissolution of the sale for shortage or excessive surplus in the extent of the immovable sold prescribe one year from the day of the sale.

Art. 2499. [Reserved]

Art. 2500. Eviction, Definition, Scope of Warranty

The seller warrants the buyer against eviction, which is the buyer's loss of, or danger of losing, the whole or part of the thing sold because of a third person's right that existed at the time of the sale. The warranty also covers encumbrances on the thing that were not declared at the time of the sale, with the exception of apparent servitudes and natural and legal nonapparent servitudes, which need not be declared.

If the right of the third person is perfected only after the sale through the negligence of the buyer, though it arises from facts that took place before, the buyer has no claim in warranty.

Art. 2501. [Reserved]

Art. 2502. Transfer of Rights to a Thing

A person may transfer to another whatever rights to a thing he may then have, without warranting the existence of any such rights. In such a case the transferor does not owe restitution of the price to the transferee in case of eviction, nor may that transfer be rescinded for lesion.

Such a transfer does not give rise to a presumption of bad faith on the part of the transferee and is a just title for the purposes of acquisitive prescription.

If the transferor acquires ownership of the thing after having transferred his rights to it, the after-acquired title of the transferor does not inure to the benefit of the transferee.

Art. 2503. Modification or Exclusion of Warranty, Seller's Liability for Personal Acts, Restitution of Price in Case of Eviction

The warranty against eviction is implied in every sale. Nevertheless, the parties may agree to increase or to limit the warranty. They may also agree to an exclusion of the warranty, but even in that case the seller must return the price to the buyer if eviction occurs, unless it is clear that the buyer was aware of the danger of eviction, or the buyer has declared that he was buying at his peril and risk, or the seller's obligation of returning the price has been expressly excluded.

In all those cases the seller is liable for an eviction that is occasioned by his own act, and any agreement to the contrary is null.

The buyer is subrogated to the rights in warranty of the seller against other persons, even when the warranty is excluded.

Art. 2504. to 2505 [Reserved]

Art. 2506. Rights of Buyer Against Seller in Case of Eviction

A buyer who avails himself of the warranty against eviction may recover from the seller the price he paid, the value of any fruits he had to return to the third person who evicted him, and also other damages sustained because of the eviction with the exception of any increase in value of the thing lost.

Art. 2507. Restitution of Full Price Despite Deterioration, Deduction of Damage when Benefit to Buyer

A seller liable for eviction must return the full price to the buyer even if, at the time of the eviction, the value of the thing has been diminished due to any cause including the buyer's neglect.

Nevertheless, if the buyer has benefited from a diminution in value caused by his own act, the amount of his benefit must be deducted from the total owed to him by the seller because of the eviction.

Art. 2508. [Reserved]

Art. 2509. Reimbursement to Buyer for Useful Improvements, Liability of Seller in Bad Faith

A seller liable for eviction must reimburse the buyer for the cost of useful improvements to the thing made by the buyer. If the seller knew at the time of the sale that the thing belonged to a third person, he must reimburse the buyer for the cost of all improvements.

Art. 2510. [Reserved]

Art. 2511. Partial Eviction, Rights of Buyer

When the buyer is evicted from only a part of the thing sold, he may obtain rescission of the sale if he would not have bought the thing without that part. If the sale is not rescinded, the buyer is entitled to a diminution of the price in the proportion that the value of the part lost bears to the value of the whole at the time of the sale.

Art. 2512. Warranty Against Eviction from Proceeds

The warranty against eviction extends also to those things that proceed from the thing sold.

Art. 2513. Scope of Warranty in Sale of Succession Rights

In a sale of a right of succession, the warranty against eviction extends only to the right to succeed the decedent, which entitles the buyer to those things that are, in fact, a part of the estate, but it does not extend to any particular thing.

Art. 2514 to 2516. [Reserved]

Art. 2517. Call in Warranty, Failure of Buyer to Call Seller in Warranty, Suit to Quiet Possession

A buyer threatened with eviction must give timely notice of the threat to the seller. If a suit for eviction has been brought against the buyer, his calling in the seller to defend that suit amounts to such notice.

A buyer who elects to bring suit against a third person who disturbs his peaceful possession of the thing sold must give timely notice of that suit to the seller.

In either case, a buyer who fails to give such notice, or who fails to give it in time for the seller to defend himself, forfeits the warranty against eviction if the seller can show that, had he been notified in time, he would have been able to prove that the third person who sued the buyer had no right.

Art. 2518 to 2519. [Reserved]

Art. 2520. Warranty Against Redhibitory Defects

The seller warrants the buyer against redhibitory defects, or vices, in the thing sold.

A defect is redhibitory when it renders the thing useless, or its use so inconvenient that it must be presumed that a buyer would not have bought the thing had he known of the defect. The existence of such a defect gives a buyer the right to obtain rescission of the sale.

A defect is redhibitory also when, without rendering the thing totally useless, it diminishes its usefulness or its value so that it must be presumed that a buyer would still have bought it but for a lesser price. The existence of such a defect limits the right of a buyer to a reduction of the price.

Art. 2521. Defects that Are Made Known to the Buyer or that Are Apparent

The seller owes no warranty for defects in the thing that were known to the buyer at the time of the sale, or for defects that should have been discovered by a reasonably prudent buyer of such things.

Art. 2522. Notice of Existence of Defect

The buyer must give the seller notice of the existence of a redhibitory defect in the thing sold. That notice must be sufficiently timely as to allow the seller the opportunity to make the required repairs. A buyer who fails to give that notice suffers diminution of the warranty to the extent the seller can show that the defect could have been repaired or that the repairs would have been less burdensome, had he received timely notice.

Such notice is not required when the seller has actual knowledge of the existence of a redhibitory defect in the thing sold.

Art. 2523. [Reserved]

Art. 2524. Thing Fit for Ordinary Use

The thing sold must be reasonably fit for its ordinary use.

When the seller has reason to know the particular use the buyer intends for the thing, or the buyer's particular purpose for buying the thing, and that the buyer is relying on the seller's skill or judgment in selecting it, the thing sold must be fit for the buyer's intended use or for his particular purpose.

If the thing is not so fit, the buyer's rights are governed by the general rules of conventional obligations.

Art. 2525 to 2528. [Reserved]

Art. 2529. Thing Not of the Kind Specified in the Contract

When the thing the seller has delivered, though in itself free from redhibitory defects, is not of the kind or quality specified in the contract or represented by the seller, the rights of the buyer are governed by other rules of sale and conventional obligations.

Art. 2530. Defect Must Exist Before Delivery

The warranty against redhibitory defects covers only defects that exist at the time of delivery. The defect shall be presumed to have existed at the time of delivery if it appears within three days from that time.

Art. 2531. Liability of Seller Who Knew Not of the Defect

A seller who did not know that the thing he sold had a defect is only bound to repair, remedy, or correct the defect. If he is unable or fails so to do, he is then bound to return the price to the buyer with interest from the time it was paid, and to reimburse him for the reasonable expenses occasioned by the sale, as well as those incurred for the preservation of the thing, less the credit to which the seller is entitled if the use made of the thing, or the fruits it has yielded, were of some value to the buyer.

A seller who is held liable for a redhibitory defect has an action against the manufacturer of the defective thing, if the defect existed at the time the thing was delivered by the manufacturer to the seller, for any loss the seller sustained because of the redhibition. Any contractual provision that attempts to limit, diminish or prevent such recovery by a seller against the manufacturer shall have no effect.

Art. 2532. Return of the Thing; Destruction of the Thing

A buyer who obtains rescission because of a redhibitory defect is bound to return the thing to the seller, for which purpose he must take care of the thing as a prudent administrator, but is not bound to deliver it back until all his claims, or judgments, arising from the defect are satisfied.

If the redhibitory defect has caused the destruction of the thing the loss is borne by the seller, and the buyer may bring his action even after the destruction has occurred. If the thing is destroyed by a fortuitous event before the buyer gives the seller notice of the existence of a redhibitory defect that would have given rise to a rescission of the sale, the loss is borne by the buyer.

After such notice is given, the loss is borne by the seller, except to the extent the buyer has insured that loss. A seller who returns the price, or a part thereof, is subrogated to the buyer's right against third persons who may be liable for the destruction of the thing.

Art. 2533. [Reserved]

Art. 2534. Prescription

A. (1) The action for redhibition against a seller who did not know of the existence of a defect in the thing sold prescribes in four years from the day delivery of such thing was made to the buyer or one year from the day the defect was discovered by the buyer, whichever occurs first.

(2) However, when the defect is of residential or commercial immovable property, an action for redhibition against a seller who did not know of the existence of the defect prescribes in one year from the day delivery of the property was made to the buyer.

B. The action for redhibition against a seller who knew, or is presumed to have known, of the existence of a defect in the thing sold prescribes in one year from the day the defect was discovered by the buyer.

C. In any case prescription is interrupted when the seller accepts the thing for repairs and commences anew from the day he tenders it back to the buyer or notifies the buyer of his refusal or inability to make the required repairs.

Art. 2535 to 2536. [Reserved]

Art. 2537. Judicial Sales

Judicial sales resulting from a seizure are not subject to the rules on redhibition.

Art. 2538. Multiple Sellers, Multiple Buyers, Successors

The warranty against redhibitory vices is owed by each of multiple sellers in proportion to his interest.

Multiple buyers must concur in an action for rescission because of a redhibitory defect. An action for reduction of the price may be brought by one of multiple buyers in proportion to his interest.

The same rules apply if a thing with a redhibitory defect is transferred, inter vivos or mortis causa, to multiple successors.

Art. 2539. [Reserved]

Art. 2540. Redhibitory Vice of One of Several Matched Things Sold Together

When more than one thing are sold together as a whole so that the buyer would not have bought one thing without the other or others, a redhibitory defect in one of such things gives rise to redhibition for the whole.

Art. 2541. Reduction of the Price

A buyer may choose to seek only reduction of the price even when the redhibitory defect is such as to give him the right to obtain rescission of the sale.

In an action for rescission because of a redhibitory defect the court may limit the remedy of the buyer to a reduction of the price.

Art. 2542 to 2544. [Reserved]

Art. 2545. Liability of Seller Who Knows of the Defect; Presumption of Knowledge

A seller who knows that the thing he sells has a defect but omits to declare it, or a seller who declares that the thing has a quality that he knows it does not have, is liable to the buyer for the return of the price with interest from the time it was paid, for the reimbursement of the reasonable expenses occasioned by the sale and those incurred for the preservation of the thing, and also for damages and reasonable attorney fees. If the use made of the thing, or the fruits it might have yielded, were of some value to the buyer, such a seller may be allowed credit for such use or fruits.

A seller is deemed to know that the thing he sells has a redhibitory defect when he is a manufacturer of that thing.

Art. 2546 to 2547. [Reserved]

Art. 2548. Exclusion or Limitation of Warranty; Subrogation

The parties may agree to an exclusion or limitation of the warranty against redhibitory defects. The terms of the exclusion or limitation must be clear and unambiguous and must be brought to the attention of the buyer.

A buyer is not bound by an otherwise effective exclusion or limitation of the warranty when the seller has declared that the thing has a quality that he knew it did not have. The buyer is subrogated to the rights in warranty of the seller against other persons, even when the warranty is excluded.

Art. 2549. Obligations of the Buyer

The buyer is bound to pay the price and to take delivery of the thing.

Art. 2550. Time and Place of Payment

Payment of the price is due at the time and place stipulated in the contract, or at the time and place of delivery if the contract contains no such stipulation.

Art. 2551 to 2552. [Reserved]

Art. 2553. Interest on Price

The buyer owes interest on the price from the time it is due.

Art. 2554. [Reserved]

Art. 2555. Liability of the Buyer Who Fails to Take Delivery

A buyer who fails to take delivery of the thing after a tender of such delivery, or who fails to pay the price, is liable for expenses incurred by the seller in preservation of the thing and for other damages sustained by the seller.

Art. 2556. [Reserved]

Art. 2557. Eviction and Threat of Eviction as Grounds for Suspension of Payment

A buyer who is evicted by the claim of a third person may withhold payment of the price until he is restored to possession, unless the seller gives security for any loss the buyer may sustain as a result of the eviction.

A seller who, in such a case, is unable or unwilling to give security may compel the buyer to deposit the price with the court until the right of the third person is adjudged. Also the buyer may deposit the price with the court, on his own initiative, to prevent the accrual of interest.

A buyer may not withhold payment of the price when the seller is not liable for a return of the price in case of eviction.

Art. 2558 to 2559. [Reserved]

Art. 2560. Payment of the Price Before Disturbance of Possession

A buyer who paid the price before being evicted of the thing may not demand that the seller return the price or give security for it.

Art. 2561. Dissolution of Sale for Nonpayment of Price

If the buyer fails to pay the price, the seller may sue for dissolution of the sale. If the seller has given credit for the price and transfers that credit to another person, the right of dissolution is transferred together with the credit. In case of multiple credit holders all must join in the suit for dissolution, but if any credit holder refuses to join, the others may subrogate themselves to his right by paying the amount due to him.

If a promissory note or other instrument has been given for the price, the right to dissolution prescribes at the same time and in the same period as the note or other instrument.

Art. 2562. Dissolution of Sale of Immovables for Non-Payment of Price; Extension of Time for Payment

When an action is brought for the dissolution of the sale of an immovable and there is no danger that the seller may lose the price and the thing, the court, according to the circumstances, may grant the buyer an extension of time, not in excess of sixty days, to make payment, and shall pronounce the sale dissolved if the buyer fails to pay within that time. When there is such a danger, the court may not grant the buyer an extension of time for payment.

Art. 2563. Payment of Price After Expiration of Term but Prior to Default

When the contract of sale of an immovable expressly provides for dissolution in case of failure to pay the price, the buyer still has the right to pay, in spite of the express dissolution clause, for as long as the seller has not given the buyer notice that he avails himself of that clause or has not filed suit for dissolution.

Art. 2564. Dissolution of Sale of Movables

If the thing is movable and the seller chooses to seek judicial dissolution of the sale because of the failure of the buyer to perform, the court may not grant to the buyer any extension of time to perform.

Art. 2565 to 2566. [Reserved]

Art. 2567. Right of Redemption, Definition

The parties to a contract of sale may agree that the seller shall have the right of redemption, which is the right to take back the thing from the buyer.

Art. 2568. Limitation on Duration

The right of redemption may not be reserved for more than ten years when the thing sold is immovable, or more than five years when the thing sold is movable. If a longer time for redemption has been stipulated in the contract that time must be reduced to either ten or five years, depending on the nature of the thing sold.

Art. 2569. Redemption, Presumption of Security

A sale with right of redemption is a simulation when the surrounding circumstances show that the true intent of the parties was to make a contract of security. When such is the case, any monies, fruits or other benefit received by the buyer as rent or otherwise may be regarded as interest subject to the usury laws.

Art. 2570. Effect of Failure to Exercise Right Within Time Stipulated

If the seller does not exercise the right of redemption within the time allowed by law, the buyer becomes unconditional owner of the thing sold.

Art. 2571. Application of Time Limit Against All Persons Including Minors

The period for redemption is peremptive and runs against all persons including minors. It may not be extended by the court.

Art. 2572. Redemption Against Second Purchaser

When the thing is immovable, the right of redemption is effective against third persons only from the time the instrument that contains it is filed for registry in the parish where the immovable is located.

When the thing is movable, the right of redemption is effective against third persons who, at the time of purchase, had actual knowledge of the existence of that right.

Art. 2573. [Reserved]

Art. 2574. Buyer's Benefit of Discussion Against Creditors of the Seller

A buyer under redemption may avail himself of the right of discussion against creditors of the seller.

Art. 2575. Ownership of Fruits and Products Pending Redemption

The fruits and products of a thing sold with right of redemption belong to the buyer.

Art. 2576. [Reserved]

Art. 2577. Ownership of Improvements and Augmentations Pending Redemption

The buyer is entitled to all improvements he made on the thing that can be removed when the seller exercises the right of redemption. If such improvements cannot be removed, the buyer is entitled to the enhancement of the value of the thing resulting from the improvements. The buyer is also entitled to the enhancement of the value of the thing resulting from ungathered fruits and unharvested crops.

If the thing sold under right of redemption is naturally increased by accession, alluvion, or accretion before the redeeming seller exercises the right, the increase belongs to the seller.

Art. 2578. Liability for Deterioration at the Time of Redemption

During the time allowed for redemption, the buyer must administer the thing sold with the degree of care of a prudent administrator. He is liable to the redeeming seller for any deterioration of the thing caused by the lack of such care.

Art. 2579 to 2583 [Reserved]

Art. 2584. Multiple Successors, Applicability of Rules Governing Lesion

If more than one seller concurred in the sale with right of redemption of an immovable, or if a seller has died leaving more than one successor, the exercise of the right of redemption is governed by the rules provided for the division of the action for lesion among multiple sellers, or among successors of the seller or of the buyer.

Art. 2585 to 2586. [Reserved]

Art. 2587. Reimbursement to Buyer on Redemption

A seller who exercises the right of redemption must reimburse the buyer for all expenses of the sale and for the cost of repairs necessary for the preservation of the thing.

Art. 2588. Encumbrances Created by Buyer

The seller who exercises the right of redemption is entitled to recover the thing free of any encumbrances placed upon it by the buyer. Nevertheless, when the thing is an immovable, the interests of third persons are governed by the laws of registry.

Art. 2589. Rescission for Lesion Beyond Moiety

The sale of an immovable may be rescinded for lesion when the price is less than one half of the fair market value of the immovable. Lesion can be claimed only by the seller and only in sales of corporeal immovables. It cannot be alleged in a sale made by order of the court.

The seller may invoke lesion even if he has renounced the right to claim it.

Art. 2590. Time of Valuation for Determination of Lesion

To determine whether there is lesion, the immovable sold must be evaluated according to the state in which it was at the time of the sale. If the sale was preceded by an option contract, or by a contract to sell, the property must be evaluated in the state in which it was at the time of that contract.

Art. 2591. Option of Buyer to Supplement Price

When a sale is subject to rescission for lesion the buyer may elect either to return the immovable to the seller, or to keep the immovable by giving to the seller a supplement equal to the difference between the price paid by the buyer and the fair market value of the immovable determined according to the preceding Article.

Art. 2592. Lesion, Return of Fruits by Buyer and Payment of Interest by Seller

If the buyer elects to return the immovable he must also return to the seller the fruits of the immovable from the time a demand for rescission was made. In such a case, the seller must return to the buyer the price with interest from the same time.

If the buyer elects to keep the immovable he must also pay to the seller interest on the supplement from the time a demand for rescission was made.

Art. 2593. [Reserved]

Art. 2594. Lesion, Action Against Vendee Who Has Resold the Immovable

When the buyer has sold the immovable, the seller may not bring an action for lesion against a third person who bought the immovable from the original buyer.

In such a case the seller may recover from the original buyer whatever profit the latter realized from the sale to the third person. That recovery may not exceed the supplement the seller would have recovered if the original buyer had chosen to keep the immovable.

Art. 2595. Peremption of Action for Lesion

The action for lesion must be brought within a peremptive period of one year from the time of the sale.

Art. 2596. Lesion, Action Against Vendee Who Has Granted a Right on the Immovable

When the buyer has granted a right on the immovable to a third person, rescission may not impair the interest of that person. The seller who receives back the immovable so encumbered is entitled to recover from the buyer any diminution in value suffered by the immovable because of the right of the third person. That recovery may not exceed the supplement the seller would have recovered if the buyer had not encumbered the immovable and had decided to keep it.

Art. 2597. Condition in Which Property is Returned to Seller; Reimbursement of Buyer for Improvements

When rescission is granted for lesion the seller must take back the immovable in the state it is at that time. The buyer is not liable to the seller for any deterioration or loss sustained by the immovable before the demand for rescission was made, unless the deterioration or loss was turned into profit for the buyer.

The seller must reimburse the buyer for the expenses of the sale and for those incurred for the improvement of the immovable, even if the improvement was made solely for the convenience of the buyer.

Art. 2598. [Reserved]

Art. 2599. Buyer's Right of Retention Pending Reimbursement

The buyer may retain possession of the immovable until the seller reimburses the buyer the price and the recoverable expenses.

Art. 2600. Divisibility of Action in Lesion Among Joint Sellers and Successors, Joinder

If more than one seller concurred in the sale of an immovable owned by them in indivision, or if each of them sold separately his share of the immovable, each seller may bring an action for lesion for his share. Likewise, if a seller died leaving more than one successor, each successor may bring an action for lesion individually for that share of the immovable corresponding to his right.

Art. 2601. Additional Terms in Acceptance of Offer to Sell a Movable

An expression of acceptance of an offer to sell a movable thing suffices to form a contract of sale if there is agreement on the thing and the price, even though the acceptance contains terms additional to, or different from, the terms of the offer, unless acceptance is made conditional on the offeror's acceptance of the additional or different terms. Where the acceptance is not so conditioned, the additional or different terms are regarded as proposals for modification and must be accepted by the offeror in order to become a part of the contract.

Between merchants, however, additional terms become part of the contract unless they alter the offer materially, or the offer expressly limits the acceptance to the terms of the offer, or the offeree is notified of the offeror's objection to the additional terms within a reasonable time, in all of which cases the additional terms do not become a part of the contract. Additional terms alter the offer materially when their nature is such that it must be presumed that the offeror would not have contracted on those terms.

Art. 2602. Contract by Conduct of the Parties

A contract of sale of movables may be established by conduct of both parties that recognizes the existence of that contract even though the communications exchanged by them do not suffice to form a contract. In such a case the contract consists of those terms on which the communications of the parties agree, together with any applicable provisions of the suppletive law.

Art. 2603. Obligation to Deliver Conforming Things

The seller must deliver to the buyer things that conform to the contract.

Things do not conform to the contract when they are different from those selected by the buyer or are of a kind, quality, or quantity different from the one agreed.

Art. 2604. Buyer' Right of Inspection

The buyer has a right to have a reasonable opportunity to inspect the things, even after delivery, for the purpose of ascertaining whether they conform to the contract.

Art. 2605. Rejection of Nonconforming Things by the Buyer

A buyer may reject nonconforming things within a reasonable time. The buyer must give reasonable notice to the seller to make the rejection effective. A buyer's failure to make an effective rejection within a reasonable time shall be regarded as an acceptance of the things.

Art. 2606. Buyer's Acceptance of Nonconforming Things

A buyer who, with knowledge, accepts nonconforming things may no longer reject those things on grounds of that nonconformity, unless the acceptance was made in the reasonable belief that the nonconformity would be cured.

Art. 2607. Buyer May Accept Part of Things Delivered

Out of a quantity of things delivered by the seller, the buyer may accept those things that conform to the contract and form a commercial unit and may reject those that do not conform. The buyer must pay at the contract rate for any things that are accepted.

Art. 2608. Merchant Buyer's Duty upon Rejection of Things

When the seller has no agent or business office at the place of delivery, a buyer who is a merchant and has rejected the things must follow any reasonable instructions received from the seller with respect to those things. If the seller gives no such instructions, and the things rejected are perishable or susceptible of rapid decline in value, the merchant buyer must make reasonable efforts to sell those things on the seller's behalf.

In all instances of rejection, a buyer who is a merchant must handle the rejected things as a prudent administrator.

Art. 2609. Purchase of Substitute Things by the Buyer

When the seller fails to render the performance required by a contract of sale of movable things, the buyer may purchase substitute things within a reasonable time and in good faith. In such a case the buyer is entitled to recover the difference between the contract price and the price of the substitute things. The buyer may recover other damages also, less the expenses saved as a result of the failure of the seller to perform.

Art. 2610. Cure of Nonconformity

Upon rejection of nonconforming things by the buyer, the seller may cure the nonconformity when the time for performance has not yet expired or when the seller had a reasonable belief that the nonconforming things would be acceptable to the buyer. In such a case the seller must give reasonable notice of his intention to cure to the buyer.

Art. 2611. Resale by the Seller

When the buyer fails to perform a contract of sale of movable things, the seller, within a reasonable time and in good faith, may resell those things that are still in his possession. In such a case the seller is entitled to recover the difference between the contract price and the resale price. The seller may recover also other damages, less the expenses saved as a result of the buyer's failure to perform.

Unless the things are perishable or subject to rapid decline in value, the seller must give the buyer reasonable notice of the public sale at which the things will be resold, or of his intention to resell the things at a private sale.

Art. 2612. Deposit of the Things by Seller

When the buyer neglects to take delivery of movable things that are the contractual object the seller may request court authority to put the things out of his possession and at the buyer's risk. The seller must give the buyer notice of the time at which the things will leave possession of the seller.

Art. 2613. Things in Transit, Ownership

When, according to the terms of the contract, the seller sends the things to the buyer through a common carrier, the form of the bill of lading determines ownership of the things while in transit.

When the bill of lading makes the things deliverable to the buyer, or to his order, ownership of the things is thereby transferred to the buyer.

When the bill of lading makes the things deliverable to the seller, or to his agent, ownership of the things thereby remains with the seller.

When the seller or his agent remains in possession of a bill of lading that makes the things deliverable to the buyer, or to the buyer's order, the seller thereby reserves the right to retain the things against a claim of the buyer who has not performed his obligations.

Art. 2614. Stoppage in Transit

The seller may stop delivery of the things in the possession of a carrier or other depositary when he learns that the buyer will not perform the obligations arising from the contract of sale or is insolvent.

Art. 2615. Judicial Dissolution

In an action for judicial dissolution of a sale of movable things the court must grant dissolution, upon proof of the defendant's failure to perform, without allowing that party any additional time to render performance.

Art. 2616. Things in Transit, Risk of Loss

When the contract requires the seller to ship the things through a carrier, but does not require him to deliver the things at any particular destination, the risk of loss is transferred to the buyer upon delivery of the things to the carrier, regardless of the form of the bill of lading.

When the contract of sale requires the seller to deliver the things at a particular destination, the risk of loss is transferred to the buyer when the things, while in possession of the carrier, are duly tendered to the buyer at the place of destination.

When the parties incorporate well established commercial symbols into their contract, the risk of loss is transferred in accordance with the customary understanding of such symbols.

Art. 2617. Payment Against Documents

In all cases where the parties have agreed that the seller will obtain a document showing that the things have been delivered to a carrier or a depositary the buyer must make payment against tender of that document and others as required. The seller may not tender, nor may the buyer demand, delivery of the things in lieu of the documents.

Art. 2618 to 2619. [Reserved]

Art. 2620. Option to Buy or Sell

An option to buy, or an option to sell, is a contract whereby a party gives to another the right to accept an offer to sell, or to buy, a thing within a stipulated time.

An option must set forth the thing and the price, and meet the formal requirements of the sale it contemplates.

Art. 2621. Acceptance, when Effective; Option Turns into Contract to Sell; Rejection

The acceptance or rejection of an offer contained in an option is effective when received by the grantor. Upon such an acceptance the parties are bound by a contract to sell. Rejection of the offer contained in an option terminates the option but a counteroffer does not.

Art. 2622. Warranty of Assignor

The assignor of an option to buy a thing warrants the existence of that option, but does not warrant that the person who granted it can be required to make a final sale. If, upon exercise of the option, the person who granted it fails to make a final sale, the assignee has against the assignor the same rights as a buyer without warranty has against the seller.

Art. 2623. Bilateral Promise of Sale; Contract to Sell

An agreement whereby one party promises to sell and the other promises to buy a thing at a later time, or upon the happening of a condition, or upon performance of some obligation by either party, is a bilateral promise of sale or contract to sell. Such an agreement gives either party the right to demand specific performance.

A contract to sell must set forth the thing and the price, and meet the formal requirements of the sale it contemplates.

Art. 2624. Deposit, Earnest Money

A sum given by the buyer to the seller in connection with a contract to sell is regarded to be a deposit on account of the price, unless the parties have expressly provided otherwise.

If the parties stipulate that a sum given by the buyer to the seller is earnest money, either party may recede from the contract, but the buyer who chooses to recede must forfeit the earnest money, and the seller who so chooses must return the earnest money plus an equal amount.

When earnest money has been given and a party fails to perform for reasons other than a fortuitous event, that party will be regarded as receding from the contract.

Art. 2625. Right of First Refusal

A party may agree that he will not sell a certain thing without first offering it to a certain person. The right given to the latter in such a case is a right of first refusal that may be enforced by specific performance.

Art. 2626. Terms of Offered Sale

The grantor of a right of first refusal may not sell to another person unless he has offered to sell the thing to the holder of the right on the same terms, or on those specified when the right was granted if the parties have so agreed.

Art. 2627. Right of First Refusal, Time for Acceptance

Unless otherwise agreed, an offer to sell the thing to the holder of a right of first refusal must be accepted within ten days from the time it is received if the thing is movable, and within thirty days from that time if the thing is immovable.

Unless the grantor concludes a final sale, or a contract to sell, with a third person within six months, the right of first refusal subsists in the grantee who failed to exercise it when an offer was made to him.

Art. 2628. Time Limitation for Option and Right of First Refusal

An option or a right of first refusal that concerns an immovable thing may not be granted for a term longer than ten years. If a longer time for an option or a right of first refusal has been stipulated in a contract, that time shall be reduced to ten years.

Nevertheless, if the option or right of first refusal is granted in connection with a contract that gives rise to obligations of continuous or periodic performance, an option or a right of first refusal may be granted for as long a period as required for the performance of those obligations.

Art. 2629. Effect Against Third Persons

An option, right of first refusal, or contract to sell that involves immovable property is effective against third persons only from the time the instrument that contains it is filed for registry in the parish where the immovable is located.

An option, right of first refusal, or contract to sell that involves movable property is effective against third persons who, at the time of acquisition of a conflicting right, had actual knowledge of that transaction.

Art. 2630. Indivisibility of Right

The right to exercise an option and the right of first refusal are indivisible. When either of such rights belongs to more than one person all of them must exercise the right.

Art. 2631 to 2641. [Reserved]

Art. 2642. Assignability of Rights

All rights may be assigned, with the exception of those pertaining to obligations that are strictly personal. The assignee is subrogated to the rights of the assignor against the debtor.

Art. 2643. Assignment Effective from the Time of Knowledge or Notice

The assignment of a right is effective against the debtor and third persons only from the time the debtor has actual knowledge, or has been given notice of the assignment.

If a partial assignment unreasonably increases the burden of the debtor he may recover from either the assignor or the assignee a reasonable amount for the increased burden.

Art. 2644. Performance by Debtor Before Knowledge of Assignment

When the debtor, without knowledge or notice of the assignment, renders performance to the assignor, such performance extinguishes the obligation of the debtor and is effective against the assignee and third persons.

Art. 2645. Accessories Included in Assignment of Right

The assignment of a right includes its accessories such as security rights.

Art. 2646. Warranty of Existence of Debt, Solvency of Debtor

The assignor of a right warrants its existence at the time of the assignment.

The assignor does not warrant the solvency of the debtor, however, unless he has agreed to give such a warranty.

Art. 2647. [Reserved]

Art. 2648. Scope of Warranty of Debtor's Solvency

An assignor who warrants the solvency of the debtor warrants that solvency at the time of the assignment only and, in the absence of agreement to the contrary, does not warrant the future solvency of the debtor.

Art. 2649. Assignor's Knowledge of The Debtor's Insolvency; Effects

When the assignor of a right did not warrant the solvency of the debtor but knew of his insolvency, the assignee without such knowledge may obtain rescission of the contract.

Art. 2650. Warranty in Assignment of Succession Rights

A person who assigns his right in the estate of a deceased person, without specifying any assets, warrants only his right of succession as heir or legatee.

Art. 2651. [Reserved]

Art. 2652. Sale of Litigious Rights

When a litigious right is assigned, the debtor may extinguish his obligation by paying to the assignee the price the assignee paid for the assignment, with interest from the time of the assignment.

A right is litigious, for that purpose, when it is contested in a suit already filed.

Nevertheless, the debtor may not thus extinguish his obligation when the assignment has been made to a co-owner of the assigned right, or to a possessor of the thing subject to the litigious right.

Art. 2653. Assignability Prohibited by Contract; Exceptions

A right cannot be assigned when the contract from which it arises prohibits the assignment of that right. Such a prohibition has no effect against an assignee who has no knowledge of its existence.

Art. 2654. Documents Evidencing the Right

The assignor of a right must deliver to the assignee all documents in his possession that evidence the right. Nevertheless, a failure by the assignor to deliver such documents does not affect the validity of the assignment.

When a right is assigned only in part, the assignor may give the assignee an original or a copy of such documents.

Art. 2655. Giving in Payment, Definition

Giving in payment is a contract whereby an obligor gives a thing to the obligee, who accepts it in payment of a debt.

Art. 2656. Delivery Essential to Giving in Payment

Delivery of the thing is essential to the perfection of a giving in payment.

Art. 2657. Giving in Partial Payment

An obligor may give a thing to the obligee in partial payment of a debt.

A giving in partial payment extinguishes the debt in the amount intended by the parties. If the parties" intent concerning the amount of the partial extinguishment cannot be ascertained, it is presumed that they intended to extinguish the debt in the amount of the fair market value of the thing given in partial payment.

Art. 2658. [Reserved]

Art. 2659. Application of General Rules of Sale

The giving in payment is governed by the rules of the contract of sale, with the differences provided for in this Chapter.

Art. 2660. Exchange, Definition

[*Amended*]

Exchange is a contract whereby each party transfers to the other the ownership of a thing other than money.

Ownership of the things exchanged is transferred between the parties as soon as there is agreement on the things, even though none of the things has been delivered.

If it is the intent of the parties that the transfer of ownership will not take place until a later time, then the contract is a contract to exchange.

(Acts 2010, No. 186, § 1.)

Art. 2661. Rights and Obligations of the Parties

[*Amended*]

Each of the parties to a contract of exchange has the rights and obligations of a seller with respect to the thing transferred by him and the rights and obligations of a buyer with respect to the thing transferred to him.

(Acts 2010, No. 186, § 1.)

Art. 2662. Rights of Party Evicted

[*Amended*]

A person evicted from a thing received in exchange may demand the value of the thing from which he was evicted or the return of the thing he gave, with damages in either case.

(Acts 2010, No. 186, § 1).

Art. 2663. Rescission for Lesion in Contracts of Exchange

[*Amended*]

A party giving a corporeal immovable in exchange for property worth less than one half of the fair market value of the immovable given by him may claim rescission on grounds of lesion beyond moiety.

(Acts 2010, No. 186, § 1).

Art. 2664. Application of the Rules of Sale

[*Amended*]

The contract of exchange is governed by the rules of the contract of sale, with the differences provided in this Title.

(Acts 2010, No. 186, § 1.)

Art. 2665 to 2667. [*Amended*] [Reserved]

(Acts 2010, No. 186, § 1.)

APPENDIX II

CASES — ILLUSTRATIONS

CHAPTER I — AGREEMENTS PREPARATORY TO A SALE OR PRE-CONTRACTS

Article I — Contract to Sell

Capo v. Bugdahl	542 So. 478 (La. 1906)
Ducuy v. Falgoust	228 La. 533 (La. 1955)
Bounds v. Makar	493 So.2d 268 (La. 3rd Cir. 1986)
Philips v. Berner	789 So.2d 41 (La. 1st Cir. 2001)
Worley v. Chandler	7 So.3d 38 (La. 2nd Cir. 2009)
Young v. Tolintino	26 So.3d 835 (La. 2nd Cir. 2009)

§ 3 — Option:

Moresi v. Burleigh	127 So. 624 (La. 1930)
Haeuser v. Castrogiovanni, Schiro	106 So.2d 306 (La. 1958)
Farris v. Interstate Enterprises, Inc.	270 So.2d 230 (La. 1st 1972)
EDCO v. Landry	371 So.2d 1367 (La. 3rd Cir. 1979)
Youngblood v. Rosedale Development Co., L.L.C.	911 So.2d 418 (La. 2nd Cir. 2005)
Solet v. Brooks	30 So.3d 96 (La. 1st Cir. 2009)

§ 4 — Right of First Refusal:

Robichaux v. Boutte	492 So.2d 521 (La. 3rd Cir. 1986)
Gorum v. The Optimist Club of Glenmora	771 So.2d 690 (La. 3rd Cir.2000)
Culp v. Eagle's Nest Church of Monroe	887 So.2d 743 (La. 2nd Cir. 2004)

CHAPTER II — PERFECTION OF A CONTRACT OF SALE

Article I — Capacity

Scott v. The Continental Insurance Co.	259 So.2d (La. 2nd Cir. 1972)
Owen v. Owen	336 So.2d 784 (La. 1976)

Tuat Nguyen v. Ngot Tran	841 So.2d 62 (La. 4th Cir. 2003)
B-G & G Investors VI, LLC v. Thibaut HG Corp.	985 So.2d 837 (La. 4th Cir. 2008)
Skannal v. Bamburg	33 So.3d 227 (La. 2nd Cir. 2010)

Article II — Consent

Marcantel v. Jefferson Door Company, Inc.	817 So.2d 236 (La. 5th Cir. 2002)
LaSalle v. The Cannata Corporation	878 So.2d 622 (La. 1st Cir. 2004)
Watkins v. Schexneider	31 So.3d 609 (La. 3rd Cir. 2010)

Article III — Thing

Barber Asphalt Paving Co. v. St Louis Cypress Co. Ltd.	46 So. 193 (La. 1908)
McDuffie v. Walker	125 La. 152 (La. 1910)
Plaquemines Equipment & Machine Co. Inc. v. The Ford Motor Co.	157 So.2d 884 (La. 1963)
Bornemann v. McKenna v. Richards	161 So.2d 741 (La. 1964)
Lafleur v. Foret	213 So.2d 141 (La. 1st 1968)
The Springs Thunder Agency, Inc. v. Odom Insurance Agency, Inc.	237 So.2d 96 (La. 1st Cir. 1970)
Saucier v. Hayes Dairy Products, Inc.	373 So.2d 102 (La. 1979)
Equibank v. IRS	749 F.2d 1176 (U.S. 5th Cir. 1985)
Philipps v. Parker	483 So.2d 972 (La. 1986)
Frank v. Motwani	513 So.2d 1170 (La. 1987)
Succession of Noah Cloud	530 So.2d 1146 (La. 1988)
State v. Piazza	668 So.2d 1125 (La. 1996)
Alvis v. CIT Group/Equipment Financing	918 So.2d 1177 (La. 3rd Cir. 2005)
Emoneyport, Inc. v. Burger King	996 So.2d 496 (La. 5th Cir. 2008)
Boone v. Conoco Phillips Company	139 So.2d 1047 (La. App. 3rd Cir. 2014)

Article IV — Price

Princeville Canning Co. v. Morris	159 So.2d 14 (La. 1st Cir. 1963)
DB Orban Co. v. Lakco Pipe & Supply, Inc.	496 So.2d 1382 (La. 3rd Cir. 1986)
Benglis Sash & Door Co. v. Leonards	87 So.2d 1171 (La. 1980)
Lessard v. Lessard Acres, Inc. and First National Bank of Port Allen	349 So.2d 293 (La. 1977)

Successions of Pelicano v. Shockley	920 So.2d 248 (La. 5th Cir. 2005)
Gulf Rice Milling, Inc., v. Sonnier	939 So.2d 1282 (La. 3rd Cir. 2006)

Article V — Lesion

O'Brien v. Legette	223 So.2d 165 (La. 1969)
Rogers v. Read	355 So.2d 46 (La. 2nd Cir. 1978)
Joiner v. Abercrombie	968 So.2d 1184 (La. 2nd Cir. 2007)

Article VI — Form

Frank v. Motwani	(see *supra*, Things)
McDuffie v. Walker	(see *supra*, Things)
S. Cosey v. L. Cosey	376 So.2d 486 (La. 1979)
Rachal v. Luzader	927 So.2d 1286 (La. 3rd Cir. 2006)
Wede v. Niche Marketing USA	52 So.3d (La. 2010)

Conclusion: When is a "sale" a "sale"?

Kegler's Inc., v. Levy	239 So.2d 450 (La. 4th Cir. 1970)
FMC Corporation v. Continental Grain Co.	355 So.2d 953 (La. 4th Cir. 1977)
Blue v. Schoen	556 So.2d 1364 (La.5th Cir. 1990)
Poree v. Elite Elevator Services Inc.	665 So.2d 133 (La. 4th Cir. 1995)
Sepulvado v. Time It Lube, Inc.	895 So.2d 729 (La. 2nd Cir. 2005)
Columbia Gulf Transmission v. Bridges	28 So.3d 1032 (La. 1st Cir. 2009)

CHAPTER III — EFFECTS OF A CONTRACT OF SALE

Article I — Transfer of Ownership

Shuff v. Morgan	9 Mart. (O.S.) 592 (La. 1821)
Kelham & Co. v. Carroll	20 La.Ann. 111 (La. 1862)
Barber Asphalt Paving Co. v. St Louis Cypress Co. Ltd.	(see *supra*, Things)
Mobile Machinery & Supply Co. v. York Oilfield Salvage Co.	171 So.872 (La. 1st Cir. 1937)
Cottam & Co. Inc.,v. Sonnier	2 So.2d 283 (La. 1st Cir. 1941)
Plaquemines Equipment & Machine Co. Inc. v. The Ford Motor Co.	(see *supra*, Things)
American Creosote Works v. Boland Machine & Mfg. Co.	35 So.2d 749 (La. 1948)
Berry v. Ginsburg	98 So.2d 548 (La. 2d Cir. 1957)
Ventre v. Pacific Indemnity Co.	419 So.2d 969 (La. 3rd Cir. 1982)

Montz v. Theard	818 So.2d 181 (La. 1st Cir. 2002)
Seals v. Sumrall	887 So.2d 91 (La. 1st Cir. 2004)
Baudin v. Spruill	931 So.2d 549 (La. 3rd Cir. 2006)

Article II — Right of Redemption

Steib v. J. Rathborne Land Co.	163 So.2d 429 (La. 4th Cir. 1964)
Potts v. Spatafora	340 So.2d 414 (La. 2nd Cir. 1976)
ACORN Community Land Association of Louisiana, Inc., v. Zeno	936 So.2d 836 (La. 4th Cir. 2006)

Article III — Risk of Loss

Kelham & Co. v. Carroll	(see *supra*, Transfer of Ownership)
American Creosote . . .	(see *supra*, Transfer of Ownership)
Goodwyn v. Pritchard	10 La.Ann. 149 (La. 1855)
Armenia Coffee Corp. v American Nat'l Fire	946 So.2d 249 (La. 4th Cir. 2006)

CHAPTER IV — OBLIGATIONS OF THE SELLER

Article I — Obligations of the Seller

§ 1 — Delivery:

Arquembourg v. Bourque	243 So.2d 92 (La.1st Cir. 1970)
Fitzgerald v. Hyland	6 So.2d 321 (La. 1942)
Lasiter v. Gaharan	670 So.2d 395 (La. 3rd Cir. 1996)

§ 2 — Warranty against Eviction:

Waterman v. Tidewater	35 So.2d 225 (La. 1947)
Board of Commissioners for the Lafourche Basin Levee District v. Dr. W. Elmer	268 So.2d 274 (La. 4th Cir. 1972)
Collins v. Slocum	317 So.2d 672 (La. 3rd Cir. 1975)
Randolph Richmond, Jr. v. Zapata Development Corp.	350 So.2d 875 (La. 1977)
Buzbee v. Fidelity National Bank	492 So.2d 15 (La. 1st Cir. 1986)
Simmesport State Bank v. Roy	614 So.2d 265 (La. 3rd Cir. 1993)
Long-Fork, L.L.C. v. Petite Riviere	987 So.2d 831 (La. 3rd Cir. 2008)

§ 4 — Warranty against Defects/Vices: Redhibition-Rescission:

R. Prather v. Massey-Ferguson	232 So.2d 80 (La. 3rd Cir. 1970)

Campo Appliance Co. v. Hurst	256 So.2d 317 (La. 1st Cir. 1971)
Del Cryer v. M. M. Manufacturing Co.	273 So.2d 818 (La. 1972-1973)
Media Production Consultants, Inc. v. Mercedes-Benz of North America	262 So.2d 377 (La. 1972)
McLain v. Cuccia	259 So.2d 337 (La. 4th Cir. 1972)
Prince v. Paretti Pontiac Co. Inc.	81 So.2d 112 (La. 1973)
Rey v. Cuccia	298 So.2d 840 (La. 1974)
Smith v. Max Thieme Chevrolet	315 So.2d 82 (La. 2nd Cir. 1975)
Meador v. Toyota	332 So.2d 433 (La. 1976)
Edwards v. Port AMC/Jeep, Inc.	337 So.2d 276 (La. 2nd Cir. 1976)
Aizpurua v. Crane Pool	449 So.2d 471 (La. 1984)
Chaudoir v. Porsche	667 So.2d 569 (La. 3rd Cir. 1996)
Pratt v. Himel Marine	823 So.2d 394 (La. 1st Cir. 2002)
Chastant, D.D.S. v. Oasys Imaging, Inc.	839 So.2d 1124 (La. 3rd Cir. 2003)
Dailey v. The Home Furnishings Store	857 So.2d 1051 (La. 4th Cir. 2003)
Tarifa v. Riess	856 So.2d 21 (La. 4th Cir. 2003)
Anzelmo v. Pelican Computer, L.L.C.	892 So.2d 659 (La. 5th Cir. 2004)
De Atley v. Victoria's Secret Catalogue, LLC.	876 So.2d 112 (La. 4th Cir. 2004)
Stevens v. Bruce	878 So.2d 734 (La. 3rd Cir. 2004)
Matt v. Agro Distributor, LLC.	904 So.2d 928 (La. 3rd Cir. 2005)
Stuck v. Dr. Long, XYZ Insurance Co.	909 So.2d 686 (La. 2nd Cir. 2005)
Slayton v. Davis	901 So.2d 1246 (La. 3rd Cir. 2005)
Aucoin v. Southern Quality Homes	984 So.2d 685 (La. 2008)
Touro Infirmary v. Sizeler Architects	900 So.2d 200 (La. 4th Cir. 2005)
Cosman v. Cabrera	28 So.3d 1075 (La. 1st Cir. 2009)
Vanek v. Seeber	29 So.3d 582 (La. 1st Cir. 2009)
Shaw v. Acadian Builders and Contractors, LLC.	130 So.3d 914 (La. 2013)
S. Stutts v. Z. Melton	130 So.3d 808 (La. 2013)

Article II — Obligations of the Buyer

Friedman Iron & Supply Co., v. J.B. Beaird Co. Inc.	63 So.2d 144 (La. 1953)
Pellegrin v. City of Thibodaux	837 So.2d 139 (La. 1st Cir. 2002)

Part II:

Louisiana Law of Lease

INTRODUCTION

1. History: 1808–2005.

The contracts of Sale and of Lease share several basic characteristics. Both are nominate contracts and both are related to Exchange, also a nominate contract which happened to be located between "sale" and "lease" in the Louisiana Civil Code.[159] In addition, the contracts of Sale and Lease are governed by common principles concerning defects in the object of the sale or the lease, delivery of the object, and the rights of third parties to the object.

On the other hand, lease is conceptually distinct from sale. A sale can be a single transaction that happens instantaneously and is not repeated. After the sale occurs, if all goes well, seller and buyer need not have any further dealings about the thing sold. As regards leases, however, additional dealings between the parties are quite normal. They arise, for example, from repairs that need to be made, from the lessor's desire to visit or inspect the thing leased, and from the lessee's obligation to make timely payments of the rent while the lease is in effect.

In Louisiana, the law of lease has gone through four major changes. First, the uncodified law of lease that governed the Territory of Orleans was written down and systematized in the Digest of 1808. The articles on lease were rewritten in the 1825 and 1870 Louisiana Civil Codes. Finally, the law was thoroughly reworked to become Title IX, Lease, in Book III of the current Code. That new version of the law was effective on January 1, 2005, and will be referred to as the "2005 Revision" or simply the "Revision".

---

[159] *See* La. C.C. arts. 2660 to 2667.

Whereas the 1870 Code dealt with leases of things in one chapter, the Revision breaks that topic down into four chapters: 1. General Provisions; 2. Essential Elements; 3. The Obligations of the Lessor and the Lessee; and 4. Termination and Dissolution. The 1870 Code had a separate chapter on the "letting out of labor or industry." The Revision renumbered that chapter as Chapter 5 of the current Code without modifying it. As the subject of that chapter has been largely eclipsed by state and federal statute, it is not analyzed in this Précis.

2. Terminology.

In a sale, there is a distinct term of art that describes each party to the contract: buyer and seller. In a lease, however, the words describing the parties differ only in one syllable, and one verb describes what both the lessor and the lessee do: they *lease* the thing. People used to say that the lessor let and the lessee hired, but those words now sound archaic. So, when clarity demands it, in this Précis the lessor "leases" and the lessee "rents." Otherwise, both parties *lease*.

On the other hand, the Précis will rarely use "landlord" to mean the lessor of an immovable but occasionally refers to the lessee of an immovable as a "tenant."

Chapter 1

LEASE: NOTION AND ELEMENTS

Article 1
Notion

Under article 2668, **"the lessor binds himself to give the lessee the use and enjoyment of a thing,"** and the lessor so binds himself **in exchange for** the lessee's undertaking to **pay a rent**. Article 1908 calls such a contract **synallagmatic**, a synonym for **bilateral**, meaning that lessor and lessee obligate themselves reciprocally and that the obligation of each is **correlative** to the obligation of the other.

In addition, lease is an **onerous** contract under article 1909, as both lessor and lessee acquire an **"advantage in exchange"** for their obligations. As a result, a lease can never be a **gratuitous** contract.[160] One who obligates himself to give another the use and enjoyment of a thing without **"obtaining any advantage in return"** cannot be called a lessor and the relationship cannot be called a lease.

Article 2
Elements of a Lease

The Civil Code of 1870 stated that three characteristics were **absolutely necessary** to create a valid lease: **thing, price,** and **consent.**[161] Today the Code handles this requirement somewhat differently. In a Chapter entitled "Essential Elements," the Code lists four elements: **thing, rent, term,** and **form**. However, despite the misleading Chapter heading, no specific article in the revised version of the Code states unequivocally that all four elements are *essential* to form a valid lease. Instead, the Code informs us what kinds of things **may be the object of a lease** and what **rent may consist of.**[162] The current Code, however, does treat one element as essential: a **lease shall be for a term.**[163] At the other end of the spectrum, it does not appear that any particular **form** at all is necessary for a lease to be valid.[164]

The deletion of **consent** from the list of essential elements to the formation of a lease should not be read to mean that consent is no longer necessary for the creation of a valid lease. Quite the contrary is true. The general rules of conventional obligations govern consent for the formation of all contracts and, of course, govern

---

160 La. C.C. art. 1910.

161 La. C.C. art. 2670 (1870).

162 La. C.C. arts. 2673 and 2675.

163 La. C.C. art. 2678.

164 La. C.C. art. 2681.

leases as well.[165] Thus, a lease will not be found to exist merely because one person was using a thing belonging to another person, either mistakenly or deliberately. The owner will not be able to collect a notionally reasonable rent as a form of compensation for the thing's use. The law of lease does not provide a remedy for such a situation.

§ 1.2.1. THE THING.

In general, **"all things, corporeal or incorporeal, that are susceptible of ownership may be the object of a lease, . . . "**[166] Therefore, in principle, anything that can form part of anyone's patrimony may be leased just as it may be sold. Nevertheless, the Code provides an exception. Things that are **consumed when used** cannot be leased. Thus, food or gasoline cannot be leased, because such items cannot be **used** without being **destroyed.**[167] One reason for the difference is that at the end of the lease, the lessee is in principle obligated to return the thing to the lessor as it was when it **"was delivered to him, except for normal wear and tear . . . "**[168] Evidently, this cannot happen if the thing no longer exists because it has been consumed in its use.[169]

Likewise, things that are incorporated into other things so as to lose their identity cannot be leased. For example, lumber, paint, bricks, and mortar cannot be leased since, when they are used or enjoyed, they become component parts of a building or other construction through integration or attachment.[170]

On the other hand, some things that are normally consumed may, on occasion, be used in a way that does not lead to their consumption. For example, someone might pay the owner of such a consumable thing for the right to use it in a display window of some kind, such as an artist's paintings in connection with a promotion, on the condition that the item be returned to the owner so that it could be sold in the ordinary course of business. Such an unusual contract should be considered a lease.

The consequence of finding that the contract under these rules is not a lease does not mean that the agreement of the parties is unenforceable. If the owner of a consumable thing **delivers** it to **another** person, **who binds himself to return an equal amount of things of the same kind and quality**, the contract is a **loan for consumption.**[171] If the recipient of the thing is merely to hold it for **safekeeping**, the contract is one of **deposit.**[172]

---

165 La. C.C. art. 2669.

166 La. C.C. art. 2673.

167 *Id.*

168 La. C.C. art. 2683(3).

169 *See* Loan for Use (La. C.C. art. 2891) and Loan for Consumption (La. C.C. art. 2904).

170 La. C.C. arts. 465 and 466.

171 La. C.C. art. 2904.

172 La. C.C. art. 2926.

If the owner of a **nonconsumable delivers** it **to another person for him to use and return**, the contract is a **loan for use.**[173] While a loan for use might appear to be the same thing as a lease, the crucial difference is that the former is **gratuitous**: the **borrower** of the thing is not presumptively bound to compensate for the benefit he derives from the loan of the thing. In a lease, of course, the lessee obligates himself to pay rent for the use and enjoyment of the thing, as is discussed in the next section.

§ 1.2.2. RENT.

In most leases, the rent is a sum of money on which the parties clearly agree, often after pointed negotiations.[174] If the lessee is not obligated to pay the rent, there is no lease. Thus, if a landowner transfers another person permission to remain on his land without any obligation to pay so long as that person would leave as soon as the landowner asked him to, this arrangement would not create a lease because there was no agreement on a rent. Instead, if there has been a delivery of the land, it would create a loan for use of a nonconsumable.[175]

The lease may authorize a **third party** to fix the rent, and it may provide for a **method** to calculate the rent. If the third party does not fix the rent or if the method to calculate it proves unworkable, there is no lease.[176] Here a lease differs from a sale, as on similar facts the court might be authorized to set the price in a contract of sale, at least with regard to movables sold by merchants.[177]

In addition to money, rent may also consist of *things* such as **commodities** or **fruits.** Even when such things are to constitute rent, the contract remains a lease, not an exchange. This is so because, in an exchange, each party **gives the ownership of one thing for the ownership of another.**[178] In a lease, the lessor does not **transfer** the ownership of the thing itself but gives **the use and enjoyment** of the thing.[179] Moreover, only those things noted in article 2675 qualify as rent in a lease. The contract of exchange has no such limitation.

Commodities have a readily identifiable market value, which implies that they must have a monetary value. A rent could consist of a **portion of the fruits yielded by the thing leased**, which in the agricultural context has a market value also.[180] In general, however, **fruits** do not have such a market value. Thus, the Revision in article 2675 has relaxed the definition of rent. In addition, rent may consist of **services** or **other performances.**[181] First, lease here differs from sale where the

---

[173] La. C.C. art. 2891.

[174] La. C.C. art. 2675.

[175] La. C.C. arts. 2891 and 537.

[176] La. C.C. art. 2676.

[177] La. C.C. arts. 2465, 2466, and 1974; *see also* Sale *supra*, pp. 19–20.

[178] La. C.C. art. 2660.

[179] La. C.C. art. 2668.

[180] La. C.C. art. 2671 (1870).

[181] La. C.C. art. 2675.

price must be paid in money.[182] Second, this formula expands on that of the prior law, which referred only to **fruits of the thing leased** or **commodities** in addition to money.[183]

These changes together justify a flexible interpretation of what validly counts as rent. The outer limit is the phrase in article 2675 that requires **other performances** to be **sufficient to support an onerous contract**. Thus, rent must satisfy be at least this minimum requirement. The lessee's promise to do work for the lessor without further quantifying or specifying what the work will be should fail this minimum test. In other words, there must be an agreement to pay rent, and the rent must be objectively quantified or quantifiable. This is especially true when the rent is not a fixed or determinable sum of money. Presumably, if the lessee earns a certain sum per hour for his services, then those services may easily function as rent. Moreover, if the lessee's services have some particular value to the lessor, the lessor, as a matter of contract, has the liberty to determine what is of value to him and even to pay a premium above the market value if he so chooses. The lessor might decide to discount the rent to a particular lessee, or the lessee might decide to pay a premium rent for a particular location.

Frequently, rent is calculated as a percentage of a sum of money that the lessee earns. For example, with a sharecropping lease, the parties agree that the rent is a stated percentage of the crop produced on the acreage leased.[184] The arrangement may be similar in a business context where the rent is calculated as a percentage of the profits of a business conducted on the premises by the lessee. In such cases, it is natural to consider the rent as the sum of money owed after applying the percentage. Strictly speaking, though, the rent should be seen as the percentage itself or, rather, the incorporeal right of the lessor to collect the money produced by applying the agreed percentage to the proceeds.

Sometimes it is not the amount of the initial rent that presents a difficulty but the amount of the rent when the lease is to be renewed or continued. In this case, the court may take a more active role in determining the rent. If a third party does not fix the rent or the method fails to work when the **redetermination** of the rent is the question, the court may fix the rent or choose a workable method.[185]

§ 1.2.3. TERM.

The Civil Code discusses **term** first in connection with Obligations in General in Title III of Book III.[186] There, **term** describes a kind of obligation subject to a specified time period rather than to the happening of an event.[187]

---

[182] La. C.C. art. 2464.

[183] La. C.C. art. 2671 (1870).

[184] La. C.C. art. 2677.

[185] La. C.C. art. 2675.

[186] On Term, see Louisiana Law of Obligations in General: A Précis p. 28 to 39.

[187] On Condition, see *id.* at p. 39–54.

In a typical urban lease of commercial property for one year, rent is payable in monthly installments on the first day of each month of the lease. The lessor cannot demand payment of next month's rent before the first day of the next month arrives. Before the term arrives on the first day of next month, the lessor may not demand performance of the lessee's obligation to pay next month's rent. The performance of the obligation to pay (or the obligation's exigibility) is suspended, delayed.

Article 2678 uses both the word "term" and the word "duration." The Code states that a **"lease shall be for a term. Its duration may be agreed to by the parties or supplied by law."**[188] That a lease must be "for a term" means no more than that a lease may only be for a limited time as opposed to perpetual. In this, the Code follows traditional civilian doctrine. This limit on the parties' freedom to contract is stated clearly in the Code. They may choose any **duration** for the term provided it does not **exceed ninety-nine years.** If they choose a longer duration, the term is cut back to that legal maximum.[189] It seems that here the Revision is employing the words "term" and "duration" interchangeably to indicate an extinctive term, or the period of time after which the lease ends.

In most negotiated leases, the parties fix both the extinctive term and the suspensive term, although they do not usually employ this vocabulary. The parties choose the overall duration of the lease (the extinctive term) as well as the date on which the lessee must pay each installment of the rent (the suspensive term). Where the parties specify a term, then the term is "fixed." To accomplish this, the parties will typically recite in their lease that **"the lease will terminate at a designated date, . . . "**[190] Less typically, they may agree that the lease will terminate **upon the occurrence of a designated event.**[191] While the exact date when that event will occur may be unknown, the parties must be certain that this event will occur. Thus, the term of a lease may be set for the life of one of the parties, or of a third party. In that case the term is treated as **fixed** but its duration cannot be known until the event occurs. **In all other cases**, the term of the lease is **indeterminate.**[192]

If the parties do not choose a term, the Civil Code will supply the term for leases according to a fairly simple set of criteria. If the lease is an **agricultural lease,** it is **from year to year; other leases of immovables** and **leases of movables used as a residence** are **from month to month. Leases of other movables shall be from**

---

[188] La. C.C. art. 2678.

[189] La. C.C. art. 2679 ¶ 1.

[190] La. C.C. art. 2678 ¶ 2.

[191] *Id.*

[192] Note that Title IX on leases classifies terms as fixed or indeterminate, and that this classification does not precisely parallel that in the Title III on obligations in general. There, article 1778 states:

> **A term for the performance of an obligation is a period of time either certain or uncertain. It is certain when it is fixed. It is uncertain when it is not fixed but is determinable either by the intent of the parties or by the occurrence of a future and certain event. It is also uncertain when it is not determinable, in which case the obligation must be performed within a reasonable time.**

Thus, a period of time that article 1778 would call uncertain but determinable, article 2678 calls fixed and avoids characterizing lease terms as certain or uncertain. *See* Alain Levasseur, Louisiana Law of Obligations in General: A Précis p. 28–39 (2006).

day to day, unless the rent was fixed by longer or shorter periods, in which case the term shall be one such period, not to exceed one month.[193] Note that for these default rules on term, the extinctive term and the suspensive term might appear to be the same period of time. A month-to-month lease would be viewed as a series of one-month leases. Nevertheless, it seems clear that revised Title IX on lease proceeds on a different theory. A month-to-month lease is a lease for an indeterminate term, that is a lease the **duration** of which has not been agreed upon. In that case, article 2680 does **establish** the duration. But article 2680 does not establish the overall duration of the lease, i.e. the extinctive term. It establishes instead the suspensive term, or the successive periods of time at the beginning of each the rent is due.[194] Thus, in a month-to-month lease, the rent would be due on the first day of each month. The overall duration of the lease — or the extinctive term — is not set by article 2680.

In addition, the Code permits the duration of the term to be set by either party; that is, the **term's duration** may be made to **depend solely on the will of the lessor or the lessee.** As explained in the *Précis on Louisiana Law of Obligations in General*, it is important to distinguish "will" from "whim."[195] The rationale behind the distinction appears to be simply that one who exercises his whim does so at no cost to himself, whereas one who exercises his will does pay some sort of cost for doing so. Here, the decision of either party to end the lease cannot be without a cost, as the benefits of the lease (the lessee's use and enjoyment of the thing, the lessor's receipt of the rent) must be given up if the lease is terminated.

If the **parties,** in addition, **have not agreed on a maximum duration**, special rules are provided.[196] The lease in effect is treated as one in which the term has not been agreed upon by the parties. Accordingly, leases like these are treated the same way as leases without an agreed-upon term in that the term is set by the Code.

If the **term's duration depends solely on the will of the lessor or the lessee,** but the parties, in addition, *have* agreed on a maximum duration, then the treatment of the lease is quite different. A lease with this term structure is "perfectly valid." When the maximum term arrives, the lease terminates and is treated as a lease with a fixed term. If the party with the power to terminate the lease wishes to do so, however, he must act in accordance with the notice requirements under article 2727.[197] Moreover, as of the exercise of the right to terminate the lease, the latter may be treated as one with an indeterminate term, despite the inclusion of the maximum term.

Special rules govern the way in which leases with indeterminate terms are brought to an end. These are discussed generally in Chapter 5 below.[198]

---

[193] La. C.C. art. 2680.

[194] La. C.C. art. 2703.

[195] Alain Levasseur, Louisiana Law of Obligations in General: A Précis p. 43–46 (2006) (discussing and critiquing the substitution of these words for the traditional vocabulary).

[196] La. C.C. art. 2679 ¶ 2.

[197] *See* Appendix I, p. 176.

[198] *See infra*, § 5.4.3, p. 161.

Chapter 2

THE OBLIGATIONS OF THE LESSOR AND THE LESSEE: DELIVERY, REPAIRS, IMPROVEMENTS

Unlike the Civil Code of 1870, which dealt with the obligations of the lessor and of the lessee in separate chapters, the Revision combines the two into one Chapter — Chapter 3 — entitled The Obligations of the Lessor and the Lessee. This Précis will treat the obligations of each party separately with the exception of repairs, where the obligations of the lessee and the lessor are linked and may be conveniently discussed together.

The lessor's principal obligations are: (1) To deliver the thing to the lessee; (2) To maintain the thing in a condition suitable for the purpose [for] which it was leased; and (3) To protect the lessee's peaceful possession for the duration of the lease. (La. C.C. art. 2682.)

Under article 2683 the lessee's principal obligations are: (1) To pay the rent in accordance with the agreed terms; (2) To use the thing as a prudent administrator and in accordance with the purpose for which it was leased; and (3) To return the thing at the end of the lease in a condition that is the same as it was when the thing was delivered to him, except for normal wear and tear or as otherwise provided hereafter.

Article 1
The Lessor's Obligation to Deliver

§ 2.1.1. TIMELINESS.

Delivery of the thing leased is one of the lessor's principal obligations. First, he **is bound to deliver the thing at the agreed time. (La. C.C. art. 2684.)** That is, he must deliver the thing in a timely fashion. Typically, the lessor will specify when he is to make the delivery, which amounts to placing the thing leased at the disposal of the lessee. If the lease is silent on this point, traditionally the civil law looks to local usages. Such usages might show that a dwelling is to be delivered or made available to the lessee on the day following a certain holiday, unless the parties agreed otherwise. While such usages (or even customs) were common several hundred years ago in (France), there are few that apply today. Therefore, if the parties neglect to specify a date of delivery, and if a dispute arises on this point, the lessor ought to be held to an obligation to deliver the thing within a reasonable time under the circumstances.

§ 2.1.2. IN GOOD CONDITION.

Second, the lessor is **bound** to deliver the thing **in good condition suitable for the purpose for which it was leased. (La. C.C. art. 2684.)** This rule may be viewed as meaning that whether the thing is in good condition will depend on its suitability for the purpose of the lease. Or it may be viewed as referring to two requirements: good condition generally speaking and suitability for the purpose it was leased. Usually not much will depend on the distinction between these two requirements. Thus, a lessee rents a building from a lessor for the lessee's use as a warehouse. The roof leaks and the flooring is not strong enough to support the type of storage that the lessor knows the lessee is planning to do in his or her warehouse. The leaking roof would mean that the lessor has failed to deliver a building that is in good condition overall. The condition of the floors would mean that the lessor has not delivered a building suitable for the purpose for which it was leased.

§ 2.1.3. DELIVERY.

The *expenses* of delivery are the obligation of the lessor. In this way, the Code's rule for leases parallels that of sales.[199] The parties may of course alter this result by agreement.

The lessor of an immovable is obligated to deliver the *entire* immovable leased. Whether he has satisfied this obligation may depend on the way in which the parties have described the surface area of the immovable. If the lessor and the lessee agree on the **extent** or superficial area of the immovable leased, and if the **extent** delivered **differs from that which was agreed upon,** the lease Revision does not have its own set of rules to solve the dispute. Instead, the revised title on lease simply incorporates the rules from Title VII on Sale dealing with the same problem. **The rights of the parties with regard to such discrepancy are governed by the provisions of the Title "Sale". (La. C.C. art. 2685.)**[200] Thus, for example, resolution of the discrepancy may depend upon whether the lease was one at a rent of so much per acre, or whether it was of a certain and limited body, and so on. The advantage of this approach is that there is no incentive to re-characterize a lease as a sale (or vice versa), if the rules governing discrepancies are more advantageous for one nominate contract than another.[201]

Article 2
The Lessee's Obligation to Use the Thing as a Prudent Administrator

The lessee's duty is to use the thing **as a prudent administrator**, which is an objective or "in abstracto" standard. In addition, he must use it **in accordance with the purpose for which it was leased**, a standard that derives from the contract between the lessor and the lessee.[202] In most cases, of course, the two standards will

---

[199] La. C.C. arts. 2475–2498; *see supra*, p. 57, on expenses of delivery.

[200] The reference is to articles 2491–2497 on Sale; *see supra*, Sale, p. 59 *et seq.*

[201] A disadvantage might be in that the rules applicable to a Sale are usually not considered to be examples of code drafting at its best.

[202] La. C.C. art. 2683.

overlap. But in some cases, the parties may contemplate that the lessee is to use the thing imprudently and in a way that is harmful to the thing. So long as this use accords with the lease, the parties may be understood either to have chosen to put aside the first standard or to have accepted that the idea of prudence must be revised in light of the purpose or cause of the lessee. The lessee of an ordinary automobile and the lessee of a racecar should not be held to the same standard; the latter is entitled to take greater risks, as the lessor must understand. Thus, proper use and misuse must be judged according to the particular lease involved.

The Code builds on these notions with a rule governing the effect of a misuse of the thing by the lessee. First, the lessee is not to **use the thing for a purpose other than that for which it was leased. (La. C.C. art. 2686.)** Note that this rule is not based on the idea that such a non-conforming use must harm the thing or create excessive wear and tear. The lessor grants the lessee the use and enjoyment of the thing, but only the use and enjoyment the parties contemplate or, in default of their shared intentions, the use and enjoyment that are consistent with local usages. Second, the lessee is not to use the thing **in a manner that may cause damage** to it. As noted above, this rule should not apply if the parties have agreed otherwise.

The Code also states that the **lessee is liable for damage to the thing caused by his fault. (La. C.C. art. 2687.)** Likewise, in addition to damage caused by his own fault, the lessee is responsible for damage caused through the fault of **a person who, with his consent, is on the premises or uses the thing**. The aim of this provision may be primarily to place on the lessee's shoulders the fault of third persons to whom he makes the leased thing available and whom the lessor would otherwise have to sue directly. In this way, the lessee effectively promises the lessor that any third person's actions with respect to the thing will be free of fault. Article 2687 does not state that the lessee and the third person should in this case be solidarily bound. Both the lessee and the third person are liable for the identical **whole performance**, and therefore the lessor should be able to treat them as solidary obligors or as indivisible obligors.[203] As a result, the lessee should be able to recover from the third person the entirety of any judgment the lessee must pay to the lessor. If the lessee, however, had some involvement in the circumstances giving rise to the harm to the thing leased, the lessee who had paid the entire judgment could only recover a virile share from the third person through contribution.

As for the lessee himself, any behavior of his that could be characterized as fault for the purposes of general civil or tort liability would be embraced by the obligations he undertakes as lessee. And if the lessor should, in the lease, choose to renounce or alter those obligations, that diminution of the lessee's responsibility should carry over to any potential delictual liability of the lessee.

As for the lessor's remedies, the Code provides that if the lessee fails to honor his obligations, the lessor may obtain injunctive relief, dissolution of the lease, and any damages he may have sustained. (La. C.C. art. 2686.) In other words, the lessor need not show irreparable harm in order to obtain injunctive relief.

---

[203] On Solidarity and Indivisibility, see Louisiana Law of Obligations in General: A Précis, p. 59–69, 80–90.

It must be acknowledged that the judge plays a role in evaluating the lessor's remedy. The lessor's path to one or all of the types of relief specified here is subject to the discretion of the judge. If the lessor cannot demonstrate harm caused by the lessee's departure from the intended use of the thing, it will be difficult for the lessor to obtain any remedy. If it is important to the lessor that the lessee strictly adhere to the intended use of the thing, the lessor may consider enhancing his possible remedies through contract, as sole reliance on the Code's protections may not be enough.

The lessee has a distinct duty to inform the lessor when certain events have occurred. First, the lessee is **bound to notify the lessor without delay when the thing has been damaged or requires repair. (La. C.C. art. 2688.)** Read strictly, this would require the lessee to notify the lessor even of some damage that it is the lessee's duty to repair. While one can imagine that the lessor will not be interested in minor damage in this category, the sense of the Code may be to let the lessor be the judge of that. Having been informed, the lessor can then inspect the repair and verify that it was done properly. If the lessee fails to give the lessor notice, article 2688 states that the lessor **is entitled to damages sustained as a result of the lessee's failure to perform this obligation. (La. C.C. art. 2688.)**

The failure to inform the lessor of a necessary repair might increase the lessor's cost of repair. Presumably, that increased cost should be an item of damage that the lessor may recover against the lessee. It has been suggested in a comment to article 2688 that the mere failure to inform may not be considered sufficient to give the lessor a right to dissolve the lease. This seems a curious limitation since, at least theoretically, the failure to notify the lessor of a needed repair, such as a leak of a dangerous substance, could create serious risks to the thing leased and to third parties. Such a failure should justify a dissolution of the lease.

It is also suggested in another comment to article 2688 that the lessee's failure to inform the lessor does not absolve the lessor of his obligation to repair, or indeed, of other obligations. Such a suggestion can be considered to be consistent with the idea that while the failure to inform may give the lessor the right to damages against the lessee, the lease and its other obligations remain otherwise intact.

The lessee must also notify the lessor **when his possession has been disturbed by a third person. (La. C.C. art. 2688.)** Thus, if the lessor of an agricultural lease is harmed because the lessee fails to inform him that a third person is encroaching on the land, the cost of dealing with the encroachment should be recoverable against the lessee. There exists here a parallel with a rule in the law of sale according to which a buyer disturbed in his possession of the thing sold must call his seller in warranty.[204]

The final obligation of the lessee is to pay all taxes, assessments, and other charges **that arise from *the use* of the thing by the lessee. (La. C.C. art. 2689.)** All other taxes, assessments, and similar charges connected to the ownership of the thing leased but not related to the use of that thing are the responsibility of the lessor.

---

[204] *See supra*, p. 70.

ARTICLE 3
THE LESSOR'S OBLIGATION NOT TO ALTER THE THING DURING THE LEASE

In general, when a lessor leases a thing, the very existence of the contract of lease deprives the lessor of the power to modify the thing. The Code states that **during the lease, the lessor may not make any alterations in the thing. (La. C.C. art. 2690.)** Thus, the lessor should not remove gutters from a residence he has leased, even if the lessee is not in fact harmed or even inconvenienced by their removal. The idea is that any portion of the thing leased that the lessor removes or merely alters interferes with the right of the lessee to use and enjoy it. The reason behind this article is clear. Having granted the use and enjoyment of the thing to the lessee, the lessor cannot interfere with its use or enjoyment without the lessee's consent. Altering or modifying the thing during the lease, even to improve it, would constitute such an interference. Of course, the parties may agree otherwise.

ARTICLE 4
REPAIRS AND IMPROVEMENTS

Taking into account the fact that the lessor may not make alterations to the thing, the Code also addresses the question of repairs to the thing. From one point of view, the lessor's obligation of warranty might seem to require that the lessor make all repairs of all kinds. Instead, however, the Code divides and allocates the responsibility to repair the thing leased between the lessor and the lessee. On the one hand, the Code places responsibility upon the lessee for certain repairs. On the other hand, the lessor is obligated only to make those repairs the lessee is not obligated to make.

§ 2.4.1. THE LESSEE'S OBLIGATION TO REPAIR.

First, the lessee must repair damage to the thing caused by his fault and, in a natural extension of this rule, he must repair damage to it caused by the fault of persons who, with his consent, are on the premises or use the thing. (La. C.C. art. 2692.) This rule applies whether the thing leased is a movable or an immovable.

Second, the lessee must **repair any deterioration** resulting from his use or from the use made by others who use the thing leased with his consent. Here, a restriction on the rule comes into play: the lessee is only obligated to repair deterioration that results from **use to the extent it exceeds the normal or agreed use of the thing. (La. C.C. art. 2692.)**

This limitation raises several issues. First, if the lessee has agreed in the lease to limit his use in some way, and he remains within that limit, the lessee has no obligation to repair any deterioration due to that permitted use. Thus, it must be decided whether the lessee has adhered to contractually imposed standards of use. Second, if the lease itself does not define such limits on use, it is possible that the lessee could have exceeded some general standard for what is an acceptable or normal level and manner of use. While a level and manner of use will rarely be established as a matter of law, it should be at least possible to prove what is normal as a matter of usage within a given trade or industry or within a certain locality. In such a case, "normal" usage would supply the term missing from the lease. Finally, it might be possible to show that the lessor and lessee themselves understood what a normal level of use would be, which could then become an implied provision of the lease.

Another difficulty flows from the rule limiting the lessee's duty to repair the "deterioration" due to exceeding the accepted norm. The deterioration caused by normal use would not be the lessee's responsibility. Making a distinction this fine, while certainly possible, will hardly be justified in most cases.

§ 2.4.2. THE LESSOR'S OBLIGATION TO REPAIR.

Outside such repairs that are on the lessee's shoulders, the lessor bears the obligation to make the repairs. The lessor must undertake **all repairs that become necessary to maintain the thing in a condition suitable for the purpose for which it was leased. (La. C.C. art. 2691.)** Thus, the lessor should not be bound to remedy all possible problems that arise with the thing leased, but only those that relate to the evident purpose for which it was leased. When that purpose is the same as the ordinary use of the thing leased, the lessor's obligation to repair seems unavoidable. When the lessee has a particular and unusual purpose for the thing, that purpose must be elevated to the "cause" of the lease.[205] In this respect, **article 2669**, in the title on Lease, states that **In all matters not provided for in this Title, the contract of lease is governed by the rules of the Titles of "Obligations in General" and "Conventional Obligations or Contracts".**

Title VII on Sale provides a closer analogy. There, the seller is bound to warrant that the thing sold is **reasonably fit for its ordinary use. (La. C.C. art. 2524.)** Analogously, the lessor has an obligation to maintain the thing leased in a condition suitable for the ordinary purpose of the thing. For the seller to be obligated to warrant that the thing sold will suit the buyer's particular needs, more is required. The seller may have **reason to know** either the buyer's **particular use** or the buyer's **particular purpose**. In addition, the seller may also have reason to know that the buyer is **relying on the seller's skill and judgment** in choosing the thing as **fit for the buyer's intended use or for his particular purpose.**[206] By analogy, the lessor should not be obligated to repair the thing leased to suit a lessee's particular use or purpose that is not the ordinary use or purpose unless the lessor has reason to know not only of that use or purpose but also of the lessee's reliance on the lessor's warranty. The corresponding article on the lessor's warranty is not clear. It states: **The lessor warrants the lessee that the thing is suitable for the purpose for which it was leased and that it is free of vices or defects that prevent its use for that purpose. (La. C.C. art. 2696-1.)** This article does not suggest that the lessor's warranty is enhanced only if the lessor has reason to know that the lessee is relying upon the lessor's judgment.

There is also a question of timing. The Code here is focusing on repairs that need to be made in order to fix problems that arise after the lessee has begun to use and to enjoy the thing. Presumably rules for pre-existing conditions are not included in

---

[205] *See* La. C.C. arts. 1966–1970 on "Cause."

[206] La. C.C. art. 2524; *see* Sale, *supra* p. 54, 72.

article 2692. Whether the lessor is obligated to repair some condition of the thing of which the lessee was aware when he entered the lease is a question that merges with the discussion of the lessor's warranties, taken up below.

Finally, the lessor and lessee may agree to alter this scheme and to shift all responsibilities for repair to one or the other. Evidently, no rule of public order forbids doing so. Such an agreement would typically occur in the documentation of the lease itself, when the lease is written. This is because, even though an oral lease of an immovable may be valid, it is difficult to prove an oral modification of a written lease and, even more so, the very existence of an oral lease. Indeed, responsibility for repairs may be adjusted by the parties as the need arises and the parties may not consider it necessary to put their understanding of these issues in a written document.

For the lessor to have a duty to repair the thing leased, it must be damaged in some way. Of course, whether or not there is actual damage to the thing is often a matter of dispute between the lessor and the lessee. Unfortunately, the jurisprudence offers little guidance on how to resolve these situations. At the other end of the spectrum, when damage to the thing leased is so great that there is total destruction of the thing, there should be no duty to repair. Instead, the lease should be terminated.

§ 2.4.3. THE LESSOR'S RIGHT TO REPAIR.

As noted above, the lessor may not make alterations to the thing during the term of the lease. One must keep in mind the distinction between an alteration of the thing, which is not a repair of it, and a repair, which restores the thing to its intended state. A repair puts the thing back the way it was; an alteration creates a new condition.

The lessor, however, may not make every kind of repair during the lease. Instead, he may only make **a repair that cannot be postponed until the end of the lease. (La. C.C. art. 2693.)** Furthermore, the lessor may make such a repair even if doing so **causes the lessee to suffer inconvenience or loss of use of the thing. *Id.***

Article 2693 states a rule about the lessor's right to repair that assumes a conflict of views between lessor and lessee. Why the lessee might resist cooperating in such a case is not difficult to see. For the lessee, the loss of use of the premises or thing leased might threaten to disrupt his living arrangements or business affairs, to the point that he would prefer to suffer the problem than get the problem repaired. This is particularly true if the end of the lease is in sight and the lessee does not plan to continue the lease. The lessor, on the other hand, will prefer to make the repair now to preserve the value of the asset itself.

As regards the lessee, the Code does provide him with substantial protection. If the lessee suffers **inconvenience** or **loss of use of the thing** leased, the lessee may be able to **obtain a reduction or abatement of the rent, or a dissolution of the lease. (La. C.C. art. 2693-2.)** These remedies will depend upon **all of the circumstances**. The factors to be considered include: 1) Was the lessor, the lessee, or both at fault in bringing about the condition that requires repair? 2) Which party is responsible for making the repairs? Normally, this responsibility belongs to the lessor, meaning that the lessee's argument for some remedy is strengthened in the typical case. 3) How long will it take to effect the repair? 4) To what degree will the lessee suffer a loss of use of the thing? In many cases, it will make sense to combine these suggested factors. A complete deprivation of use should be tolerable for a short time, a minor deprivation for a longer time, and so on.

Application of fault as a factor seems puzzling. If the repair is one for which the lessee is responsible because the lessee is at fault in creating the need for it, then it is hard to see why the lessee should ever obtain an abatement of the rent, say, because the lessee must leave the premises while the lessor repairs it. The lessee has the obligation to repair in this case under article 2692, yet the lessor has also the right to do so.

The Code states the lessee's right to repair as one that depends upon the lessor's failure to fulfill that obligation. Thus, if the lessor fails to perform his obligation to make necessary repairs within a reasonable time after demand by the lessee, the lessee may cause them to be made. (La. C.C. art. 2694.) Key to this provision is the demand by the lessee, which must be made before the repairs are undertaken. If that is the case, then the lessee has a choice. He may demand immediate reimbursement of the amount expended for the repair. *Id.* Typically, this amount is not large enough to justify the expenses of a formal dispute. Fortunately for the lessee, the Code permits him a sort of compensation, and he may apply that amount to the payment of rent. *Id.* So as not to leave the lessor defenseless, the Code confines the lessee's repair-and-reduce remedy to the extent that the repair was necessary and the expended amount was reasonable. *Id.*

These remedies only apply when the lessor has the obligation to repair. It should not be forgotten that the lessee may bear the obligation to make repairs when the lessee is at fault in bringing about the need for them under article 2692. It follows that, having the obligation, he must also have the right to repair in this case also. This result, although not stated in the Code articles, is logical.

§ 2.4.4. IMPROVEMENTS TO THE THING LEASED.

During the lease, lessees often adapt or wish to adapt the thing leased to their own needs. Occasionally, lessees add improvements to the thing leased, such as buildings and other substantial structures when an immovable is the object of the lease. When such a lease is over, and when it does not provide an answer to the fate of the improvements, the law must decide who is the owner of such improvements: the lessee who made them or the lessor who owns the immovable where they are located?

The problem occurs in various contexts. A good faith or a bad faith possessor builds on the land of another.[207] A husband builds upon an immovable that is the separate property of his wife.[208] A purchaser of an immovable makes improvements to it, knowing that his seller had mortgaged it to secure his own debt, and the

---

207 *See* La. C.C. arts. 493, 498.

208 *See* La. C.C. art. 2366.

mortgagee forecloses.[209] The Revision of Lease is the most recent formulation of a solution to this problem.

One first preliminary question is the type of property concerned. The Code refers to **attachments, additions, or other improvements**. The word "improvements" is a term of art, as an improvement need not in fact improve or increase the value of the principal thing involved.[210] Elsewhere, the Code assumes that improvements in this technical sense may even cause **harm.**[211]

A second preliminary question is the role of the parties" autonomy. May the parties themselves choose their own rules to govern this situation? Clearly, they may do so. The parties to a lease may provide their own rules for the treatment of improvements when the lease ends. Failing such an agreement, the Code provides a set of suppletive rules and procedures.[212]

The first rule is that, at the termination of the lease, the lessee **may remove all improvements that he made to the leased thing. (La. C.C. art. 2695 (1).)** Emphasis should be placed on the word "all." It should mean both improvements that are made with the lessor's consent, and those made without it (reasoning *a generali sensu*). When the lessee acts without the lessor's consent, the lessee may place himself in breach of his obligations, of course,[213] but the process under article 2695, however, is the same in both cases.

Second, the lessee must remove the improvements so as to **restore the thing to its former condition**. The Civil Code of 1870 provided a somewhat different formula, namely that the lessee had to **leave** the thing **in the state in which he received it.**[214] Current article 495, which deals with the ownership of improvements generally, also speaks of an obligation of the possessor **to restore the property to its former condition**. At a minimum, the lessor is to be no worse off than at the inception of the lease. And if this occurs, not only is the lease terminated successfully, but no dispute can arise based on any claim by the lessor that he was entitled to the improvements or their value.

The Civil Code addresses the situation where the lessee does not remove the improvements. Now it is the lessor's turn to act. He has two choices. First, he may **appropriate ownership of the improvements by reimbursing the lessee for their costs or for the enhanced value of the leased thing, whichever is less. (La. C.C. art. 2695 (2)(a).)** Alternatively, the lessor may **demand that the lessee remove the improvements within a reasonable time and restore the leased thing to its former condition. (La. C.C. art. 2695 (2)(b).)**

If the lessor takes the second route and demands that the lessee remove-and-restore, and the lessee takes those actions, then the matter ends. If, however, the lessee does not act in accordance with the lessor's demand, then the lessor faces

---

[209] *See* La. C.C. art. 3318.

[210] La. C.C. art. 2695, comment (a).

[211] La. C.C. art. 495.

[212] La. C.C. art. 2695.

[213] La. C.C. art. 2686.

[214] La. C.C. art. 2726 (1870).

another pair of choices. Faced with the lessee's inaction, the lessor's first alternative is to remove the improvements and restore the leased thing to its former condition at the expense of the lessee. (La. C.C. art. 2695(2)(b).) This means that the lessor must both undertake to do the work of removal or to contract for it, and then pursue the lessee for reimbursement. Unless the lessor can obtain some sort of security for the lessee's eventual obligation to reimburse him, the lessor may find this alternative too risky. The lessor's second alternative might appear more tempting, as he may **appropriate ownership of the improvements without any obligation of reimbursement to the lessee. *Id.*** In order to do so, he must notify the lessee by certified mail of his decision to appropriate them. The article states: **Appropriation of the improvement by the lessor may only be accomplished by providing additional notice by certified mail to the lessee after expiration of the time given the lessee to remove the improvements. (La. C.C. art. 2695 (2)(b).)**

While this seems clear enough, there are important concerns that appear to have been omitted from the article. For example, article 2695 refers to the notification at this point as an **"additional notice"**, but the article does not refer to the **"demand"** in part (2)(b) quoted above as a notice. Nor does article 2695 require that a demand be written or in any particular form. Moreover, the article does not mention any need for the lessor to specify a time within which the lessee is to act. In comparison, article 493 does have these elements. That article requires the owner of the land, whose position is like the lessor's here, to mail a written demand that the other party remove the improvements. If the other party does not do so in ninety days, only then is a second notice required, this time by certified mail, telling the recipient that ownership of the improvements has transferred.

Chapter 3

THE LESSOR'S WARRANTIES

ARTICLE 1
WARRANTY AGAINST VICES OR DEFECTS

§ 3.1.1. LESSOR'S WARRANTY AND SELLER'S WARRANTY.

The warranty owed by the lessor can be seen as a cousin of the warranty owed by the seller.[215] Just as the seller warrants that the thing sold is free of redhibitory defects, the lessor warrants that the thing he leases is free of vices and defects. While the law of sale and the law of lease deal with the same problem, they don't devote the same amount of space to it. The Lease Revision devotes just four articles to the problem, whereas the Civil Code on Sale has some fifteen provisions on redhibition alone. The comparatively unequal treatment is easily explained by the analogy between the obligation of a seller and the obligation of a lessor insomuch that redhibition in sale and the warranty against vices and defects in lease are the same concept. The foundation in both instances is a presumption of error; it is presumed that the obligee (the buyer, the lessee) would not have contracted had he known of the vice. The law likewise presumes that the obligor (the seller, the lessor) would not have entered a contract had he known of the vice either. Thus, as the case is one of mutual error, the obligee (the buyer, the lessee) may seek rescission of the contract based on error. Another basis for the warranty in both sale and lease is that they are onerous contracts. For a contract to be onerous, the buyer or lessee must **obtain an advantage in exchange for his obligation.**[216] If the buyer or the lessee obtains a thing or a lessee obtains the use and enjoyment of a thing that is radically defective, it is clear that neither secures an advantage as a counter-performance to his own obligation.

It follows that the parties are free to contract in light of the vice or defect as they see fit. The lessee may decide to rent a thing, knowing of the defect. In that case, there is no ground for an action based on the defect. Furthermore, because of the nature of warranty against vices and defects, the lessee may validly waive any right he might have for the lessor's failure to satisfy the warranty. However, because a lessor may be tempted to use its typically stronger bargaining power to extract waivers from a lessee who might otherwise not waive its warranty rights, the Code provides the lessee with some protections.

---

[215] On Warranty in a contract of Sale, see *supra*.

[216] La. C.C. art. 1909.

§ 3.1.2. THE LESSOR'S WARRANTY: LEGAL REGIME.

A. Elements.

The Code states clearly the elements of the lessor's warranty. The lessor warrants the lessee that the thing is suitable for the purpose for which it was leased and that it is free of vices or defects that prevent its use for that purpose. (La. C.C. art. 2696.) The idea of a defect in the thing is linked to the purpose for which the thing is leased. Thus, the lessor first warrants that the thing is right for the lessee's acknowledged purpose or cause.

Assume the lessee rents a piece of equipment that is substantially underpowered for the work that the lessor knows the lessee will use it for. The lessor has failed to satisfy this warranty. Changing the situation slightly, assume that the lessee rents a piece of equipment that is suitably powered for the same job, but the equipment shuts down unpredictably due to a fault in the electrical system. Further, the lessor does not know of the problem, nor should he have known. Again, the lessor has not satisfied his obligation of warranty. The Code states that the **warranty provided in the preceding article also encompasses vices or defects that are not known to the lessor. (La. C.C. art. 2697.)** And Louisiana Civil Code article 2696-2 provides that **this warranty also extends to vices or defects that arise after the delivery of the thing and are not attributable to the fault of the lessee.** In both these situations, the defect existed at the time of the lease.

If the thing that the lessor delivers is not of the kind specified in the contract, evidently the proper remedy is to be found in the rules of conventional obligations or contracts. The connection is explicit as regards the contract of Sale.[217] While no explicit cross-reference to conventional obligations is made in the law of lease, the connection is fully justified nevertheless. Article 2669 does make the connection to Title III on Obligations in General and to Title IV on Conventional Obligations or Contracts for **all matters not provided for** in Title IX on Lease.

If the lessee knows of such vices or defects and fails to notify the lessor, the lessee's recovery for breach of warranty may be reduced accordingly. (La. C.C. art. 2697.) This rule reduces, in a sense, the lessor's responsibility. A typical case is the occurrence of an event causing damage that is a defect within the meaning of article 2697, such as storm damage to the roof and attic of a building. Furthermore, assume that this damage engages the lessor's responsibility to repair. The lessee's failure to notify may increase the costs to repair the damage to the roof and attic, as the roof damage could allow ordinary rainfall and wind to cause further damage to the building that already requires repair. The lessee's recovery should be reduced by the extent of the cost of the additional repairs. This concept is consistent with the lessee's obligation to mitigate damages.[218] Moreover, this defense for the lessor is in addition to the claim granted to him against the lessee

[217] La. C.C. art. 2524-3.

[218] La. C.C. art. 2002.

for failure to inform.[219]

Generally in contracts, only the obligee's intent is protected through the contract. However, special situations can be demonstrated such as those that affect a third party beneficiary to the contract. In residential leases exceptionally, persons other than the lessee as obligee are protected. In such leases, the warranty against vices and defects owed by the lessor **applies to all persons who reside in the premises in accordance with the lease. (La. C.C. art. 2698.)**

B. Waiver of Warranty for Vices or Defects.

As noted above, the Code provides some protections to lessees even in those instances where lessors suggest or demand waivers of liability in relation to this warranty against vices or defects. In principle, the warranty certainly **may be waived. (La. C.C. art. 2699.)** Such waivers, however, may only occur through **clear and unambiguous language that is brought to the attention of the lessee. (*Id.*)** The idea here is that not only must the language of the waiver be clear and unambiguous, but it must also be explained to the lessee. As a practical matter, this necessitates a written waiver. It is difficult to imagine the lessor requiring the lessee to make an oral waiver and later then bringing what the lessee said to the attention of the lessee. It seems intuitive that what the law contemplates is the lessor presenting the lessee with a written waiver for the lessee to sign, usually incorporated in the documentation of the lease. The law requires not merely that the lessee sign the lease, but that the lessee particularly focuses his attention on the waiver within the lease. That fact in practice is usually handled with a separate signature line or box at that point in the document. Thus, whereas leases generally do not require written form in order to be valid, either the lease itself or some other writing must include the waiver of this warranty in order for it to be effective.

There are further restrictions surrounding waivers of warranty. The Code states first that a waiver of warranty is ineffective: (1) To the extent it pertains to vices or defects of which the lessee did not know and the lessor knew or should have known. (La. C.C. art. 2699.) First, if the lessee knows of the defect, he may effectively waive the warranty pertaining to that defect. This is consistent with the idea of presumed error. The lessee who is aware of the problem may go forward into the lease. Second, if the lessee is ignorant of the defect and the lessor knows about it, the waiver is ineffective. There may be other remedies against the lessor, as his failure to disclose the existence of defects might amount to fraud under articles 1953 and 1954 of the Civil Code. Third, if both the lessee and the lessor are ignorant of the defect, but it can be shown that the lessor *ought* to have known of the defect, the waiver is ineffective. This is the typical posture of attempts to exclude waivers of the warranty.

A waiver of the warranty for vices and defects is also ineffective in a residential or consumer lease, to the extent it purports to waive the warranty for vices or defects that seriously affect health or safety. (**La. C.C. art. 2699(3)**.) Such concerns relate to public order.

---

[219] *See* La. C.C. art. 2688 *infra*.

Finally, waivers are also ineffective if they are **contrary to the provisions of article 2004. (La. C.C. art. 2699(2).)** Article 2004 provides:

"Any clause is null that, in advance, excludes or limits the liability of one party for intentional or gross fault that causes damage to the other party.

Any clause is null that, in advance, excludes or limits the liability of one party for causing physical injury to the other party."

Thus, while the rule on intentional or gross fault is not likely to apply to leases, if the lease purports to limit any liability the lessor might incur for physical injury to the lessee caused by a defect the lessor knows or should know to exist in the thing, that clause will be ineffective.[220]

C. Shifting Premises Liability.

The provisions of the Civil Code Ancillaries are also important in the law of lease. Section 3221 of Title 9 provides:

"Notwithstanding the provisions of Louisiana Civil Code Article 2699, the owner of premises leased under a contract whereby the lessee assumes responsibility for their condition is not liable for injury caused by any defect therein to the lessee or anyone on the premises who derives his right to be thereon from the lessee, unless the owner knew or should have known of the defect or had received notice thereof and failed to remedy the defect within a reasonable time."

What this statute accomplishes is the shifting of potential delictual liability due to defects in the premises to the lessee and to most third parties. In the business context, a lease that shifts such potential liability to the lessee in effect places the responsibility upon him to secure proper insurance for the risk that may occur. For our purposes, section 3221 is another method, in addition to waiver of the warranty, for the lessor to avoid responsibility under the warranty. Evidently, if the owner knows or ought to know of the existence of the defect, this creates a significant limitation on the ability to shift responsibility.

Another statute from the Civil Code ancillaries provides protection from suits arising out of the recreational use of immovables.[221] The statute states that an owner of land, in principle, is not liable if he permits others to use his land for recreational purposes. An owner is liable only for **willful or malicious failure to warn against a dangerous condition, use, structure, or activity**. The relevance for lease is that "owner" under this statute is a term of art and is defined to include lessees as well as anyone who is in **control** of the immovable concerned. Thus, this statute does not so much shift potential liability from lessor to lessee as diminish the liability of both to third persons.

---

[220] *See infra.*

[221] La. Rev. Stat. 9:2795.

Article 2
The Lessor's Warranty of Peaceful Possession

The lessor warrants the lessee's peaceful possession of the leased thing against any disturbance caused by a person who asserts ownership, or right to possession of, or any other right in the thing. (La. C.C. art. 2700.) While this rule may appear clear on its face, it conceals several significant issues which, when clarified, help advance our understanding of the law of lease.

§ 3.2.1. THE LESSEE'S POSSESSION OF THE THING LEASED, THE RIGHT TO POSSESS, AND THIRD PERSON TRESPASSERS.

The first issue is the nature of the lessee's interest that article 2700 protects. Peaceful possession, which is the formula used by article 2700 for the lessee's interest, on initial examination might seem an easy enough idea to comprehend. We can immediately visualize the lessee using and enjoying the thing leased, physically holding or controlling it, therefore possessing it. In the next scene, another person arrives who unsettles this state of affairs by claiming some right in the thing, and that claim constitutes the sort of **disturbance** that this article intends to prevent or remedy.

But, in fact, possession may not be the best word to describe the lessee's interest here. The word **possession** in the Civil Code is used in two ways: it may denote **physical possession** of a thing, but **possession** has also the core legal meaning of the ***right* to possess**. These concepts are explained in Book III, Title XXIII Occupancy and Possession, particularly in Chapter 2 Possession, which begins at article 3421.

Article 2700 may be read to mean that the lessor does not warrant the lessee against those who interfere as a matter of fact with the lessee's use and enjoyment of the thing leased. For example, a third person dumps a load of trash on the land rented by the lessee and then speeds away. The lessor is not bound by article 2700 to remove the trash. One explanation is that this third person has made no claim of any right whatsoever to the land. The article requires that the third person claim **ownership** of the thing, or the **right to possess** the thing, or some **other right in the thing**. From this, we might conclude that the act of a third person that qualifies as a disturbance under article 2700 interferes with the lessee's right to possess as such. But this is not truly so because the lessee does not have that right.

Note that in the definition of lease, it is not the **possession** of the thing that the lessor grants the lessee, but the **use and enjoyment** of the thing. The distinction is not one that should be overlooked. The law governing possession of things is careful to distinguish between the possessor of a thing and a mere holder, that is, one who merely holds or controls a thing physically. One who holds a thing in this sense, and does so "as would an owner" for one year, gains the right to possess. And it is clear that the true owner in physical possession of a thing has the right to possess unless he has lost it.

This rule has practical consequences. For example, assume that *A* as the true owner of a parcel of undeveloped land also has the right to possess it. Assume next that a non-owner, *B*, physically detains this immovable under the mistaken belief that he owns it, having purchased it from *X*, another person who claims ownership of the property. *B* behaves as if he owns it by cutting down trees and digging ditches in preparation for the building of a house. Ten months after these activities have begun, the true owner *A* brings a possessory action[222] against *B*. *B* will lose the possessory action. He cannot defend the suit on the ground that *X* had a better title than *A*. *B* must give up his detention of the property and bring his own petitory action[223] against *A* later. On the other hand, if *A* brings the petitory action against *B* more than a year after *B* has taken physical control of the property, then *A* loses the right to possess, that is, he loses possession in the legal sense. If that occurs, *A* must bring the petitory action against *B* and must prove his ownership against *B* in order to recover the property.

The connection with lease can now be made. The lessee does physically control the property leased and thus resembles the mere holder mentioned above. But while the mere holder physically possesses for himself, this is not true of the lessee. The lessee exerts control over the thing not for himself but for the lessor; the lessee is a precarious possessor. That is, the lessee possesses the property — possesses it physically — for the lessor. If, for example, the lessor is not the owner but has begun acquisitive prescription,[224] the lessee continues the possession *of* the lessor and *for* the lessor for the purpose of accrual of acquisitive prescription. The *right* to possess is not transferred to the lessee because the ownership of the thing does not pass to the lessee. The lessee, of course, may take all kinds of actions that any owner could take on the property. But, in law, the lessee's *physical possession* is entirely dependent on the lessor.

Another result of the lessee's precarious possession is that the lessee cannot acquire the right to possess adversely to the lessor unless the character of his possession changes. Using the facts in the previous example, assume that *A* is not the true owner; *X* is. When *A*'s lessee *B* learns this he buys the property from *X*. From that point forward he no longer possesses for *A* but for himself. This fact is even clearer if *B* should now bring a petitory action against *A* to establish *B*'s ownership.[225]

Note that a strict application of the lessee's precarious possession would mean that the lessee could not even sue a trespasser or expel a squatter. Taking the dependence of the lessee's right to control the thing leased to its logical limit would mean that only the lessor could take legal action to fend off intrusions by a third person without claim of right, as if the lessee were a stranger to the property leased.

All in all, although the Civil Code does not solve the riddle of the "true" legal nature of the lessee's interest, it appears that the lessee's interest or right is a

---

[222] The possessory action is found in article 3655 of the Louisiana Code of Civil Procedure.

[223] The petitory action is found in article 3651 of the Louisiana Code of Civil Procedure.

[224] La. C.C. art. 3446.

[225] La. C.C. arts. 3437, 3438.

"personal right," a right against the person of the lessor, and not a "real right."[226] The Civil Code does provide, however, that the lessee **may file any appropriate action** to deal with a **person who does not claim a right in the leased thing**, but who is in fact disturbing the lessee's **peaceful possession.**[227] As noted above, because we know that the lessee does not have the right to possess as such, it is clear that when the Code articles speak of the lessee's possession, they should be read as referring to the lessee's right to use and to enjoy the thing, which entails the lessee's right to detain the thing and engage in acts of physical possession. Thus, it is clear that the lessee has the power to protect his interests under the lease against actions of third persons. For example, the lessee, as precarious possessor, may bring the possessory action, despite the fact that he lacks any real right in the thing leased.[228]

With respect to third persons who do not claim a right in the thing at all but merely trespass or intrude, the Civil Code does not provide that the lessee may call upon the assistance of the lessor to deal with such intruders; in fact, it says the opposite: **the lessor is not bound to protect the lessee's possession against a disturbance caused by a person who does not claim a right in the leased thing. (La. C.C. art. 2702.)**

§ 3.2.2. DISTURBANCES IN FACT AND IN LAW.

When a third person interferes physically with the lessee's possession but makes no claim of right, such physical disturbances are traditionally called disturbances in fact. When a third person, however, makes a claim of right, such as ownership, this is usually called a disturbance of law. A third person might claim that he is owner and that the lessor has no authority to lease the premises. He might furthermore bring legal action against the lessee to eject the lessee from the premises. Up to this point, there is no physical interference with the lessee's enjoyment, but the lessee is suffering a disturbance in law.

This terminology is parallel to that of the law of sale.[229] In sale, the buyer may suffer a disturbance in law sufficient to evict him if he learns that someone other than his seller is the true owner of the thing he has purchased. This is not sufficient, however, for a lessee to suffer an eviction. For example, the Code clearly contemplates that the lessor may not be the owner when the lessor is himself a lessee. The lessee is not "evicted" on the basis of such facts. A contrary result would make even an ordinary sublease impossible. Where the third person sues the lessee to remove him, that certainly suffices as a disturbance in law.

The distinction between the two kinds of disturbance is expressed in the Code of Civil Procedure in article 3659:

"Disturbances of possession which give rise to the possessory action are of two kinds: disturbance in fact and disturbance in law.

---

[226] La. C.C. art. 1763, 1765; *See* Louisiana Law of Obligations in General: A Précis p. 21–28.

[227] La. C.C. art. 2702.

[228] La. C.C. art. 3440.

[229] See the discussion of disturbances in fact and of law in the Sales Précis *supra*.

"A disturbance in fact is an eviction, or any other physical act which prevents the possessor of immovable property or of a real right therein from enjoying his possession quietly, or which throws any obstacle in the way of that enjoyment.

"A disturbance in law is the execution, recordation, registry, or continuing existence of record of any instrument which asserts or implies a right of ownership or to the possession of immovable property or of a real right therein, or any claim or pretension of ownership or right to the possession thereof except in an action or proceeding, adversely to the possessor of such property or right."

This article is a good example of the use of the word possession both as a legal right (as in the first and third paragraphs) and as a physical act (as in the second).

§ 3.2.3. THE LESSOR'S DUTY NOT TO INTERFERE WITH THE LESSEE'S POSSESSION.

The warranty of peaceful possession owed by a lessor to a lessee concerns acts of third persons. As for the relationship between the lessee and a third person, it is of course not contractual in nature. Interferences by the lessor himself, however, would violate the lessor's duties under the lease, and those duties do arise under contract. Such violations therefore are handled under the general rules of contract in Titles III and IV of the Code, especially those dealing with failure to perform in Title IV, particularly Chapter 8 General Effects of Contracts and Chapter 9 Dissolution. Those rules are adequate for lease and therefore no additional and special provisions need be added to Title IX.

§ 3.2.4. RESIDENTIAL LEASE: DISTURBANCES BY INVITEES AND ADJACENT LESSEES.

The Revision provides a special rule for the protection of lessees of residences. For such leases the warranty of peaceful possession extends to **a disturbance caused by a person who, with the lessor's consent, has access to the thing or occupies adjacent property belonging to the lessor**. **(La. C.C. art. 2700, ¶ 2.)** This rule articulates the results of court decisions allowing residential lessees to obtain a remedy against lessors who had leased adjoining premises to other lessees who made a habit of celebrating noisily through the night. This liability of the lessor is contractual in nature. The lessor's responsibility here would derive from his ability to grant access to the thing leased or to adjacent property only to persons who will not disturb the lessee.

The rule is tailored to solve a particular sort of problem. Indeed, the Revision included it, thereby codifying results formulated in the jurisprudence. Because the lessor's liability in fact derives from his contract with the lessee as well as the law, this Code article should not be narrowly construed. Instead, there is no reason why the principle should not be applied by analogy (*ubi eadem ratio idem lex*) in contexts outside residential leases.

As noted above, the warranty of peaceful possession protects the lessee from certain kinds of interferences with his use and enjoyment of the thing leased. Those interferences are described by a single term of art: **disturbances.** Such disturbances by the terms of Civil Code article 2700 may be of three kinds. One such disturbance may result from third persons claiming ownership of the thing. Thus, in the hypothetical above we have the owner *A*, then *B* who claims ownership against *A*, and *X* who is the person from whom *B* derives his claim of ownership against *A*. Assume that *A* has leased the immovable to *T* and that *B* is attempting to oust *T* by suing him for trespass. Note that this disturbance by *B* may be a disturbance in fact, if *B* is taking steps that physically interfere with *T* whose acts of precarious possession are being frustrated. But strictly speaking it is not *T*'s *possession* that is being disturbed, it is *T*'s use and enjoyment of the thing; it is *A*'s possession that is being disturbed. That possession is being disturbed both in fact and in law. While the former is an annoyance, the latter undermines *A*'s rights to the thing more fundamentally.

It is important to recall the way that warranty against eviction works in sale. Third parties who behave as *X* has in this hypothetical will disturb a buyer both in fact and in law. But a buyer may also be disturbed in law **without** being disturbed in fact. That is, the existence of a bona fide third-party claim of ownership of the thing that the buyer has bought prima facie evicts the buyer. Such is not the case with respect to the lessee. If a third party lays legal claim to the immovable the lessee has rented, but where that third party takes no steps to challenge the lessee, arguably the lessee is not disturbed.

§ 3.2.5. THE CALL IN WARRANTY.

If a third party claimant interferes with the lessee's use and enjoyment of the thing, the lessee's natural course is to notify the lessor of the problem and call upon him to dispose of it. **Article 2701** of the Revision states:

"The lessor is bound to take all steps necessary to protect the lessee's possession against any disturbance covered by the preceding Article, as soon as the lessor is informed of such a disturbance. If the lessor fails to do so, the lessee may, without prejudice to his rights against the lessor, file any appropriate action against the person who caused the disturbance.

"If a third party brings against the lessee an action asserting a right in the thing or contesting the lessee's right to possess it, the lessee may join the lessor as a party to the action and shall be dismissed from the action, if the lessee so demands."

This article must be read in conjunction with article 2688 which states that the lessee **is bound to notify the lessor without delay when his possession has been disturbed by a third person**. Article 2688 also provides the effect of a failure to notify the lessor of the disturbance. A failure to notify entitles the lessor to **damages sustained as a result of the lessee's failure to perform this obligation.**

Revised **article 2701** does not state the effect of the lessee's failure to notify on the *lessee's* claim against the lessor. In the law of sale, **a buyer who fails to give such notice, or who fails to give it in time for the seller to defend himself, forfeits the warranty against eviction if the seller can show that, had he been notified in time, he would have been able to prove that the third person who**

sued the buyer had no right. (La. C.C. art. 2517, ¶ 3.)[230] The law of lease should obtain a similar result. The lessee who fails to notify the lessor should not be able to recover under the warranty of peaceful possession if the lessor can show that with notice he could have protected the lessee's rights under the lease.

If the call in warranty is properly made and the lessor fails to defend against the third person's claim, the law is clear that the lessee **may, without prejudice to his rights against the lessor, file any appropriate action against the person who caused the disturbance. (La. C.C. art. 2701.)** The sense of the article is that the lessee may recover against the lessor for the costs of litigation with the third party. This result was explicit in the prior law of lease.[231] Eliminating that text should not change the rule, as the result is both obvious and necessary under the general principles stated in Titles III and IV of Book III of the Civil Code.

A potential basis of litigation with the third party could be a possessory action. If the lessor knows of the disturbance and **is informed** according to **article 2701**, it should not be necessary for the lessee to take the unnecessary step of delivering a formal notification of the problem in order to protect his rights.

This way of handling the lessee's call in warranty in the Revision is somewhat curious. The lessee's obligation to notify the lessor of a disturbance by a third person is conceptually distinct from the obligation to notify him of a needed repair and should be included together with the other rules pertaining to the warranty of peaceful possession.

§ 3.2.6. DEGREE OF DISTURBANCE.

The *degree of disturbance* needed to trigger the lessor's warranty is sometimes clear. Thus, where the action of the third party is sufficient to evict the lessee from the thing leased, this is doubtless sufficient to engage the lessor's responsibility. On the other hand, the lessee may be disturbed by third party actions that are not so severe, raising the question whether the lessee may proceed against the lessor.

For example, the jurisprudence has found that hunters going on a tract of land, an immovable under an oral hunting lease with the owner, do not disturb the possession granted by the same owner to one *possessing* the land for purposes of the latter's accrual of acquisitive prescription. On the other hand, if the possessor were instead a *lessee* of the land, the actions of the hunters should be sufficient to trigger the lessor's responsibility under the warranty of peaceful possession, if the hunters claimed the right to go on the land from one claiming in turn a real right in the land.[232]

It is useful to compare the protection of the lessee under the warranty of peaceful possession with the protection of the buyer under the warranty against eviction. One example has already been given, that of failure to give notice under the call in

---

230 *See* Sale *supra*.

231 La. C.C. art. 2696 (1870).

232 A traditional view is that the owner's exercise of his right to hunt on property leased to a farmer does not disturb the lessee, provided no crops are damaged. *Pothier, Traité du Contrat de Louage et Traité des Cheptels* § 75 (Hutteau, ed. 1806).

warranty. Another example is the difference between the seller's liability for his own act that evicts the buyer and the lessor's disturbance of his lessee's possession. Generally, after selling the thing, the seller has no further right to avail himself of the thing sold.[233] Under the law of lease, however, the lessor does have that right. Indeed, as the provisions on repair show, sometimes the lessor has an obligation to take actions that one might argue interfere with the lessee's use and enjoyment of the thing. But from another point of view, the repairs that the lessor makes may aid the lessee's use and enjoyment. Whether they aid the lessee's use or hinder it is a question of fact.

---

233 Exceptionally, the seller may exercise control over the thing sold under article 2487. *See* Précis on Sale *supra*.

Chapter 4

THE LESSOR'S RIGHTS: RENT AND SECURITIES

ARTICLE 1
THE LESSEE'S OBLIGATION TO PAY RENT

The Code requires the lessee to perform his obligation to pay rent at a certain time and in a certain place. The lease sets the amount of the rent the lessee is obligated to pay. As regards the moment of payment of the rent, it is generally to be paid **at the beginning of the term.** If the rent is **payable by intervals shorter than the term, the rent is due at the beginning of each interval. (La. C.C. art. 2703(1).)** As to the place of payment, the rent is generally **payable at the address provided by the lessor**. If the lessor does not give an address or has none, then the rent is payable **at the address of the lessee. (La. C.C. art. 2703(2).)**

The parties, of course, are free to agree otherwise, and often agree that the rent will be payable to a mandatary or employee of the lessor, or under the form of payment authorized by the lessee from his bank account to the lessor's bank account.

The Revision also suggests that either **usage** or **custom** may direct where and when the rent is to be paid. The word choice of "usage" in this context makes good sense, as questions of where and when rent is due may vary by locality, for rural versus urban areas, and so on. It seems unlikely, however, that any **custom** in the sense of **article 2** could develop on these matters.

The following is a frequently disputed issue. Assume a written lease decrees that the rent must be paid by a date certain, such as the first of the month. Assume also that the lease states clearly any amendment to the lease shall be in writing. For many months, the lessor accepts payments on the tenth of the month without any protest. Then the lessor refuses the next payment on the tenth and sues to dissolve the lease for breach. The lessee argues that the parties by their actions have tacitly amended the provisions of the written lease, moving the date of payment of the rent from the first to the tenth. The lessee's position is that because a lease, even of an immovable, may be oral, the revision of a written lease may likewise be oral. The lessor's position on the contrary is that the parties agreed to restrict their freedom to amend this particular lease and to do so only in writing. Without attempting a full survey of the jurisprudence, the lessee's argument seems more successful since it could be said that the lessor, as obligee/creditor of the lessee's obligation to pay the rent, has "waived" his right to a benefit he had attempted to secure for himself in the written contract.

The failure of the lessee to pay the rent, obviously, entitles the lessor to a remedy.

If the lessee fails to pay the rent when due, the lessor may, in accordance with the provisions of the Title "Conventional Obligations or Contracts," dissolve the lease and may regain possession in the manner provided by law. (La. C.C. art. 2704.) Again, the Title on Lease relies upon the general rules governing breach of contracts to address the situation.

A special problem occurs with agricultural leases. If the crop fails, it usually means that the lessee will be unable to pay the rent. And where the rent is in the form of crops, the loss of the crop means a loss of the rent itself. Here, the law of lease is an example of the defense of impossibility, set out in **articles 1873 through 1877** of the Civil Code. The general rule governing this defense is that **an obligor is not liable for his failure to perform when it is caused by a fortuitous event that makes performance impossible.**[234] The major exception to this rule is the obligor's assumption of the risk of the fortuitous event.

In agricultural leases, if **an unforeseeable and extraordinary event** destroys **at least one-half of the value of the crops,** then the lessee may claim an **abatement** or reduction of the rent.[235] **(La. C.C. art. 2705.)** Limiting the lessee's right to claim an abatement to such a large loss in value might be criticized as unfair. Perhaps the Revision assumed that any loss up to fifty per cent is foreseeable, but the assumption is open to question. Only **unharvested crops** qualify. Compensation from other sources for the loss, which the lessee **has received or may receive, such as insurance proceeds or government subsidies, shall be taken into account in determining the amount of abatement.**[236] If lessor and lessee have made **a contrary agreement** — for example, that the lessee will take the risks of such events, then the lessee of course cannot obtain an abatement of the rent.

If the lessee and the lessor have agreed that the rent will consist of a portion of the crops, the rule differs. In this case, *any* loss of the crops shall be borne by both parties in accordance with their respective shares. (La. C.C. art. 2706.) Naturally, if the fault of the lessor or the lessee is the cause of the loss, the rule does not apply. Indeed, in that case, the loss is not due to a fortuitous event at all.

Article 2
The Lessor's Security Rights

The law of lease provides several protections for the lessor as creditor of the lessee's obligation to pay rent and the lessee's other obligations under the lease. First, for the lease of an immovable, the **lessor has a privilege on the lessee's movables that are found in or upon the leased property. (La. C.C. art. 2707.)** In addition, **in an agricultural lease, the lessor's privilege also encompasses the fruits produced by the land.**[237] The lessor enjoys here a right to provoke a public sale of the things in which he has a privilege and to be paid from the money that the sale produces. Indeed, any creditor enjoys this right, but a privileged creditor is **preferred** to other creditors in the sense that he is paid first. If his claim exhausts

---

[234] La. C.C. art. 1873.

[235] La. C.C. art. 2705.

[236] *Id.*

[237] *Id.*

the money generated by the sale, then the other creditors take nothing. **(La. C.C. art. 3182 and 3186.)** The several varieties of privileged creditors are themselves ranked and rules governing the place of the lessor are stated by the Code.[238] A privilege may cover all the property of a debtor, in which case it is general as to the debtor's movables and immovables.[239] The lessor's privilege is one that affects only particular movables, those on the leased premises, and is known as a special privilege.[240]

Not only does the lessor enjoy a privilege over the lessee's movables, he may also have a privilege over movables of a sublessee. This aspect of the privilege is limited and is only effective **to the extent that the sublessee is indebted to his sublessor at the time the lessor exercises his right. (La. C.C. art. 2708.)**

The lessor exercising rights under his privilege may be most concerned about seizing movables that belong to a third party. Here the law offers some comfort, as the **lessor may lawfully seize a movable that belongs to a third person if it is located in or upon the leased property, unless the lessor knows that the movable is not the property of the lessee. (La. C.C. art. 2709.)** Note that the standard is not whether the lessor *ought* to know but whether he, in fact, knows that the movable does not belong to the lessee. The third person does not automatically lose rights in his property, of course. He **may recover the movable by establishing his ownership prior to the judicial sale.**[241] But if does not do so, the judicial sale will divest him of ownership, as **the movable may be sold as though it belonged to the lessee.**[242]

To enforce the privilege, the lessor may assert the privilege against the movables **while they are in or upon the leased property.** In addition, he may also have them seized **for fifteen days after they have been removed,** provided the lessee still owns them and they **can be identified.**[243] Under the Civil Code of 1870, the lessor lost his privilege if he agreed to permit the lessee to remove the movables from the leased premises.[244] Thus, Title IX as revised might be read to permit the lessor to seize them after their removal notwithstanding his consent, but the Revision in fact has created a gap by removing the lessor's consent from the text of the Code.

If the movables have already been seized by the sheriff for some other reason (such as where they have been seized by another creditor), the lessor may exercise his privilege against them **without the necessity of a further seizure thereof, as long as the movables or the proceeds therefrom remain in the custody of the officer. (La. C.C. art. 2710, ¶ 2.)**

It is important to recall that Chapter 9 of Title 10 of the Louisiana Revised Statutes governs the use of movables as real security. As a general rule, to obtain

---

238 La. C.C. arts. 3256–3260.

239 La. C.C. arts. 3189 and 3252.

240 La. C.C. art. 3219.

241 *Id.*

242 *Id.*

243 La. C.C. art. 2710-1.

244 La. C.C. art. 2709 (1870).

real security in a movable the creditor must either have possession of the movable or must see to the creation and perfection of a security interest in the movable. "Creation" and "perfection" are terms of art used in Chapter 9 of Title 10 which enacts the corresponding title of the Uniform Commercial Code. What this means for the lessor's privilege is not that the lessor's privilege is invalid, but that another creditor of the lessee who has a perfected security interest in a movable on the leased premises will be paid from the proceeds of the sale of the movable before the lessor is paid. It is possible for a lessor himself to take advantage of the provisions of Chapter 9 and to perfect his lessor's privilege. The limitations on doing so appear to be only practical.

Under the prior law, the jurisprudence was clear that the lessor could not enforce the privilege through self-help, that is, by taking possession of the lessee's movables or changing the locks on the leased premises. However, if the lessee abandons the premises, the lessor may take possession of the lessee's property, if only to move it off the premises. There is no reason to interpret the Revision of the law of Lease as having changed that rule.

Chapter 5

TERMINATION AND DISSOLUTION

Article 1
Transfer of Interest by Lessor or Lessee

If the lessor sells the thing he has leased, in general the lease does not end unless lessor and lessee agreed otherwise.[245] In fact, the rule is somewhat broader. It applies not only to sales, and not only to sales by the lessor, since the Revision refers to a **transfer of the leased thing.** Thus, where the lessor is not the owner, and where the owner transfers the lease, the general rule is that this transfer **does not terminate the lease.**

Where immovables are concerned, the rules of recordation govern. Although lease is still understood not to create a real right, a lease may be recorded as if it did. Indeed, it is possible and often desirable merely to record an extract of the lease. Thus, a lessee may assert and record in the public records the fact that he has rented an immovable and his rights under the lease will be protected against the subsequent interests of third parties in the immovable. On the other hand, **a third person who acquires an immovable that is subject to an unrecorded lease is not bound by the lease.** (La. C.C. art. 2712.) Even if the lease is unrecorded, the lessor may not interfere with the lessee's use and enjoyment of the immovable by transferring it to a third person. This is a feature of the warranty of peaceful possession as discussed above.[246] In addition, the rule is emphasized in Section 8 of Title IX dealing with "Transfer of interest bye the lessor or the lessee": **In the absence of a contrary provision in the lease contract, the lessee has an action against the lessor for any loss the lessee sustained as a result of the transfer. (La. C.C. art. 2712, ¶ 2.)**

Finally, after having dealt with the rights of the lessor to transfer, the Code addresses the rights of the lessee to handle his own interest in the lease. Generally, **the lessee has the right to sublease the leased thing or to assign or encumber his rights in the lease. (La. C.C. art. 2713.)** It is often the case, however, that the lease will prohibit the lessee from capitalizing on his interest in the lease. The lessee's exploitation of his interest, however, must be **expressly prohibited by the contract of lease.**[247] Still, if the lease expressly **prohibits one of these rights**, it is **deemed to prohibit the others.**[248] The lease, of course, may state expressly that only one or only two of the transactions is prohibited. With that exception,

---

[245] La. C.C. art. 2711.

[246] *See supra* p. 148.

[247] *Id.*

[248] *Id.*

prohibitions in the lease of **subleasing, assigning, or encumbering** must be **strictly construed against the lessor.**[249]

Article 2
Total Loss of the Thing

It is a basic principle of the law of obligations that an obligor is not liable for his failure to perform when it is caused by a fortuitous event that makes performance impossible. (La. C.C. art 1873.) That rule does not apply when the obligor has assumed the risk of such a fortuitous event, or when such an event occurs after he has been put in default.[250] Besides, the obligor is liable when the fortuitous event that caused his failure to perform has been preceded by his fault, without which the failure would not have occurred.[251] Here, the fortuitous event and the fault of the obligor are linked, so that the failure to perform can be attributed to the obligor.

These basic rules and the exceptions are carried over to lease. If the thing leased is **totally destroyed without the fault of either party,** the lease **terminates.** And the Code makes clear that in this case **neither party owes damages to the other. (La. C.C. art. 2714.)** Here, the principle of article 1873 applies both to the lessor, who bears the obligations of delivery and warranty, and to the lessee, who is obligated to pay rent and use the thing prudently. Article 2714 makes clear that total destruction of the thing leased absolves lessor and lessee of their respective obligations under the lease.

Article 2714 has the same effect if the thing is **lost**, which is a term that hails from the 1870 Code. The term "lost" may have been used because, in the early days, the dominant form of destruction for the typical objects of a lease would have entailed a complete loss. At the time, firefighting was largely ineffective, and the wooden buildings of Louisiana towns and cities were famously vulnerable to fire that often caused a complete loss. Barring collusion or arson, such losses would be without the fault of either lessor or lessee.

Another way in which the thing leased may become unavailable for the lease is by expropriation, when the state or a political subdivision forces a sale of the thing from the owner, even against his will. When the state or a political subdivision becomes owner, the lessee in most cases will no longer be able to use or enjoy it. The result is that the lease terminates in the same way it would if the thing leased had been lost or destroyed. One difference is that in some cases it should be possible for the lessee to recover for the expropriation of his interest in the lease. An exception to the principle that the lessee's right under the lease is merely personal and exists solely against the lessor would be justified here. The right to compensation ordinarily belongs to the owner alone, when the "capital", the "asset" itself is destroyed. In the case of an expropriation, the "capital, asset" remains in existence in the hands of somebody else. Thus the former owner should receive some compensation for having been deprived of his ownership of the "capital, asset" but the lessee should also receive some compensation for having been deprived of the

---

249 *Id.*

250 *Id.*

251 *Id.*

use and enjoyment of that "capital, asset."

Article 3
Partial Loss of the Thing

When the loss, destruction, or expropriation is not complete, the lessee may **obtain a diminution of the rent or dissolution of the lease. (La. C.C. art. 2715.)** Whether the lessee may succeed here depends on **the circumstances of both parties** and on which remedy — reducing the rent or dissolving the lease — is **more appropriate under the circumstances.**[252] This quite clearly invites the judgment of the court and fact finder.

An additional complication is that another factor may influence the decision, namely whether the thing's **use is otherwise substantially impaired.** Indeed, this factor of substantial impairment of use potentially authorizes adjustment of the terms of the lease even when the impairment of the use by the lessee is much less in degree than the impairment of the use that would result from partial loss, destruction, or expropriation. The inconvenience to the business of the lessee, for example, of government works on roads or similar infrastructure near the premises leased ordinarily would not amount to even a partial taking. Likewise, without a contractual shifting of the risk that such works will affect the lessee's business, the lessee should not be able to recover from the lessor through a diminution of rent. This would not accord with the stability of contractual arrangements that the parties have made.

Finally, the fault of the lessee or the lessor should be considered. If the lessee bears some fault for the partial loss or substantial impairment of the use, he may not obtain some remedy from the lessor on that account. If the lessor is at fault, however, not only may the lessee obtain the relief that article 2715 describes, but the lessee should also obtain damages.

Article 2715 concludes by considering the effect of another sort of cause for substantial impairment of the use of the thing to the lessee. If such impairment occurs because of **circumstances external to the leased thing**, the lessee may obtain **a dissolution of the lease**, but he may **not** obtain a **diminution of the rent**. A comment to the article gives two examples of such circumstances.[253] In the first, a neighbor raises his walls and "intercepts the light" coming to the "house" that the lessee rented. In the second, a zoning rule or "other governmental restriction imposes substantial restrictions on the use of the leased thing." While neither the text of the article nor the comment is explicit on the point, it seems that the article only contemplates restrictions that occur after the lease is in effect, not restrictions that affect the thing at the time the lease goes into effect.

The reason for granting the lessee only the remedy of dissolution in this case may simply be a continuation, in part, of a distinction that existed in the 1870 Code. Article 2697 of that Code gave the remedies of diminution of rent or dissolution of the lease in case of partial destruction. Article 2699 dealt with the equivalent of

---

[252] *Id.*

[253] La. C.C. art. 2715, comment c.

substantial impairment of the use and only granted dissolution. The jurisprudence nevertheless granted a reduction in rent under article 2699, reasoning that the stronger remedy of dissolution included the remedy of diminution of the rent.[254]

Clearly, under the Revision, diminution of rent is not available in certain cases — cases in which the reasons for the impairment of the use are **external** to the thing leased itself. Generalizing from the examples given above, an external cause is something a third party does that diminishes the utility of the thing leased without harming the thing itself. Harms to the thing itself would include those that occur because of some defect in it, for which the lessor presumably would also be responsible in warranty. The causes for such harm, and thus the resulting impairment in utility, could be described as internal, not external. Such internal harms to the thing itself are addressed in the first paragraph of article 2715, and for them diminution in rent is clearly available. If a flood destroys one of two roads to the leased premises and substantially impairs their use, presumably the cause for the impairment is external and the lessee has only dissolution as a possible remedy. If the flood partially destroys the leased premises, the lessee will have the choice to seek diminution in rent or dissolution of the lease.

Article 4
Other Instances of Termination

§ 5.4.1. USUFRUCT.

The Code provides other instances of termination of a lease that are less problematic. For example, a usufructuary may grant a lease, which presents a situation in which a non-owner may properly grant a lease.[255] In that case, such a lease **terminates upon the termination of the usufruct. (La. C.C. art. 2716.)** If the lessor did not inform the lessee of the truth and **failed to disclose his status as a usufructuary,** the lessor will be **liable to the lessee for any loss caused by such termination.**[256] If the lessor discloses his usufruct of the thing that the lessee rents from him, the lessee then will have no remedy. If the lessee accepts a lease whose term is beyond the time of the death of his lessor (which ends the usufruct and therefore terminates the lease under article 2716), there will be no remedy against the lessor or his succession on that account. An attempt by the usufructuary to create a lease that will continue after the usufruct ends will fail because a lease granted by a usufructuary automatically terminates when the usufruct ends. If, however, the naked owners were to intervene in such a lease, the lease should be valid and continue after the usufruct ceases.

---

[254] La. C.C. art. 2715, comment a.

[255] On usufruct see Louisiana Civil Code articles 535 *et seq.*

[256] *Id.*

§ 5.4.2. DEATH.

In case of the death of either party to the lease, the lease's validity and continuation are not affected. In the event of the lessor's death or the lessee's death, the **lease does not terminate. (La. C.C. art. 2717.)** Moreover, if either party to the lease is a juridical person, such as a corporation or a partnership, the **cessation** of their **existence** likewise does not terminate the lease. Naturally, the parties may alter this rule.

§ 5.4.3. RIGHT TO TERMINATE.

If the lease has a fixed term, but the parties **have reserved the right to terminate the lease before the end of the term,**[257] then in order to terminate the lease pursuant to that right, a party must give notice to the other. If the mechanism for the notice of termination was agreed upon in the lease, that mechanism must be used. If the lease is silent as to how notice is to be given, then the parties must use the mechanism provided for termination of leases with indeterminate terms.[258] In addition, the lease may provide for timing for notice that is longer than that provided in the Code, but it cannot be shorter. The party who is to be notified of termination benefits from the longer period. Moreover, the right to receive notice is an imperative rule; it **may not be renounced in advance.**[259]

§ 5.4.4. OTHER CAUSES OF DISSOLUTION OF LEASES.

Article 2719 contains a simple reminder that leases may be dissolved, like all contracts, when a party to the lease is in breach. When a party to the lease fails to perform his obligations under the lease or under this Title, the other party may obtain dissolution of the lease pursuant to the provisions of the Title of "Conventional Obligations or Contracts".

Article 5
Leases With A Fixed Term

§ 5.5.1. IN GENERAL.

As one would expect, when the parties have entered a **lease with a fixed term,** the lease **terminates upon the expiration of that term, without need of notice, . . . (La. C.C. art. 2720).** The parties must take some action in order for the lease to continue beyond the point of expiration, and the Code provides explicitly for how this may occur.

Prolonging a lease can happen in two ways. First, the Code provides for the tacit reconduction of the lease. For a reconduction of the lease to occur, the parties need simply continue as before, with the lessee using and enjoying the thing, and the

---

[257] La. C.C. art. 2718.

[258] *See infra,* Louisiana Civil Code articles 2727 to 2729 p. 176–77.

[259] La. C.C. art. 2718.

lessor receiving the rent as the lessee pays it. The Code expresses this simple idea a bit more formally. Such a lease is **reconducted if, after the expiration of the term, and without notice to vacate or terminate or other opposition by the lessor or the lessee, the lessee remains in possession. (La. C.C. art. 2721.)** Moreover, the lessee's continued possession must go on for a certain length of time, depending on the original term and type of lease: **(1) For thirty days in the case of an agricultural lease; (2) For one week in the case of other leases with a fixed term that is longer than a week; or (3) For one day in the case of a lease with a fixed term that is equal to or shorter than a week. (La. C.C. art. 2721.)**

The Code of 1870 and the supporting jurisprudence endorsed the idea that reconduction could occur almost against the will of the lessee or even both parties. The Revision clarifies this matter and states that this is no longer the case. Thus, if either the lessor or the lessee makes clear his intention not to continue the lease, reconduction will not occur. This makes sense, because the basis of tacit reconduction is the inference of intent on the part of the lessor and the lessee to continue the lease — intent of the lessee evidenced by his maintaining possession and that of the lessor by continuing to permit the lessee to maintain possession. If one or both of the parties make clear that this is not the meaning that may be attached to their situation, then the contract of lease must terminate. This is the reason for the phrase **"without notice to vacate or terminate or other opposition by the lessor or the lessee."**[260] If the lessor has given the lessee notice to vacate, there can exist no doubt as to the intention of the lessor. The same is true if the lessee or the lessor makes clear that he opposes a continuation of the lease.

This leaves the problem of characterizing the nature of the relationship between a former lessor and lessee when the latter maintains possession of the leased thing. Likewise, it is necessary to characterize the nature of the lessee's possession when it continues past the expiration of the lease but not long enough for tacit reconduction to occur. For example, before the expiration of the lease, the lessee possessed the thing precariously for the lessor. Does his precarious possession continue after the lease expires? For our purposes, it is clear that the relationship between the lessor and the lessee is a "former relationship" and is no longer governed by the law of lease.

Another point should be mentioned. Under the Revision, it is now clear that the lease of a movable can be reconducted. This is a change from a prior rule to the contrary, which had been set by judicial decision.

§ 5.5.2. AGRICULTURAL AND NONAGRICULTURAL LEASES.

When an agricultural lease is reconducted, the new term is **from year to year.** The Code allows the parties a limited choice here. The new term will be from year to year, **"unless the parties intended a different term which, according to local custom or usage, is observed in leases of the same type." (La. C.C. art 2722.)**

[260] La. C.C. art. 2721.

The intent of the Revision seems to have been to permit reconduction of an agricultural lease based either on the duration of the initial term or — maybe more likely — on the length of time it takes a farmer to "harvest" a "yearly" crop. Revised article 2722 allows for the possibility that the term of the reconducted lease may be something other than from year to year, if it is shown that **"the parties intended a different term which, according to local custom or usage, is observed in leases of the same type."** This provision may prove useful when the initial term was shorter than a year — such as "one farming season" — but also when it was longer than a year.[261]

Thus, the word "intention" seems to have been understood with reference to the parties' intention about the term when they concluded the initial lease. Article 2722 can be interpreted to mean that the parties may state their intention at the time reconduction can occur. The parties might have intended a lease term of three years at the outset, but intend a lease term of two years for the reconduction. Nevertheless, custom or usage may serve as a check on their intentions, whether manifested at the outset of the initial lease or at the time of reconduction. If the term they intend is not recognized either by custom or usage, then the new term will be from year to year, despite their contrary intention. Furthermore, their own pattern of practice over time is not enough to assure a term for the reconducted lease that they want but that may be inconsistent with custom or usage.

And yet custom is a source of law. (La. C.C. arts. 1, 3.) Usages are not law; they only serve to aid the court when legislation and custom provide **"no rule for a particular situation."** (La. C.C. art. 4.) Usages provide this assistance when, in default of legislation and custom, the court must proceed according to equity. A decision according to equity requires the examination of **"justice, reason, and prevailing usages."** (La. C.C. art. 4.)

Thus if custom decrees a certain term, the parties are deemed to follow it, unless they clearly intend to depart from it.

Tacit reconduction ought to be seen as merely a presumption that the parties intend to continue a lease with all provisions unchanged other than the expired term. Since the law of tacit reconduction presumes that they adopt a certain new term as specified in the Code, the parties ought to be able to adopt whatever term they choose. Such a lease with a "new term" adopted by agreement between the parties could possibly be treated as a reconducted lease with all the other provisions of the lease remaining the same. However, the fact that the parties have adopted a new term may justify considering the lease as a new lease and not a reconducted lease. In that case, the lessor should be concerned about the survival of his security rights he had acquired under the prior lease.

As regards nonagricultural leases and their reconduction, Louisiana Civil Code article 2723 provides that "[t]he term of a reconducted nonagricultural lease is:

(1) From month to month in the case of a lease whose term is a month or longer;

(2) From day to day in the case of a lease whose term is at least a day but shorter than a month; and

---

[261] La. C.C. art. 2722, comment (c).

(3) For periods equal to the expired term in the case of a lease whose term is less than a day."

The prior law provided only for the reconduction of the lease of a "house or room."[262] Evidently, the Revision has expanded the rule substantially.

§ 5.5.3. RECONDUCTION-CONTINUITY

The most important legal feature of reconduction is the following: a reconducted lease is *not* a new lease but a *continuation of the old one*. The language of the Code does not say this in these precise words. It does say that reconduction means **all provisions of the lease continue for the term provided in article 2722 or 2723. (La. C.C. art. 2724.)** This idea of the lease being "continued" must be justified, since not all provisions of the lease "continue" in effect; the term has changed. The term of the initial lease was fixed or determinate; the term of the reconducted lease is "indeterminate." Accordingly, **a reconducted lease is terminated by giving the notice directed in articles 2727 through 2729,** which lay down the rules that apply to leases with indeterminate terms. **(La. C.C. art. 2724, ¶ 2.)**

The idea that the reconducted lease is not a new one is firmly anchored. It follows that a lessor's privilege under the initial lease should continue without break under the reconducted lease. To hold that the reconducted lease is a new lease could trigger inconvenient results, such as the lessee's obligation to remove improvements at the end of the lease. Still, the institution of reconduction of the lease is a bit awkward.

§ 5.5.4. EXTENSION.

Reconduction of a lease is distinguished by the Code from an extension of a lease. Here, the parties plan ahead and provide in their initial lease that one of them, usually the lessee, will have **an option to extend the term.** If, later, the **option is exercised, the lease continues for the term** that the parties set in the option.[263] Here again, just as with reconduction, the lease as extended by the new term is treated as one with the original lease. With extensions, however, all other provisions of the lease do not necessarily remain the same, except for the term. The Code provides that the lease continues **under the other provisions stipulated in the option. (La. C.C. art. 2725.)** When an option to extend is agreed to during the negotiation of the initial lease, much care is devoted to such an "other provision," probably more than is devoted to the duration of the extended term. Chiefly, both lessor and lessee will carefully weigh how the rent is to be set upon exercise of the option to extend the lease. Rent is certainly not a minor provision of a lease, and as the parties see it, ideas that the parties may have on the amount of the rent and how it will be paid will almost certainly differ. Other changes might also be included among the stipulated provisions, albeit within certain limits. For example, if the lessee were given an option to renew the lease but on a different parcel of property,

262 La. C.C. art. 2689 (1870).

263 La. C.C. art. 2725.

this should not be acceptable as an extension of the original lease but should be considered to be a new lease.

The Code has adopted the concept of "extension" as its term of art for this situation. It did so deliberately in order to emphasize that an "extended lease" is a "continuation of the old lease," not a new one. In practice, however, what the Code calls an extension is usually labeled a "renewal," a word that the drafters of the Revision feared might create the misimpression that a new lease would be created in this situation.[264]

§ 5.5.5. AMENDMENT.

The Revision deals finally with the concept of an amendment of a lease. In this instance, the Code states that an amendment to a provision of the lease contract that is made without the intent of effecting a novation does not create a new lease. (La. C.C. art. 2726).

One cannot discuss the concepts of reconduction and extension of leases without also discussing the concept of novation.[265] The Code states that one form of novation occurs **when, by agreement of the parties, a new performance is substituted for that previously owed, or a new cause is substituted for that of the original obligation. If any substantial part of the original performance is still owed, there is no novation. (La. C.C. art. 1881 ¶ 1.)** Read literally, one might conclude that any change to the provisions of a contract would cause a novation; however the Code states that this is not so. The same Code article further states that a **mere modification of an obligation, made without intention to extinguish it, does not effect a novation. (La. C.C. art. 1881 ¶ 3.)** Furthermore, the parties must manifest an **intention to extinguish the original obligation** for novation to occur, and this intention **must be clear and unequivocal**. Accordingly, **novation may not be presumed. (La. C.C. art. 1880.)**

The Revision in article 2726 is therefore applying the basic principles of novation to the amendment of a lease. While article 2726 is new, it is applying a traditional civil-law concept, and therefore it does not make new law. One cannot state abstractly the extent to which parties must amend a lease before the intent to novate it is undeniable. Surely, they can go too far. The point of article 2726 is that minor changes will not accomplish this result when novation is not desired.

Article 6
Leases With an Indeterminate Term

When the term of a lease is indeterminate, either party to the lease may end the lease through a simple process of notification. Such a lease, the Code states, **terminates by notice** of that fact **given to the other party. (La. C.C. art. 2727.)** This rule applies not only to leases with explicitly indeterminate terms but also to leases that have been reconducted. It also governs a lease whose term is supplied by the law. This occurs when the parties do not agree to the duration of the term.

---

[264] La. C.C. art. 2725, comment a.

[265] On Novation, see Louisiana Law of Obligations in General: A Précis, p. 142 *et seq.*

Such a legal term depends on the kind of lease involved. Thus, agricultural leases are year to year, leases of other immovables and movables used as residences, are month to month, and leases of other movables are generally day to day.[266] Because article 2680 categorizes the potential terms of leases where the parties are silent, the possibilities for notice are much simpler than they might be otherwise.

The timing of the notification sufficient to terminate a lease depends on the length of the period the parties use to measure the lease term. The Code here is using the fact that the parties will typically measure the lease term for their own purposes. That is, they will specify when the lessee is to pay rent: daily, weekly, monthly, or yearly. If the lease term thus is **measured by a period longer than a month**, notice must be given **at or before thirty calendar days before the end of that period.** If the lease term is month-to-month, notice must be given **at or before ten calendar days before the end of that month**. If the term **is** measured by a period equal to or longer than a week but shorter than a month, then notice must be given at or before five calendar days before the end of that period. Finally, if the term is measured by a period shorter than a week, notice must be given at any time prior to the expiration of that period. (La. C.C. art. 2728).

There is an alternate way to look at the phrase **"at or before the time specified"** in article 2728. First, this phrase does not work for leases whose term is shorter than a week. A formulation that would be clearer could be as follows: "in a year-to-year lease, the notice must be given **at least** thirty days before the end of the year."[267] For a month-to-month lease, "**at least** ten days before the end of the month." To terminate a week-to-week lease a notice of termination must occur "**at least** five days before the end of the week." "No later than" also captures the idea. The rule may be stated the other way around, namely, a notice of termination may be given up to thirty days before the end of the year, and so on.

If notice is properly given and timed, then it **terminates the lease at the end of the period specified in the notice**. If the notice does not specify a date when the lease terminates following the notice, then it ends **at the end of the first period for which the notice is timely.**[268] Thus, assume a month-to-month lease of an apartment, with possession and rent due on the first of the month. On March 27, the lessor gives the lessee notice of termination. The notice is too late to be effective to compel the lessee's departure at the end of March, but it will be timely for a departure at the end of April.

Formality for the notice is minimal. For **an immovable** and for **a movable used as a residence,** notice must be in writing. Outside of these two situations, notice **may be oral.**[269] Finally, for all types of things leased, **surrender of possession to the lessor** is equivalent to notice of termination.[270] Thus, it is not necessary for the lessee to give the lessor written notice of termination of the lease with an indeterminate term, so long as the lessee surrenders possession timely, that is,

---

[266] La. C.C. art. 2680.

[267] La. C.C. art. 2728 comment (b).

[268] La. C.C. art. 2728.

[269] La. C.C. art. 2729.

[270] *Id.*

within the time limits stated in article 2728. This does not seem to work for the lessor. If the lessor timely but orally advises the lessee that a month-to-month lease will terminate at the end of the month, an agreement by the lessee that he will quit the premises immediately does not seem sufficient by itself to constitute notice by surrender of possession. Unless the lessee can in fact remove himself, and his movables, from the premises very quickly, it seems he cannot surrender possession of the premises to the lessor in a timely fashion. The lessor, therefore, ought always to take advantage of the protection of written notice.

APPENDIX I

LOUISIANA CIVIL CODE 2015

Art. 2668. Contract of Lease Defined

Lease is a synallagmatic contract by which one party, the lessor, binds himself to give to the other party, the lessee, the use and enjoyment of a thing for a term in exchange for a rent that the lessee binds himself to pay.

The consent of the parties as to the thing and the rent is essential but not necessarily sufficient for a contract of lease.

Art. 2669. Relation with Other Titles

In all matters not provided for in this Title, the contract of lease is governed by the rules of the Titles of "Obligations in General" and "Conventional Obligations or Contracts".

Art. 2670. Contract of Lease

A contract to enter into a lease at a future time is enforceable by either party if there was agreement as to the thing to be leased and the rent, unless the parties understood that the contract would not be binding until reduced to writing or until its other terms were agreed upon.

Art. 2671. Types of Leases

Depending on the agreed use of the leased thing, a lease is characterized as: residential, when the thing is to be occupied as a dwelling; agricultural, when the thing is a predial estate that is to be used for agricultural purposes; mineral, when the thing is to be used for the production of minerals; commercial, when the thing is to be used for business or commercial purposes; or consumer, when the thing is a movable intended for the lessee's personal or familial use outside his trade or profession. This enumeration is not exclusive.

When the thing is leased for more than one of the above or for other purposes, the dominant or more substantial purpose determines the type of lease for purposes of regulation.

Art. 2672. Mineral Lease

A mineral lease is governed by the Mineral Code.

Art. 2673. The Thing

All things, corporeal or incorporeal, that are susceptible of ownership may be the object of a lease, except those that cannot be used without being destroyed by that very use, or those the lease of which is prohibited by law.

Art. 2674. Ownership of the Thing

A lease of a thing that does not belong to the lessor may nevertheless be binding on the parties.

Art. 2675. The Rent

The rent may consist of money, commodities, fruits, services, or other performances sufficient to support an onerous contract.

Art. 2676. Agreement as to the Rent

The rent shall be fixed by the parties in a sum either certain or determinable through a method agreed by them. It may also be fixed by a third person designated by them.

If the agreed method proves unworkable or the designated third person is unwilling or unable to fix the rent, then there is no lease.

If the rent has been established and thereafter is subject to redetermination either by a designated third person or through a method agreed to by the parties, but the third person is unwilling or unable to fix the rent or the agreed method proves unworkable, the court may either fix the rent or provide a similar method in accordance with the intent of the parties.

Art. 2677. Crop Rent

When the parties to an agricultural lease agree that the rent will consist of a portion of the crops, that portion is considered at all times the property of the lessor.

Art. 2678. Term

The lease shall be for a term. Its duration may be agreed to by the parties or supplied by law.

The term may be fixed or indeterminate. It is fixed when the parties agree that the lease will terminate at a designated date or upon the occurrence of a designated event.

It is indeterminate in all other cases.

Art. 2679. Limits of Contractual Freedom in Fixing the Term

The duration of a term may not exceed ninety-nine years. If the lease provides for a longer term or contains an option to extend the term to more than ninety-nine years, the term shall be reduced to ninety-nine years.

If the term's duration depends solely on the will of the lessor or the lessee and the parties have not agreed on a maximum duration, the duration is determined in accordance with the following Article.

Art. 2680. Duration Supplied by Law; Legal Term

If the parties have not agreed on the duration of the term, the duration is established in accordance with the following rules:

(1) An agricultural lease shall be from year to year.

(2) Any other lease of an immovable, or a lease of a movable to be used as a residence, shall be from month to month.

(3) A lease of other movables shall be from day to day, unless the rent was fixed by longer or shorter periods, in which case the term shall be one such period, not to exceed one month.

Art. 2681. Form

A lease may be made orally or in writing. A lease of an immovable is not effective against third persons until filed for recordation in the manner prescribed by legislation.

Art. 2682. The Lessor's Principal Obligation

The lessor is bound:

(1) To deliver the thing to the lessee;

(2) To maintain the thing in a condition suitable for the purpose of which it was leased; and

(3) To protect the lessee's peaceful possession for the duration of the lease.

Art. 2683. The Lessee's Principal Obligation

The lessee is bound:

(1) To pay the rent in accordance with the agreed terms;

(2) To use the thing as a prudent administrator and in accordance with the purpose for which it was leased; and

(3) To return the thing at the end of the lease in a condition that is the same as it was when the thing was delivered to him, except for normal wear and tear or as otherwise provided hereafter.

Art. 2684. Obligations to Deliver the Thing at the Agreed Time and in Good Condition

The lessor is bound to deliver the thing at the agreed time and in good condition suitable for the purpose for which it was leased.

Art. 2685. Discrepancy Between Agreed and Delivered Quantity

If the leased thing is an immovable and its extent differs from that which was agreed upon, the rights of the parties with regard to such discrepancy are governed by the provisions of the Title "Sale".

Art. 2686. Misuse of the Thing

If the lessee uses the thing for a purpose other than that for which it was leased or in a manner that may cause damage to the thing, the lessor may obtain injunctive relief, dissolution of the lease, and any damages he may have sustained.

Art. 2687. Damage Caused by Fault

The lessee is liable for damage to the thing caused by his fault or that of a person who, with his consent, is on the premises or uses the thing.

Art. 2688. Obligation to Inform Lessor

The lessee is bound to notify the lessor without delay when the thing has been damaged or requires repair, or when his possession has been disturbed by a third person. The lessor is entitled to damages sustained as a result of the lessee's failure to perform this obligation.

Art. 2689. Payment of Taxes and Other Charges

The lessor is bound to pay all taxes, assessments, and other charges that burden the thing, except those that arise from the use of the thing by the lessee.

Art. 2690. Alterations by the Lessor Prohibited

During the lease, the lessor may not make any alterations in the thing.

Art. 2691. Lessor's Obligation for Repairs

During the lease, the lessor is bound to make all repairs that become necessary to maintain the thing in a condition suitable for the purpose for which it was leased, except those for which the lessee is responsible.

Art. 2692. Lessee's Obligation to Make Repairs

The lessee is bound to repair damage to the thing caused by his fault or that of persons who, with his consent, are on the premises or use the thing, and to repair any deterioration resulting from his or their use to the extent it exceeds the normal or agreed use of the thing.

Art. 2693. Lessor's Right to Make Repairs

If during the lease the thing requires a repair that cannot be postponed until the end of the lease, the lessor has the right to make that repair even if this causes the lessee to suffer inconvenience or loss of use of the thing.

In such a case, the lessee may obtain a reduction or abatement of the rent, or a dissolution of the lease, depending on all of the circumstances, including each party's fault or responsibility for the repair, the length of the repair period, and the extent of the loss of use.

Art. 2694. Lessee's Right to Make Repairs

If the lessor fails to perform his obligation to make necessary repairs within a reasonable time after demand by the lessee, the lessee may cause them to be made. The lessee may demand immediate reimbursement of the amount expended for the repair or apply that amount to the payment of rent, but only to the extent that the repair was necessary and the expended amount was reasonable.

Art. 2695. Attachments, Additions, or Other Improvements to Leased Thing

In the absence of contrary agreement, upon termination of the lease, the rights and obligations of the parties with regard to attachments, additions, or other improvements made to the leased thing by the lessee are as follows:

(1) The lessee may remove all improvements that he made to the leased thing, provided that he restore the thing to its former condition.

(2) If the lessee does not remove the improvements, the lessor may:

(a) Appropriate ownership of the improvements by reimbursing the lessee for their costs or for the enhanced value of the leased thing whichever is less; or

(b) Demand that the lessee remove the improvements within a reasonable time and restore the leased thing to its former condition. If the lessee fails to do so, the lessor may remove the improvements and restore the leased thing to its former condition at the expense of the lessee or appropriate ownership of the improvements without any obligation of reimbursement to the lessee. Appropriation of the improvement by the lessor may only be accomplished by providing additional notice by certified mail to the lessee after expiration of the time given the lessee to remove the improvements.

(c) Until such time as the lessor appropriates the improvement, the improvements shall remain the property of the lessee and the lessee shall be solely responsible for any harm caused by the improvements.

Art. 2696. Warranty Against Vices or Defects

The lessor warrants the lessee that the thing is suitable for the purpose for which it was leased and that it is free of vices or defects that prevent its use for that purpose. This warranty also extends to vices or defects that arise after the delivery of the thing and are not attributable to the fault of the lessee.

Art. 2697. Warranty for Unknown Vices or Defects

The warranty provided in the preceding Article also encompasses vices or defects that are not known to the lessor.

However, if the lessee knows of such vices or defects and fails to notify the lessor, the lessee's recovery for breach of warranty may be reduced accordingly.

Art. 2698. Persons Protected by Warranty

In a residential lease, the warranty provided in the preceding Articles applies to all persons who reside in the premises in accordance with the lease.

Art. 2699. Waiver of Warranty for Vices or Defects

The warranty provided in the preceding Articles may be waived, but only by clear and unambiguous language that is brought to the attention of the lessee.

Nevertheless, a waiver of warranty is ineffective:

(1) To the extent it pertains to vices or defects of which the lessee did not know and the lessor knew or should have known;

(2) To the extent it is contrary to the provisions of Article 2004; or

(3) In a residential or consumer lease, to the extent it purports to waive the warranty for vices or defects that seriously affect health or safety.

Art. 2700. Warranty of Peaceful Possession

The lessor warrants the lessee's peaceful possession of the leased thing against any disturbance caused by a person who asserts ownership, or right to possession of, or any other right in the thing.

In a residential lease, this warranty encompasses a disturbance caused by a person who, with the lessor's consent, has access to the thing or occupies adjacent property belonging to the lessor.

Art. 2701. Call in Warranty

The lessor is bound to take all steps necessary to protect the lessee's possession against any disturbance covered by the preceding Article, as soon as the lessor is informed of such a disturbance. If the lessor fails to do so, the lessee may, without prejudice to his rights against the lessor, file any appropriate action against the person who caused the disturbance.

If a third party brings against the lessee an action asserting a right in the thing or contesting the lessee's right to possess it, the lessee may join the lessor as a party to the action and shall be dismissed from the action, if the lessee so demands.

Art. 2702. Disturbance by Third Persons Without Claim of Right

Except as otherwise provided in Article 2700, the lessor is not bound to protect the lessee's possession against a disturbance caused by a person who does not claim a right in the leased thing. In such a case, the lessee may file any appropriate action against that person.

Art. 2703. When and Where Rent is Due

In the absence of a contrary agreement, usage, or custom:

(1) The rent is due at the beginning of the term. If the rent is payable by intervals shorter than the term, the rent is due at the beginning of each interval.

(2) The rent is payable at the address provided by the lessor and in the absence thereof at the address of the lessee.

Art. 2704. Nonpayment of Rent

If the lessee fails to pay the rent when due, the lessor may, in accordance with the provisions of the Title "Conventional Obligations or Contracts", dissolve the lease and may regain possession in the manner provided by law.

Art. 2705. Abatement of Rent for Unforeseen Loss of Crops

In the absence of a contrary agreement, the agricultural lessee may not claim an abatement of the rent for the loss of his unharvested crops unless the loss was due to an unforeseeable and extraordinary event that destroyed at least one-half of the value of the crops. Any compensation that the lessee has received or may receive in connection with the loss, such as insurance proceeds or government subsidies, shall be taken into account in determining the amount of abatement.

Art. 2706. Loss of Crop Rent

When the rent consists of a portion of the crops, then any loss of the crops that is not caused by the fault of the lessor or the lessee shall be borne by both parties in accordance with their respective shares.

Art. 2707. Lessor's Privilege

To secure the payment of rent and other obligations arising from the lease of an immovable, the lessor has a privilege on the lessee's movables that are found in or upon the leased property.

In an agricultural lease, the lessor's privilege also encompasses the fruits produced by the land.

Art. 2708. Lessor's Privilege over Sublessee's Movables

The lessor's privilege extends to the movables of the sublessee but only to the extent that the sublessee is indebted to his sublessor at the time the lessor exercises his right.

Art. 2709. Lessor's Right to Seize Movables of Third Persons

The lessor may lawfully seize a movable that belongs to a third person if it is located in or upon the leased property, unless the lessor knows that the movable is not the property of the lessee.

The third person may recover the movable by establishing his ownership prior to the judicial sale in the manner provided by Article 1092 of the Code of Civil Procedure. If he fails to do so, the movable may be sold as though it belonged to the lessee.

Art. 2710. Enforcement of the Lessor's Privilege

The lessor may seize the movables on which he has a privilege while they are in or upon the leased property, and for fifteen days after they have been removed if they remain the property of the lessee and can be identified.

The lessor may enforce his privilege against movables that have been seized by the sheriff or other officer of the court, without the necessity of a further seizure thereof, as long as the movables or the proceeds therefrom remain in the custody of the officer.

Art. 2711. Transfer of Thing Does Not Terminate Lease

The transfer of the leased thing does not terminate the lease, unless the contrary had been agreed between the lessor and the lessee.

Art. 2712. Transfer of Immovable Subject to Unrecorded Lease

A third person who acquires an immovable that is subject to an unrecorded lease is not bound by the lease.

In the absence of a contrary provision in the lease contract, the lessee has an action against the lessor for any loss the lessee sustained as a result of the transfer.

Art. 2713. Lessee's Right to Sublease, Assign, or Encumber

The lessee has the right to sublease the leased thing or to assign or encumber his rights in the lease, unless expressly prohibited by the contract of lease. A provision that prohibits one of these rights is deemed to prohibit the others, unless a contrary intent is expressed. In all other respects, a provision that prohibits subleasing, assigning, or encumbering is to be strictly construed against the lessor.

Art. 2714. Expropriation; Loss or Destruction

If the leased thing is lost or totally destroyed, without the fault of either party, or if it is expropriated, the lease terminates and neither party owes damages to the other.

Art. 2715. Partial Destruction, Loss, Expropriation, or Other Substantial Impairment of Use

If, without the fault of the lessee, the thing is partially destroyed, lost, or expropriated, or its use is otherwise substantially impaired, the lessee may, according to the circumstances of both parties, obtain a diminution of the rent or dissolution of the lease, whichever is more appropriate under the circumstances. If the lessor was at fault, the lessee may also demand damages.

If the impairment of the use of the leased thing was caused by circumstances external to the leased thing, the lessee is entitled to a dissolution of the lease, but is not entitled to diminution of the rent.

Art. 2716. Termination of Lease Granted by a Usufructuary

A lease granted by a usufructuary terminates upon the termination of the usufruct.

The lessor is liable to the lessee for any loss caused by such termination, if the lessor failed to disclose his status as a usufructuary.

Art. 2717. Death of Lessor or Lessee

A lease does not terminate by the death of the lessor or the lessee or by the cessation of existence of a juridical person that is party to the lease.

Art. 2718. Leases with Reservation of Right to Terminate

A lease in which one or both parties have reserved the right to terminate the lease before the end of the term may be so terminated by giving the notice specified in the lease contract or the notice provided in Articles 2727 through 2729, whichever period is longer. The right to receive this notice may not be renounced in advance.

Art. 2719. Dissolution for Other Causes

When a party to the lease fails to perform his obligations under the lease or under this Title, the other party may obtain dissolution of the lease pursuant to the provisions of the Title of "Conventional Obligations or Contracts".

Art. 2720. Termination of Lease with a Fixed Term

A lease with a fixed term terminates upon the expiration of that term, without need of notice, unless the lease is reconducted or extended as provided in the following Articles.

Art. 2721. Reconduction

A lease with a fixed term is reconducted if, after the expiration of the term, and without notice to vacate or terminate or other opposition by the lessor or the lessee, the lessee remains in possession:

(1) For thirty days in the case of an agricultural lease;

(2) For one week in the case of other leases with a fixed term that is longer than a week; or

(3) For one day in the case of a lease with a fixed term that is equal to or shorter than a week.

Art. 2722. Term of Reconducted Agricultural Lease

The term of a reconducted agricultural lease is from year to year, unless the parties intended a different term which, according to local custom or usage, is observed in leases of the same type.

Art. 2723. Term of Reconducted Nonagricultural Lease

The term of a reconducted nonagricultural lease is:

(1) From month to month in the case of a lease whose term is a month or longer;

(2) From day to day in the case of a lease whose term is at least a day but shorter than a month; and

(3) For periods equal to the expired term in the case of a lease whose term is less than a day.

Art. 2724. Continuity of the Reconducted Lease

When reconduction occurs, all provisions of the lease continue for the term provided in Article 2722 or 2723. A reconducted lease is terminated by giving the notice directed in Articles 2727 through 2729.

Art. 2725. Extension

If the lease contract contains an option to extend the term and the option is exercised, the lease continues for the term and under the other provisions stipulated in the option.

Art. 2726. Amendment

An amendment to a provision of the lease contract that is made without an intent to effect a novation does not create a new lease.

Art. 2727. Termination of Lease with an Indeterminate Term

A lease with an indeterminate term, including a reconducted lease or a lease whose term has been established through Article 2680, terminates by notice to that effect given to the other party by the party desiring to terminate the lease, as provided in the following Articles.

Art. 2728. Notice of Termination; Timing

The notice of termination required by the preceding Article shall be given at or before the time specified below:

(1) In a lease whose term is measured by a period longer than a month, thirty calendar days before the end of that period;

(2) In a month-to-month lease, ten calendar days before the end of that month;

(3) In a lease whose term is measured by a period equal to or longer than a week but shorter than a month, five calendar days before the end of that period; and

(4) In a lease whose term is measured by a period shorter than a week, at any time prior to the expiration of that period. A notice given according to the preceding Paragraph terminates the lease at the end of the period specified in the notice, and, if none is specified, at the end of the first period for which the notice is timely.

Art. 2729. Notice of Termination; Form

If the leased thing is an immovable or is a movable used as residence, the notice of termination shall be in writing. It may be oral in all other cases.

In all cases, surrender of possession to the lessor at the time at which notice of termination shall be given under Article 2728 shall constitute notice of termination by the lessee.

APPENDIX II

Cases — Illustrations

CHAPTER I — LEASE: NOTION AND ELEMENTS

Article I — Notion

Gauthier v. Allright New Orleans, Inc.	417 So.2d 375 (La. 4th Cir. 1982)
Thomas v. Lewis	475 So.2d 52 (La. 2nd Cir. 1985)
Debbie Holt v. Bethany Land Company and Durel Cup	843 So.2d 606 (La. 2nd Cir. 2003)
Richard v. Hall	874 So.2d 131 (La. 2004)
Bruscato v. Oswalt	975 So.2d 120 (La. 2nd Cir. 2008)

Article II — Elements of a Lease

§ 1 — The Thing

Arata v. Louisiana Stadium and Exposition Dist.	225 So.2d 362, cert. denied 396 U.S. 279 (1969)

§ 2 — Rent

Louisiana Ass'n for Mental Health v. Edwards	322 So.2d 761 (La. 1975)
Willis v. Ventrella	674 So.2d 991 (La. 1st Cir. 1996), rehearing denied, writ denied 681 So.2d 1266, 1996-1937 (La. 1996)
C. Zakrzewski Daigle v. M. Vanderpool	858 So.2d 552 (La. 1st Cir. 2003)

§ 3 — Term

Kite v. Carter	856 So.2d 1271 (La. 3rd Cir. 2003)
Metairie PJ's, Inc. v. Richards Clearview, L.L.C.	963 So.2d 548 (La. 5th Cir. 2007)

CHAPTER II — THE OBLIGATIONS OF THE LESSOR AND THE LESSEE: DELIVERY, REPAIRS, IMPROVEMENTS

Price v. Scott	107 So.2d 808 (Orl. Cir. 1959)

Article I — The Lessor's Obligation to Deliver

Bennett v. Southern Scrap Material Co.	46 So.2d 211 (1908)

Article II — The Lessee's Obligation to Use the Thing as a Prudent Administrator

New Orleans & Carrollton Ry. v. Darms	2 So. 230 (La. 1887)
Karno v. Bourbon Burlesque Club, Inc.	931 So.2d 1111 (La. 4th Cir. 2006)

Article III — The Lessor's Obligation Not to Alter the Thing During the Lease

Article IV — Repairs and Improvements

Reed v. Classified Parking System	232 So.2d 103 (La. 2nd Cir. 1970)
Friendly Finance, Inc. v. Cefalu Reality Investment, Inc	303 So.2d 558 (La. 1st Cir. 1974)
Pistorious v. Eschette	814 So.2d 13 (La. 1st Cir. 2002)
Karno v. Joseph Fein Caterer, Inc.	846 So.2d 105 (La. 4th Cir. 2003)
Hai Nam Chinese Restaurant Partnership v. B & B Construction of New Iberia	942 So.2d 97 (La. 3rd Cir. 2006)
Weinmann v. Duhon	997 So.2d 647 (La. 5th Cir. 2008)

CHAPTER III — THE LESSOR'S WARRANTIES

Article I — Warranty Against Vices or Defects

Cornelio v. Viola	161 So. 196 (Orl. Cir. 1935)
Tassin v. Slidell Mini-Storage, Inc.	396 So.2d 1261 (La. 1981)
C. Martinez v. P.F. Coleman, Lotus Reality	786 So.2d 170 (La. 5th Cir. 2001)

Article II — The Lessor's Warranty of Peaceful Possession

Coleman v. Haight	14 La.Ann. 564 (1859)
Kenney v. Cox	649 So.2d 15 (La. 4th Cir. 1994)
Potter v. First Federal Savings and Loan	615 So.2d 318 (La. 1993)
Shubert v. Tonti Development Corp.	30 So.3d 977 (La. 5th Cir. 2009)

CHAPTER IV — THE LESSOR'S RIGHTS: RENT AND SECURITIES

Fisk v. Moores	11 Rob. (La) 279 (La. 1845)
Edwards v. Standard Oil Co. of La.	144 So. 430 (La. 1932)
Wolf v. Cuccia	144 La. 336, 80 So. 581 (1919)

CHAPTER V — TERMINATION AND DISSOLUTION

Article I — Transfer of Interest by Lessor or Lessee

T.D. Bickham Corp. v. Hebert	432 So.2d 228 (La. 1983)
Martinez v. Louisiana Department of Wild Life and Fisheries	514 So.2d 140 (La App 4th Cir. 1987)
Means v. Comcast, Inc.	17 So.3d 1012 (La. App. 2nd Cir. 2009)

Article II — Total Loss of the Thing

Article III — Partial Loss of the Thing

Kuebel v. Charvet's Garden Center, Inc.	30 So.3d 885 (La. 5th Cir. 2009)

Article IV — Other Instances of Termination

The Bossier Center, Inc. v. Palais Royal, Inc.	385 So.2d (La. 2nd Cir. 1980)
Truschinger v. Pak	513 So.2d 1151 (La. 1987)
City of Donaldsonville v. Thiac	542 So.2d 1111 (La. 1st Cir. 1989)
Mansur v. Cox	898 So.2d 446 (La. 1st Cir. 2004)
Smith v. State, Dept. of Transp. & Development	899 So.2d 516 (La. 2005)
Charles Robert Carter Properties, Inc. and Studio Properties, L.L.C. v. Ecoscience Resource Group, L.L.C.	35 So.3d 1114 (La. 1st Cir. 2010)

Article V — Leases with a Fixed Term

Granger v. Tri-Tech, LLC	981 So.2d 88 (La. 3rd Cir. 2007)
Jamison v. D'Amico	955 So.2d 161 (La. 4th Cir. 2007)

Article VI — Leases with an Indeterminate Term

The Bossier Center, Inc. v. Palais Royal, Inc.	385 So.2d (La. 2nd Cir. 1980)
Truschinger v. Pak	513 So.2d 1151 (La. 1987)
City of Donaldsonville v. Thiac	542 So.2d 1111 (La. 1st Cir. 1989)
Sid-Mars Restaurant & Lounge, Inc. v. Gardner	844 So.2d 178 (La. 5th Cir. 2003)
Mansur v. Cox	898 So.2d 446 (La. 1st Cir. 2004)
Smith v. State, Dept. of Transp. & Development	899 So.2d 516 (La. 2005)

Index

E

F

G

H

I

J

L

M